DEAR SELMA

Dear Selma

A WORLD WAR II
LOVE LETTER ROMANCE

BERNARD D. BROWN

Compiled by his daughter Shelley N.Brown

LUMINARE PRESS
WWW.LUMINAREPRESS.COM

Dear Selma
A WORLD WAR II LOVE LETTER ROMANCE
Copyright © 2020 by Bernard D. Brown

Printed in the United States of America

Cover Design by Claire Flint Last

Luminare Press
442 Charnelton St.
Eugene, OR 97401
www.luminarepress.com

LCCN: 2020912917
ISBN: 978-1-64388-493-6

Table of Contents

Introduction

I always knew my parents fell in love over the letters they exchanged while my father was in the army during World War II but I didn't realize the details of their enduring long-distance relationship until I sat down and read each one. When my mother passed away in 2017 my siblings and I helped my dad move out of our family home in Salem, Oregon. It was then that we started reading the letters and realized what a treasure we had.

As the Americans took Germany, my father was on the front lines fighting from fox holes. It's chilling to think that each letter could have been his last. I want to believe that these letters gave my dad the drive and determination to get through the war and back to the woman he had known most of his life and was now falling in love with.

I hope you enjoy the heartfelt expressions of a young man (really a boy), homesick but also determined to fulfill his duty. We dedicate this book to all those who didn't make it back.

—Shelley

The Beginning

OREGON

Childhood friends:
Selma Nepom, Bobby Buchwach, Marvin Nepom,
Bobby (Bernard) Brown,
Normie Nepom and friend
Rockaway Beach, 1936

BERNARD "BOB" BROWNE
1710 SOUTH WINTER ST.
SALEM, OREGON

SELMA NEPOM
716 S.W. HARRISON
PORTLAND, OREGON

October 16, 1941

Dear Selma,

Golly was I ever surprised to hear from you, I had to read the card three times before I really realized it.

Selma I want to thank you an awful lot for your invitation. I am not positive yet, but I am pretty sure that I will be able to come, with the <u>car.</u> You see Selma, I am not sure about getting off of work Saturday morning. If I do come, I will stay at Hesh's Friday night (if we ever go to bed) and leave for Salem Saturday morning. But anyhow Selma, you count on me, and if I can't go I'll let you know before Sunday, October 18th, but I don't think I'll have to. Selma, what time do you want me to come in? I don't think I'll be able to leave Salem (the <u>joint</u>) until about 7 o'clock P.M., but I can get into Portland easily at 8 o'clock. I hope that that isn't too late.

Not much doing in Salem lately. It is still as dead as ever. School five days a week, Demolay meets Thursday night, Hi Y meets Wed. night, football game Friday night, and work all day Saturday, and take-it-easy all day Sunday. Every week I do that same thing, and Selma believe me, it gets so-o-o-o monotonous.

Now how about you. What do you hear from Ruth? How are the Folks and Normie and Betty? How is school coming along, are you having fun? Portland's a wonderful city Selma take it from somebody who knows. I really miss the place. Say hello to everybody including that girl from New York, I forgot her name, darn it.

Well that's about it for now Selma.

Love,
Bob

5

*Photo of Bernard and
Selma in high school*

BERNARD "BOB" BROWNE
1710 SOUTH WINTER ST.
SALEM, OREGON

SELMA NEPOM
716 S.W. HARRISON
PORTLAND, OREGON

June 11, 1943

Dear Selma,

Received your very nice letter a couple of days ago and was very glad to hear that you also finally made it, I'll bet you really had to work hard. Nice going kid.

Selma, I want to thank you and the rest of your swell family for the graduation present you sent me. I really do appreciate it.

Regards to the rest of the family from the folks and myself.

Bob

Enlistment and Boot Camp

FORT BENNING, GEORGIA

Photo taken on weekend leave
in Columbus, GA

BERNARD D. BROWNE
1ST CO. 1ST PLATOON ASTP
6TH TAG. REG. FORT BENNING, GA.

MISS SELMA NEPOM
716 S.W. HARRISON
PORTLAND, 1, OREGON

November 21, 1943

Dear Selma,

Golly I'll bet your really surprised to hear from me. As yet I don't know whether your address is correct, or not, it's just a guess. I hope you don't mind me writing to you, but I just thought I would like to hear from you and write to you.

I'm here taking my basic training—thirteen weeks of it. I've already had 11 weeks. Last week and this coming week we're out on bivouac. The only reason we hiked into camp today was to get some clean clothes and take a real shower. Boy this field stuff is really rugged, especially in these Southern woods. Only two more weeks and we'll be through thank goodness. From here I don't know where I'll go but anyplace will be better than Georgia. Georgia is one awful state believe me. I came through 14 states coming down here and I'll still take Oregon any day. By the way, Al Lebenzon is also stationed down here. We've seen one another a couple of times but being that he is in a different regiment we don't have much time at all to see each other. It was good to see him though.

I imagine you're working for your father. Be sure to say hello to the rest of the family for me and tell your Mom she's still my best girlfriend. How are they all? What have you been doing for excitement lately? Anything new in town? I imagine you're still writing to Heshy—how's he doing anyhow?

Well Sel, that's about it for now. I hope to hear from you soon—that is if this letter ever gets to you with this address on it.

Bob

BERNARD D. BROWNE
1ST CO. 1ST PLATOON ASTP
6TH TAG. REG. FORT BENNING, GA.

MISS SELMA NEPOM
716 S.W. HARRISON
PORTLAND, 1, OREGON

December 4, 1943

Dear Selma,

Boy was I glad to get your letter. For a while I thought my letter didn't get to you or you were either too busy. Anyhow I'm much happier now.

Yes Selma, I do write to Buck. He's one guy that I'll always be writing to I guess. You watch, he'll be a lieutenant within a year or so, because he's really in a good deal. He'll make the best of it too. About me, I'll try to explain it all. When they put me in the Army, they sent me to Ft. Benning to take my basic training. When I got here, they gave me a whole bunch of exams. Everything from math to psychology. They then put me into the A-12 program, so I took basic at an A.S.T.P. unit here. We had our final review this morning which officially completes our 13 weeks of training. They're sending me to college and as I see it they're going to try to make an engineer out of me. Guess what college I'm going to Selma? This will kill you—it's Oklahoma A & M and I leave for there sometime next week but can't say just when. Of all places to send me, they have to send me there. I was hoping to get sent someplace near home, but I guess that just doesn't go in the Army. Wait till that furlough comes kid, I'll tell you all about it. I sure wish it wasn't Oklahoma though because I doubt very much if I'll like it there.

This fellow from Washington D.C. sounds O.K. kid, he really does. All Bob's are good kids—it says here but remember there's more than one.

Golly I sure hope Frieda has a boy. I'm almost excited as her husband. It's too bad about Lew and Sylvia but as you said, that's life. I'm glad to hear that Betty and Eric are getting along fine. Golly I never thought they were married that long.

Congratulations on your birthday. I wish I would have known about it a little bit sooner. Golly isn't it funny the way we grow up though. It just seems like yesterday that we were all a bunch of kids.

Selma, I'm ashamed of you asking if I want any addresses. I'm writing to you, that's all I really care about. I imagine it sounds funny to hear me talk that way, but a guy doesn't realize certain things until he gets away from home. Nuff Said!

You're right about me being a private and I'll probably be one for quite a while. This A-12 program isn't too good for promotions. After two years of college (if you don't flunk out) you're made a Pfc, and after completion of school you're made a corporal. So you see just how it stands.

Well Selma, that's about the works for now. Hope to hear from you soon. Write to me in Oklahoma. Temporary address:

Pvt. "me"
Basic Eng. #1
Oklahoma A & M
Stillwater, Oklahoma

Don't worry about these Georgia peaches. You can't beat a girl from the West Coast, I know that now. I went to Shul over the holidays and it's the funniest thing to hear a combination of Jewish and a Southern accent. I went to Shul though and that's all that counted.

Goodbye for now Sel.

Bob

Army Specialized
Training Program

⸺⧟⸺

STILLWATER, OKLAHOMA

MISS SELMA NEPOM
716 S.W. HARRISON ST.
PORTLAND, 1, OREGON

December 15, 1943

Dear Selma,

I received your letter today and was sure glad to hear from you. As far as Oklahoma goes, it's got the South beat by an awful lot. It's not as good as Oregon though. It is awfully cold here now and they expect snow any day now, so you see what a swell time I'm going to have skiing down the streets of Stillwater—ha, ha.

The school itself is a very nice school. They have 2500 air cadets, 2500 of us, and 2800 sailors studying Radar. There are some civilians here even though it is a service school.

The main idea of the Army to send us here is to find out what we're best qualified for. We go to school here from 1 month up to 2 years. You can be sent to any type of outfit— Engineers, Air Corp, Infantry, Signal Corp— etc. within that span of time so I just hope I don't qualify for anything so that I can stay in school longer. It's really a very complicated set-up. As yet I don't understand it myself. I originally thought that they were sending us here to make engineers out of us but I found out different when I got here.

We carry 27 hours a week of actual class & lab. work. Not having any college before I find it quite stiff, in fact plenty tough. We study English, History, Math.—combined algebra-trig & calculus, Chemistry, Physics, Military Science, Military drill, & Phy. Ed. It's a tough course but I guess that's the best way they can find out what we can specialize in. I hope it's not the infantry.

I wrote Lewie tonight and told him just what you told me. He'll appreciate that a lot Sel. I knew that he was going to get married to her, but I didn't think he would pull a surprise on us. He was planning to come home Xmas and bring her with him but he couldn't get his furlough so I guess they decided to get married there.

I'm looking very much forward to a furlough Selma, but I won't get it until sometime in March—darn it. That's an awful long time to wait.

I'll be there one of these days though and when I do you just tell your soldier boy he'd better leave town. It was nice of him to give you an orchid though. He sounds like an O.K. guy—darn it!! I'm glad to hear that you read my letter to your mother. Believe me—I don't mind at all. She's tops Sel. I'm just trying to be tactful—you know—get on the good side of the parents first—ha! ha!

Well Sel, that's about it for now. Give my regards to the family and stay and help out your Pop if he needs you. Don't go to college, you might meet some other nice guys. I act as if I own you, don't I? "Jus Foolin" Write soon kid.

Love,
Bob

P.S. Permanent address is on back of envelope.

STILLWATER, OKLA.

MISS SELMA NEPOM
716 S.W. HARRISON ST.
PORTLAND, 1, OREGON

December 26, 1943

Dear Selma,

I just got back from Oklahoma City, where I was invited to spend Christmas weekend, and I found your letter with a bunch of others laying on my bunk. I was sure glad to hear from you Sel, you write very interesting letters.

Oklahoma City is one of the most quaint places I've ever been in. Right on the courthouse grounds they have a large oil well, and the same occurs throughout the city. It is about the same size as Portland (Pre-War) but is all flat. No hills at all. This girl's father is an oil man and he showed me all through his wells. I've never seen so much oil in all my life. They call it black-gold. I wonder why—ha, ha. I think 90% of the people here live off of the oil. It's an enormous industry here.

Stillwater is a different story. It is very small, about the size of Forest Grove. The population is about 8,000. It is one of these small towns built around a big college. Reminds me somewhat of Corvallis. The people here are typical Westerners and are very friendly. We get off every Saturday at 2:00 P.M. and are free until 12:00 PM. Sunday. Christmas we got off from Thursday 12:00 Noon until tonight at 12:00 midnight. The free weekends are a good deal, but we always have too many studies to do so you can see where most of it goes, believe it or not.

I'm glad to hear you're reading my Uncle's latest book. You're right kid—I haven't read it. But I would if I had the time and the book. How did you like the sarcasm he used? I heard he used quite a bit in this book.

We are having a New Year's Eve Party here at school New Year's Eve. It's going to be a formal deal and our A-12 band is going to play for the dance. It's sure going to be good to see a formal again. It's been a <u>long</u> time. How about you Sel? I'm glad to hear Sol is coming home. I didn't know him very well, but he seemed to be a very nice fella. Now that I see I have so much competition I'll have to act the big brother type until some of those wolves move out. What do you think of your new brother Selma? Here goes anyhow.

As long as you're playing the field and they're all after you—give 'em all a run for their money. Treat em all the same—show no partiality until you find one that you like better than all the rest. You may not find him for a while but when you do—you'll know it. Ha, ha, just listen to me talk. Why in the heck I work against myself, I don't know.

Well Sel, that's about it for now. Treat Sol good, because if he thinks he's got a crush on you, keep him going. You might find out you have one on him one of these days. Oy—there I go again—talking against myself.

Happy New Year's Sel. Hope to hear from you soon.
Regards to the family—Please write.

Bob

Oklahoma A&M University

PVT. BERNARD D. BROWNE
39337016 – Co. E – 3872 A.S.T.U.
OKLAHOMA A & M COLLEGE
STILLWATER, OKLAHOMA

MISS SELMA NEPOM
716 S.W. HARRISON ST.
PORTLAND, 1, OREGON

January 8, 1944

Dear Selma,

You'll have to excuse this penmanship because I'm sitting on my bunk and there are about 10 fellows around trying to find out what I'm writing to you.

I received your very welcomed letter and enjoyed reading it. I suppose you know Sel that you write very interesting letters.

I'm glad to hear you had such a good time over New Years. Golly kid, you really did it up right. That's the best way to enjoy it though.

By the way Sel, don't let this oil man deal fool you. Some of the biggest oil men in this state have less money than some of the poor farmers. And again, most of the Indians in this state are wealthier than the white men. I think there are more Indians in this state than any other place in the country. Contrary to belief the Indian is quite the man around here.

This girl I was telling you about is a very nice girl, but it's nothing to worry about. For one thing, she's not a Jewish girl and I just don't think I could really like her. She's a good kid to take out on weekends though. Good dancer, good personality and all that, but as far as green streaks go, I think I have more to worry about than you. I'm glad to hear that you're having a lot of fellas over to the house. You don't know how good it makes them feel. But be careful kid, don't go falling for some jerk who feeds you a beautiful line. A lot of these fellas aren't the best in the world. That's from your brother for this letter. Aren't I crazy though?

Well Sel, that's about all I have time for now. Take care and write me real soon.

Love,
Bob

P.S. I'm glad to hear you had a good time with Sol, damn it!
P.S.(2) Note change in return address.

21

PVT. BERNARD D. BROWNE
39337016 – Co. E – 3872 A.S.T.U.
OKLAHOMA A & M COLLEGE
STILLWATER, OKLAHOMA

MISS SELMA NEPOM
716 S.W. HARRISON ST.
PORTLAND, 1, OREGON

January 18, 1944

Dear Selma,

I got your letter this afternoon and enjoyed it very much. Funny thing kid, I seem to look forward to your letters, wonderful isn't it? Now listen here you, I want you to know one thing, the only reason I'm acting like a big brother is because with all those wolves in Portland I am helpless. Being that I'm so far away I don't have any ground to stand on, but just wait till I get home, if I ever do. By the way, some of those wolves should be pretty nice fellows. Never swear off of men Selma. You'd be very bored if you didn't go out with some guy once in awhile. Have a good time with em Honey. Before you know it they'll be sending all kinds of presents and everything (suckers aren't they?) But don't be too nice to them—remember me—this war won't last (see what happens) forever.

Selma I'm awfully glad to hear you're joining the Cadet Nurse Corp. It's a very good training for anyone and I'm sure you'll like it. I'm glad to hear your folks don't mind. I think it's a good thing.

I imagine you're quite surprised getting monogramed stationery from me all the time, but here's the story. Lewis's wife sent this to me just a week ago. She seems to be a really swell kid.

Well Honey the studies here are still keeping me really busy. They sure know how to lay it on. I don't see how we can ever learn anything the way they cram it into us. I guess they know what they're doing though.

I got a letter from Banny yesterday and she told me that Frieda is still waiting for her baby. Of all things to write me about. Anyhow I've got something to look forward to—hope it's a girl—fooled you, didn't I?

Well kid, that's about it for now. Write soon and tell me all about those water pipes—I hope they got fixed. Regards to the family.

Bob

Pvt. Bernard D. Browne
39337016 – Co. E – 3872 A.S.T.U.
Oklahoma A & M College
Stillwater, Oklahoma

Miss Selma Nepom
716 S.W. Harrison St.
Portland, 1, Oregon

January 26, 1944

Dear Selma,

I received your letter yesterday and today is the first chance I got to answer it so here goes.

I'm sorry my last letter was so short but no foolin, they keep us so busy around here that we don't have time for anything. I'll try to make up for it now though. Let me know how I do.

You really had quite a week, didn't you? I'm sort of glad that you didn't get into the Nurse Corp deal. Why should you go to a dumpy hospital to live when you have such a swell home and such wonderful parents—I can just see your Mom smiling now as she reads this. Besides Sel you don't want to be cooped up for three years. I would feel much safer though. A fine way for a brother to talk.

I'm glad to hear Bob got home for a couple of days. I sure wish I could. About a furlough Sel, I don't know any more about it than you do. No foolin, they don't let you in on a thing. They say though, that after we complete our 3-month course here, we get a seven day furlough. A lot I could do with such an extended furlough. With best train connections the most I could be home would be about a day and a half. The plane will give me reservation to Portland, but they don't guarantee passage back. When the time comes though I'll go cry to the C.O. and maybe fix it to take my finals a little early. It should be sometime in March if it comes at all.

I'm glad to hear you went out with a gentile fella—I'll bet Tillie isn't smiling now—but really, I think it does you a lot of good, but when you come right down to it—you just can't beat a <u>good</u> Jewish boy or girl. I'll bet you think I've changed a lot, don't you? It's the truth though Sel—there isn't anything better, so stick your chin up kid.

I'm glad to hear about Frieda's baby. See, I wanted a girl and she had one. Wouldn't it be wonderful if I could get everything I wanted? Just between you and I sis, I'm working hard—how'm I doing? Aren't brothers wonderful?

Well Sel, I'd better call it quits for now. I'm all out. Please write soon and take care of that cold. By the way, if you have an old wrinkled up (1st step) snapshot of yourself floating around I would sure like to have it, also the fellows around here are beginning to wonder what you look like—

All the fellows here send their regards to Bernie's (that's me) girl-friend—especially Johnny my bunk mate. Regards to the family Selma.

Your G.I. Oakie,

Bob

P.S. I'm sending you some pictures of the campus

PVT. BERNARD D. BROWNE
39337016 – Co. E – 3872 A.S.T.U.
OKLAHOMA A & M COLLEGE
STILLWATER, OKLAHOMA

MISS SELMA NEPOM
716 S.W. HARRISON ST.
PORTLAND, 1, OREGON

February 6, 1944

𝒟*ear* 𝒮*elma,*

I got your two letters and was awfully glad to get them both. I like to hear from you very much.

I'm sorry I didn't write sooner but no fooling I've been awfully busy studying for exams which we had this last weekend. Boy were they tough. All I do now is wait and pray. Anyhow that's the reason I didn't write any sooner. The folks even started to wonder what was the matter? Anyhow, now that it's all over with I feel much better. I just hope I passed everything.

Say kid, those murders remind of old times. Remember the way things used to pop around our neck of the city. Those good ole days.

I'm glad to hear you got those pictures O.K. I can't find any film at all around here for my camera, so I guess I won't be able to take any snapshots for a while. I'm looking very much forward in getting one of you though. Believe it or not, I still think I remember what you look like. After all, I've known you long enough.

I talked to the C.O. about my furlough and he says he can't do anything because he doesn't know when the furloughs are coming through. So, I guess all I can do at present is wait and see what will happen. Pray for me Honey.

We had quite a time at school this week. Everybody on the campus seemed to be cramming. We were all so mixed up between Chemistry and Physics that we (I) doubt very much getting passing grades. We have only 4 wks left, that is if we pass these last finals. College is great stuff Sel, no fooling.

I'm sorry to hear about Bob going to be transferred but that is the Army. You're at one place for a while and just as you get used to it, you ship out to another. Great life, this Army.

I got a letter from Bobby today and he sent me a picture of himself. He sure looks swell in a cadet uniform.

Well Sel, that's about it for now. I'm sorry this letter isn't longer, but I just can't think of anything. Take care of yourself and give my regards to the family.

Love,
Bob

PVT. BERNARD D. BROWNE
39337016 – Co. E – 3872 A.S.T.U.
OKLAHOMA A & M COLLEGE
STILLWATER, OKLAHOMA

MISS SELMA NEPOM
716 S.W. HARRISON ST.
PORTLAND, 1, OREGON

February 15, 1944

Dear Selma,

I received your letter today. Happy to get it Honey.

You ought to be ashamed of yourself going to bed so early. With all the excitement going on in Portland and you have to go to bed so early. Give some of those fellows a break, Sel, but not too many.

I'm glad to hear that your father went to the Springs. It does a person good every once in a while to go someplace and relax. I'll bet you and Ruth really have a job now. Keep up the good work. Regards to Ruth.

My eight-week exams turned out O.K. They beat my four weeks average which made me feel pretty good. All I have to do now is hope to pass my twelve-week finals. After they're over with I'll probably be sent to some regular outfit. From here I don't know where I go, but I hope it's closer to home. If so I should get a furlough. It's hard to tell just what goes in the Army.

It started to snow yesterday, and everything is white outside now. It sure is pretty. It's only about two inches deep and will only last about a week or so. They don't ski or anything here because the state is so flat. All they do here is make snowmen and have snow fights. The campus really looks nice with everything white. Some of the buildings here are really beautiful.

Selma, last Friday I went to an A & M basketball game and between halves they had an Indian war dance put on by real Oklahoma Indians—feathers and all. Golly it was really interesting. They are supposed to be the real thing—and they sure looked like it. As you probably know the State is full of Indians. Not many around here but they are really plentiful around the larger cities.

I met a fellow who was just sent here from San Diego to study Radar. He is in the Navy and we both went to high school together. He hates Okla. compared to the West Coast. I know just how he feels.

You're right about the Air Mail deal Selma. It is very bad from here. I often thought of changing but never put it into use. I want to get these letters to you as soon as possible because you're one girl I really want to keep in touch with. Listen to me Sel, don't I sound awful? I mean it though.

Well kid, that's about it for now. Write soon Honey.

Love,
Bob

Regards to everybody

Pvt. Bernard D. Browne
39337016 – Co. E – 3872 A.S.T.U.
Oklahoma A & M College
Stillwater, Oklahoma

Miss Selma Nepom
716 S.W. Harrison St.
Portland, 1, Oregon

February 24, 1944

Dear Selma,

I got your swell letter today and I liked it. I have the habit of looking forward to your letters now which is something different for me. See what your letters do to me.

Sel, I guess you know it already, but if you don't, I let you in on a very disappointing secret. The A.S.T.P. program is being dissolved totally and by April 1st all trainees (including me) will be back in the troops. I sort of thought this deal was too good to last. I was actually getting something out of the Army. They say that they can't get enough men in the service through selective service, so they have to cut out our program. Our term ends March the fourth and we won't start a new term. What a deal. There sure are a lot of sad looking fellows around here.

I'm trying to get into the Air Corp. I just hope I pass my mental and physical tests. Anything's better than the infantry Sel, and I figure the Air Corp will do me more good than anything else. I just hope I get in.

We've all been promised a seven-day furlough after this term is over-with. The only trouble is, is that it's not enough time for me to get home and back. I can't get a plane because I don't have any priority. I sure do get the good deals. Anyway, my folks are planning to come up and see me before I'm shipped out again (wish you were coming with them). I'm expecting them sometime this weekend. They'll probably stay a few days and on the way back, will stop at L.A. and visit with Lewie and Junne.

I'm glad you liked the valentine—I was hoping you would. The clerk who sold it to me said that you must be a wonderful girl. I assured her that you were. Keep that chin up now Selma.

About me writing to you—it was very funny the way it started. Nobody told me about you or anything—it was just a hit on the head,

I guess. I'll save it and tell you just how it happened the first time I see you. Sure do hope it will be soon.

Yes, we do have a bowling alley here, a big one. We go bowling on an average of twice a week. I like it an awful lot.

I'm glad to hear that big Sol is coming home but I wish he wouldn't stay so long. I see where I'm going to have trouble with that guy. He's really a swell guy but you can do much better than that. Let him show you a good time though. Golly I'm awful the way I talk, aren't I. I'm sorry—maybe I'm a little jealous. Sure wish he would stay away though.

I'm glad to hear about the other Sol though. He's really a swell guy. We practically spent my last summer in civilian life together at Rockaway. Ask him, he'll tell you all about it. He is in a very good deal—I'm sure he'll like Willamette. Sure wish I was going there. Maybe someday Honey.

Selma you say that you are trying to figure me out. I want you to keep trying. I'm hoping someday you will.

Enclosed you will find some snapshots that we happened to take around the barracks when we had some spare time (weekends). No. 1 is a picture of a typical Oklahoman and myself. He was born in Oklahoma and reminds me of Mortemer Sneard. He sure is funny but really is a swell guy. He sure is a brain too. As you can see, he has his fatigues on. No. 2 is guess who? Don't I look mean though—I'm really not, they just took it at the wrong time. No. 3 is me in a G.I. sak. It's Johnnie's overcoat, as you can see it doesn't fit at all. I had to use his because mine was in the barracks and I was too lazy to get it. You see, it doesn't pay to be lazy. No. 4 is a snap of Johnny and me. He is also an Oklahoman who I've gone through basic training with. He's rather a wealthy boy and doesn't act much like a typical Oakie. He's a swell fellow. He's always asking me about my girl from home—guess who that is.

Well Sel, that's about it for now. Take care and give my regards to the family. Write soon.

With Love on Valentine's Day
I think this little greeting
Should help to make it clear
I think that you're a darling,
I think that you're a dear,
And I think I'll tell you
Something else—
I think it would be fine
If you would think it over
And would be my Valentine.

Love,
Bob

Advanced Infantry Training

CAMP HOWZE, TEXAS

Dear Selma,   3/10/44

I got your letter in Stillwater but didn't get a chance to answer it because we were shipping out so soon. We arrived here yesterday afternoon, and boy what a disappointment compared to a dorm and a college campus. I'm in the army though, and that can almost mean anything. We were classified on the train and 1800 of us got put into the infantry. It's far from anything I like but I guess it's up to me to do my best wherever they put me.

So far what I've seen of Texas isn't worth much. It's all flat and dry. This so called camp that we're at just sits right out on the open prairie. We're ten miles from the closest town — population 9,000 Texans. I'm sure I'm going to like it here.

I'm glad you liked those snapshots Sel — they weren't much. I've often thought of taking a photograph but I've not had the time to wait for those long appointments. Now that I'm stuck in this hole I doubt whether I'll ever get the chance again. I'll surprise you though one of these days. And on the other hand — this may be a little sudden — but how about a photograph of you. You know sort of a morale lifter. I could sure use one Hon — I would nothing better to have one of you. Sound like a love struck kid, don't

I do? Crazy what an Army Camp can do to a fellow. I hope have a picture of Elma because I certainly would like one.

I'm glad to hear Bobby got another chance to get home. He's really sick. I now wish I would have done something like that, but I saw a chance to get some college, and this is where I end up. Well here's hoping the war ends soon. Boy will I come home fast.

I hope you drove Bob to Salem. How do you like the ole place. I hope you dropped in on the folks.

The folks were with me in Stillwater for a few days. There wasn't much doing but it was nice just being with them. When it comes to excitement you have to make your own in that place.

Well Sis, that's about all I have time for now. Please write soon. I still don't know how the mail gets in and out of this hole.

Love,
Bob

address is — Pvt. Bernard D. Browne 39337016
Co. I - 410th Infantry A.P.O. - 470
Camp Howze, Texas

35

Pvt. Bernard D. Browne – 39337016
Co. I – 410th Inf. A.P.O. – 470
Camp Howze, Texas

Miss Selma Nepom
716 S.W. Harrison St.
Portland, 1, Oregon

March 10, 1944

Dear Selma,

I got your letter in Stillwater but didn't get a chance to answer it because we were shipping out so soon. We arrived here yesterday afternoon and boy what a disappointment compared to a dorm and a college campus. I'm in the army though and that can almost mean anything. We were classified on the train and 1800 of us got put into the infantry. It's far from anything I like but I guess it's up to me to do my best wherever they put me.

So far what I've seen of Texas isn't worth much. It's all flat and dry. This socalled camp that we're at just sits right out on the open prairie. We're ten miles from the closest town—population 9,000 Texans. I'm sure I'm going to like it here.

I'm glad you liked those snapshots Sel—they weren't much. I've often thought of taking a photograph, but I've not had the time to wait for those long appointments. Now that I'm stuck in this hole, I doubt whether I'll ever get the chance again. I'll surprise you though one of these days. And on the other hand—this may be a little sudden—but how about a photograph of you. You know sort of a morale lifter. I could sure use one Honey—I would like nothing better to have one of you. Sound like a love-struck kid, don't I Sel? Crazy what an Army Camp can do to a fellow. I hope you have a picture Selma because I certainly would like one.

I'm glad to hear Bobby got another chance to get home. He's really set. I now wish I would have done something like that, but I saw a chance to get some college and this is where I end up. Well here's hoping the war ends soon. Boy will I come home fast.

I hope you drove Sol to Salem. How do you like the ole place? I hope you dropped in on the folks.

36

The folks were with me in Stillwater for a few days. There wasn't much doing but it was nice just being with them. When it comes to excitement you have to make your own in that place.

Well Sel, that's about all I have time for now. Please write soon. I still don't know how the mail gets in and out of this hole.

Love,
Bob

Address is —Pvt. Bernard D. Browne 39337016
Co. I – 410th Inf. A.P.O. – 470
Camp Howze, Texas

PVT. BERNARD D. BROWNE
A.S.N. 39337016
CO. I – 410TH INFANTRY A.P.O. – 470
CAMP HOWZE, TEXAS

MISS SELMA NEPOM
716 S.W. HARRISON ST.
PORTLAND, 1, OREGON

.... *March 21, 1944*

Dear Selma,

I received your awaited letter today. Believe it or not it takes letters 4 days to arrive from the West Coast. Airmail doesn't help either, because the mail has to be switched to two different air lines. That's Texas for you Sel, everything is wrong. The post here, they tell me, is one of the worst in the country and I believe it. Plenty of flat land and heat.

We do everything around here. I've been put into the machine gun section and boy do I have fun packing that thing around. You know what they say about infantrymen (hard head, strong body, and no brains). Altogether there are 1800 A.S.T.P. fellows here from Texas A. & M., Oklahoma A. & M., and Oklahoma University. We were all put into the good old infantry and you should see us when we all get together. Everybody feels like crawling into a hole and hide. They're all plenty disgusted, and I don't blame them. I guess we're here though for good, because we've been assigned to companies for further training. It's far from what I wanted to get out of the Army, but I guess all I should do now is do my best and pray for this mess to end soon.

We're closest to the small town of Gainesville, Texas, population 15,000. The closest large city is Dallas, Texas. It's close to the size of Portland and is 83 miles from here. There are a few other Jewish fellows here in the Company and we more or less stick together. They're really a swell bunch of fellows. One of them is from Chicago and the others from New York and vicinity. We're all planning to get out of this hole as soon as we can get a pass of some kind. I don't think we'll be able to get a pass for a little while yet because we're just new here.

The outfit here (103rd Division) really has quite a record. They've been activated since November 1942 and have been training for combat ever since. They really know their stuff. They went to the Louisiana Maneuvers in 1943 for 15 weeks and by all indications I think they'll be going again in June or July. I imagine I'll be going along too—boy will that be sport, ha, ha.

Selma, I'm sure glad to hear about your new job. It really sounds O.K. Golly you've really got a lot to do. Don't get too stuck on your job now, that will be bad. I'll bet it's interesting to work at a Grammar School. Be careful for those young wolves now—they grow up young these days. But seriously Sel, it really sounds like a good deal. I'm glad for you.

Well, I guess that's about it for now. Take care, don't work too hard and write soon, I look forward to your letters.

Your Texas Doughboy,

Love,
Bob

Miss Selma Nepom

% Joseph Lane School

7200 S.E. 60th. St.

Portland, 6, Oregon

BROWN'S JEWELERS-OPTOMETRISTS
LIBERTY AND COURT STS.
SALEM, OREGON

MISS SELMA NEPOM
c/o JOSEPH LANE SCHOOL
7200 S.E. 60TH ST.
PORTLAND, 6, OREGON

April 3, 1944

Dear Selma,

Just a line to let you know we finally got home and here I am this afternoon trying to hack a letter off to you, how am I hacking Honey?

Sel, I leave from Portland Wednesday at 6:30 p.m. on the Portland Rose. Selma if you manage to get down in time meet me at the information desk. I think there's only one. Part of the family will probably be there so you shouldn't have any trouble finding me. I hope you'll be through work in time. The train leaves at 6:30 on the nose so we'll probably be there a little early.

Selma, I certainly had a swell time with you over the weekend. I sure hope you had a good time. You're really a swell kid Sel and also a lot of fun. Always stay happy like you are, and you'll always have jerks like me falling for you. I'm sure looking forward to my next furlough, sure hope it comes soon.

The reason I mailed this letter to school is because I thought it would get there sooner.

Hope to see you Wednesday night Sel.
Love,
Bob

Pvt. Bernard D. Browne 39337016
Co. I 410th Inf. A.P.O. 470
Camp Howze, Texas

Miss Selma Nepom
c/o Joseph Lane School
7200 S.E. 60th St.
Portland, 6, Oregon

April 5, 1944

Honey,

Sure was swell of you to see me off. I would have been disappointed if you hadn't of been there. I already miss you Sel, wonder what it's going to be like in two weeks or so. I'll write you every time I get the chance.

Take good care of yourself.

Love,
Bob

Pvt. Bernard D. Browne 39337016
Co. I 410th Inf. A.P.O. 470
Camp Howze, Texas

Miss Selma Nepom
c/o Joseph Lane School
7200 S.E. 60th St.
Portland, 6, Oregon

April 7, 1944

Honey,

Still at it and it's now starting to get boring again. No pretty country anymore. It's all flat.

We arrive at Denver in a couple of hours for a 5 hr. layover. I miss you Honey.

Saw Elaine's husband at breakfast. He's a nice guy. I'll write again tomorrow.

Love,
Bob

PVT. BERNARD D. BROWNE 39337016
Co. I 410TH INF. A.P.O. 470
CAMP HOWZE, TEXAS

MISS SELMA NEPOM
c/o JOSEPH LANE SCHOOL
7200 S.E. 60TH ST.
PORTLAND, 6, OREGON

April 8, 1944

Still at it Honey. We're 5 hrs. late now but we should be caught up by the time we get there—I hope its tomorrow morning. Miss you a lot Sel. I'll write you a letter after I get there. This traveling business sure does get monotonous. Take care Sel and I'll write tomorrow.

Love,
Bob

WESTERN UNION

CLASS OF SERVICE

This is a full-rate Telegram or Cablegram unless its deferred character is indicated by a suitable symbol above or preceding the address.

1201

A. N. WILLIAMS
PRESIDENT

NEWCOMB CARLTON
CHAIRMAN OF THE BOARD

J. C. WILLEVER
FIRST VICE-PRESIDENT

SYMBOLS

DL=Day Letter

NT=Overnight Telegram

LC=Deferred Cable

NLT=Cable Night Letter

Ship Radiogram

The filing time shown in the date line on telegrams and day letters is STANDARD TIME at point of origin. Time of receipt is STANDARD TIME at point of destination

VA317 NL=GAINESVILLE TEX 9   1944 APR 9 PM 5 33

MISS SELMA NEPON=

:CARE JOSEPH LANE SCHOOL 7200 SOUTHEAST 60 ST

PORTLAND ORG=

SWEETHEART ARRIVED OK EVERYTHING IS FINE WILL WRITE YOU

TODAY LOVE=

:BOB.

THE COMPANY WILL APPRECIATE SUGGESTIONS FROM ITS PATRONS CONCERNING ITS SERVICE

44

PVT. BERNARD D. BROWNE 39337016
CO. I 410TH INF. A.P.O. 470
CAMP HOWZE, TEXAS

MISS SELMA NEPOM
c/o JOSEPH LANE SCHOOL
7200 S.E. 60TH ST.
PORTLAND, 6, OREGON

.... *April 9, 1944*

Sweetheart,

Well I finally got here and I want you to know that I would much rather be home with you. Selma, I learned one thing when I went home and I think you know what it is, but if you don't, I'll tell you. Selma I convinced myself that I like you an awful lot. We seem to understand each other so well.

I'm awfully glad you came to the depot to see me off. You're wonderful. Better watch out Honey, you're going to have a persistent boyfriend on your hands.

Sel, I got a letter from Hesh—very nice of him to write, but straighten me out on one thing and that's just what goes on between you and him? Just where do I stand compared to him. Please tell me the truth because I'm going to believe whatever you tell me.

I imagine you got my picture by now. I sure hope you like it. It's not too good, but it's supposed to look like me. I'm looking very much forward in getting your picture in fact I can hardly wait.

Texas is the same as ever Honey, except it's a little warmer. Boy I'll bet it's sure going to be hot this summer.

Sweetheart, I want you to take good care of yourself. Don't get too interested in your job. I don't want a schoolteacher on my hands. I'm sure glad you're going to college. Wish I was going with you. Maybe someday we'll be together.

Sel, I have a t.l. for you. Bob, that boy I introduced you to, thought you were a very nice- looking girl. You are Selma. You sure looked swell at the station. Golly listen to me rave about you.

Well sweetheart that's about it for now. Take care Sel, write soon and think of me a lot. Regards to the family.

Love ya,
Bob

Pvt. Bernard D. Browne 39337016
Co. I 410th Inf. A.P.O. 470
Camp Howze, Texas

Miss Selma Nepom
c/o Joseph Lane School
7200 S.E. 60th St.
Portland, 6, Oregon

April 11, 1944

Sweetheart,

Excuse the fancy stationery but it's all I can get my hands on at the present time. I just got off of K.P. and I'm sure tired. Great stuff Sel, I swear I washed 500 dishes, cups, etc. Proud of me Honey?

I got your swell letter this afternoon and boy, you're in. I'm glad to hear that you like Mom. Whether you know it or not, she thinks you're pretty swell too. Golly, already I'm having competition in my own family.

We had a night problem last night. It sure was a honey. We left camp at 7:30 P.M. and returned at 1:45 A.M. We were the enemy and we really did a good job of it. Our machine gun was fired so much it almost got red-hot. We weren't captured though.

I'm glad you liked my picture Sel. I want you to know that you are the only person that has a picture like that of me outside of the family. I feel very much flattered when you say that it outshines all the others—I'm glad though. Sure wish I had yours. We're only allowed to keep one picture out for daily inspection and—well, I'm waiting.

Selma, I miss you a lot. In fact, if I was more sure of the future I would go so far to say that I love you. I'm being silly now aren't I Honey? Sweetheart, take care of yourself and remember that I'm thinking of you always. Golly listen to me—sounds bad doesn't it. Take care Sel and write often.

Love ya,
Bob

Pvt. Bernard D. Browne 39337016
Co. I 410th Inf. A.P.O. 470
Camp Howze, Texas

Miss Selma Nepom
716 S.W. Harrison St.
Portland, 1, Oregon

April 13, 1944

Dear Selma,

Well here I am again. Are you tired of me yet? You'd better not be.

I got your letter this afternoon and listen you, you'd better go to a doctor right away and if you need a rest (which you probably do) take one. Go someplace where it's real quiet and do nothing but relax. I was sure sorry to hear about you being sick. Maybe it's your job Sel. Please feel better and take care of yourself.

We're having a big inspection next Thursday by the commanding General (1 star) of the post. All we do during our spare time is prepare for it. We are only allowed to have issued equipment for inspection, so we have to figure out a place to put all our civilian stuff. They say it's really going to be a toughie.

Last night our company ran the infiltration course. Boy what a course. We have to crawl on our stomachs for 150 yards while machine gun bullets go 18 inches over our heads. What a sensation to see tracer bullets go whizzing over your head. They were really close too. Something else to chalk up to experience.

It got a little cool last night but during the days it's still pretty warm. I'll bet it's really going to be a scorcher this summer.

Quite a few fellows left today on furlough and I'm sure looking forward to mine again. If I have things figured right, I'll be home in August or September. I seem to live from furlough to furlough now—guess why?

Well Honey, I'd better sign off now because lights will be going out soon. Take care of yourself Sweetheart and write real soon.

Love ya,
Bob

PVT. BERNARD D. BROWNE 39337016
CO. I 410TH INF. A.P.O. 470
CAMP HOWZE, TEXAS

MISS SELMA NEPOM
c/o JOSEPH LANE SCHOOL
7200 S.E. 60TH ST.
PORTLAND, 6, OREGON

April 16, 1944

Dear Selma,

Well today is Sunday—just a week ago I got back here and just a week before that I was with you. Boy, the time sure flies doesn't it?

Golly Sel, with all the current news you gave me I'm right up with the gossip column in Portland. You're a swell kid Selma—now don't get swell-head on me.

I'm sorry to hear about Charlotte and her tonsillitis. Tell her she'll get to eat all the ice cream she wants in the hospital. I hope she likes ice cream.

I'm sorry to hear about Bob (Camp Adair). He must like you a lot or he wouldn't keep coming to see you. Don't treat him bad because it's awfully hard on a fella when the girl he likes tries to give him the brush off. On the other hand, don't treat him too nice. I need some agents to watch out for my interest—don't I? Selma believe me it's the same way up here. When I go out with other girls, I don't care how beautiful or nice they are—I'm thinking of you. I'm being frank with you Honey because I think that's the only way to be. I do go out with other girls—I told you that when I was home, but you're still tops. It's the truth. So you see when you go out with other fellows remember that you've got a doughboy in Texas.

I'm glad to hear about Joe Olshen getting a discharge. Golly I haven't seen him in a long time. I'll bet he's really grown up. Tell that wolf to stay away. It sure is awful the way I try to tie you down isn't it. If the guy's a service man, it's alright because they'll leave eventually to some other part of the country. But this permanent stuff is bad. I'm glad he's going to school anyhow.

Not much new around here Selma. We were restricted last night because we have a <u>big</u> inspection coming off next Thursday and we had to start preparing for it. Boy it's really going to be a rough one too.

We had machine gun practice yesterday and I am now asst. gunner in the company. I carry a pistol now instead of a rifle. On problems I also have to carry the machine gun (42 lbs.) which isn't so good. Oh well that's the army, I guess. It's better than being an ordinary rifleman anyhow.

The weather here is really warm. We're now in Sun-tans but it's still warm. I should get used to it soon.

Well Sel, that's about it for now.
Take care and write soon.

Love ya,
Bob

Give my regards to the family.

PVT. BERNARD D. BROWNE 39337016
CO. I 410TH INF. A.P.O. 470
CAMP HOWZE, TEXAS

MISS SELMA NEPOM
c/o LANE SCHOOL
7200 S.E. 60TH ST.
PORTLAND, 6, OREGON

April 17, 1944

Dear Selma,

I got your letter this afternoon and just got back about an hour ago from sending you a wire. I hope you got it alright.

Sel your letter was a killer. Boy I was breathless all the way through it. You sure do use your words beautifully. You're tops kid. You sure did straighten me out on a lot of things—for the better of course. I seem to understand you so much better. Honey, Hesh didn't say a thing to me in his letter about you. I was just curious and wanted to know. Thanks a lot Sweetheart—you sure did a swell job. By the way—don't let type written letters bother you. I like em all just so they're from you. Please don't be nervous Sel—that's bad for a girl your age—maybe you're smoking too much. Take care of yourself Honey.

Honey, I very strongly agree with you on this family business. Parents should be blessed more and more. Let me tell you Sel—you have one wonderful family. Give your mother a big kiss for me. I also agree with you when you say you want a man whom you could share with his family. Technically speaking the family is part of the bargain. You may marry the daughter, but you also have another family in the deal. In a way that's one of the better points of marriage, especially when you get a good family— Boy, listen to me preach—wow!!

Golly Honey, I can't get over your letter—it was a masterpiece. I'll hold onto it—believe me I will. You're wonderful Sweetheart. It seems so funny that I didn't realize it sooner than I did. I wish I knew why. I'm sure glad I'm not too late—I still have to keep on my toes though I guess.

About the picture Sel—send me a 5x7 in a book type folder. That size will be perfect for my shelf. Sure wish it was here. I can hardly wait for it.

That was sure sweet of you to ask me if I needed anything—You're sure swell. Really though Hon, I don't need a thing. To tell you the truth we're restricted so badly that there is very little that I can have. I just ordered some stationery in town Saturday with our divisional patch on it. The quality isn't too sharp but it's about the best you can do in a small army town of 12,000 people. So you see Sel I have plenty of stationery. Sweetheart there's really nothing I need. I had to take a bunch of stuff (civilian) in and check it at the U.S.O. for this big inspection coming off. Great life Honey.

Well Sweet, I'd better sign off now because lights will be out in about 3 minutes. Thinking of you Sel. Write soon and I'll write you tomorrow if I get the chance. Take care Sweet.

Love ya,
Bob

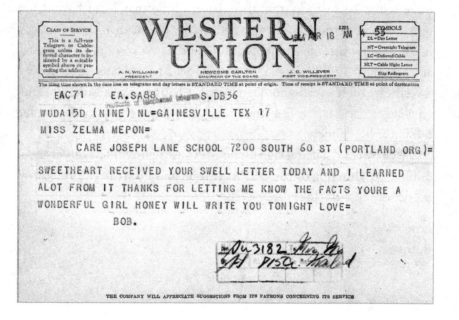

Pvt. Bernard D. Browne 39337016
Co. I 410th Inf. A.P.O. 470
Camp Howze, Texas

Miss Selma Nepom
c/o Lane School
7200 S.E. 60th St.
Portland, 6, Oregon

April 19, 1944

Dear Selma,

I just have a little free time now so I thought I would write to you and let you know that the big inspection is over with. It lasted about 2-1/2 hours and was really tough. I passed it alright personally, but our barracks got gigged for many reasons. I sure am glad it's overwith.

We have a night problem tonight Honey. It will probably last until one or two in the morning. I'll write you and tell you what it's all about. You're probably not too interested in infantry tactics but as a matter of fact I don't like them so well myself.

How are things going Sel? How are you and how is your job? I hope everything is O.K. How are the folks and the rest of the family?

I've got to run now Sweetheart, but I'll write again tomorrow if I get the chance. Please excuse the terrible penmanship. It's one of those bunk deals. Write soon.

Love,
Bob

Pvt. Bernard D. Browne 39337016
Co. I 410th Inf. A.P.O. 470
Camp Howze, Texas

Miss Selma Nepom
c/o Lane School
7200 S.E. 60th St.
Portland, 6, Oregon

April 21, 1944

Dearest Selma,

I got your letter today, but I feel rather selfish because I just can't seem to get you a letter every day. I'll tell you why Sel. We are now going through a night problem stage in training and we have on an average of 4-night problems a week. We really keep busy too. During the day it is almost impossible to write letters. Regardless though Honey, I want you to know that I'm always thinking of you. You're a wonderful person and I still can't figure out why in the heck I didn't realize that a lot sooner. Oh well, I know it now anyhow, I just hope I'm not too late, if you know what I mean. I'm ready for competition just so it doesn't gang up on me.

I like Ruth's stationery very much—I seem to see things while reading your letter. You don't know how much I look forward to your letters. I sure wish I was stationed at Adair. Nothing could stop me then.

I'm glad to hear you got my wire. I sure had a hard time of thinking what to say in it. That letter you wrote really was swell.

I'm also glad to hear that you went to the doctor for a check-up. If there's anything wrong, they'll know what it is.

I got a letter from Lew today and he and his wife spent last weekend with Besse & Dave. They sure had a swell time laying around on the beach. Wouldn't that be swell if I could come home so that we could go to the beach this summer. Boy we should really look forward to something like that. We sure could have a swell time. Just wait till this mess is over with. I'll prove it to you.

Not much new in this part of the country—I don't think it will ever change. We had a pretty rough day today and to tell you the truth—I'm a little bit tired.

I hope you're not changing your mind about college Honey. You'll have plenty opportunity to work later in life—why do it now? Go to school Sel. With your brain you'll really get a lot out of it. I hope you don't meet any real nice fellas though. There I go again, being selfish. I think you know what I mean though.

Well Sweetheart, I hate to cut this letter short but I'd better if I want to make retreat in time. I'll write again tomorrow for sure. Take care Honey and think of me because I'm thinking an awful lot of you.

Regards to all and my congratulations to Charlotte.

Loads of love,
Bob

USO

7/23/44

Dearest Selma,

Guess what I just saw about two
hours ago? It was a typical Texan Rodeo.
Five of us fellows came to Denton, Texas (30
miles away) this morning to see it. Boy
it was really the ~~well~~ real thing. They
had everything from cow milking to steer
roping. Great people these Texans when it
comes to Rodeos.

How are things with you Sel? Anything
new happening around town?

We went to a U.S.O. dance last night
and had a pretty nice time. They sure do
treat you swell. I met a hostess there (married
and 28 years old) who use to live in Portland
so we had a lovely time talking all about
Portland. Guess who I was thinking of all

THE YOUNG MEN'S CHRISTIAN ASSOCIATIONS • THE NATIONAL CATHOLIC COMMUNITY SERVICE
THE SALVATION ARMY • THE YOUNG WOMEN'S CHRISTIAN ASSOCIATIONS
THE JEWISH WELFARE BOARD • THE NATIONAL TRAVELERS AID ASSOCIATION

that time. You - remember?

Nothing new Sel, everything is the same as ever except that it's getting hot as h---. It's a sticky heat and all during the day and night it seems to be damp and sticky.

We're starting back for the Post as soon as I finish this letter. These guys won't leave me alone. All they keep teasing me about is Selma. They seem to think alot of you because I told them all about you. Great bunch of fellas Sel - they're all Jewish and we really have a great time together.

Well Henry, I'd better sign off for now. Take care of yourself and don't work too hard.

Love, ya,
Bob

THE YOUNG MEN'S CHRISTIAN ASSOCIATIONS • THE NATIONAL CATHOLIC COMMUNITY SERVICE
THE SALVATION ARMY • THE YOUNG WOMEN'S CHRISTIAN ASSOCIATIONS
THE JEWISH WELFARE BOARD • THE NATIONAL TRAVELERS AID ASSOCIATION

Pvt. Bernard D. Browne 39337016
Co. I 410th Inf. A.P.O. 470
Camp Howze, Texas

Miss Selma Nepom
c/o Lane School
7200 S.E. 60th St.
Portland, 6, Oregon

April 23, 1944

Dearest Selma,

Guess what I just saw about two hours ago? It was a typical Texan Rodeo. Five of us fellows came to Denton, Texas (30 miles away) this morning to see it. Boy it was really the real thing. They had everything from cow milking to steer roping. Great people these Texans when it comes to Rodeos.

How are things with you Sel? Anything new happening around town?

We went to a U.S.O. dance last night and had a pretty nice time. They sure do treat you swell. I met a hostess there (married and 28 years old) who use to live in Portland, so we had a lovely time talking all about Portland. Guess who I was thinking of all that time. You—remember? Nothing new Sel, everything is the same as ever except that it's getting hot as h---. It's a sticky heat and all during the day and night it seems to be damp and sticky.

We're starting back for the Post as soon as I finish this letter. These guys won't leave me alone. All they keep teasing me about is Selma. They seem to think a lot of you because I told them all about you. Great bunch of fellas Sel—they're all Jewish and we really have a great time together.

Well Honey, I'd better sign off for now. Take care of yourself and don't work too hard.

Love ya,
Bob

PVT. BERNARD D. BROWNE 39337016
CO. I 410TH INF. A.P.O. 470
CAMP HOWZE, TEXAS

MISS SELMA NEPOM
c/o LANE SCHOOL
7200 S.E. 60TH ST.
PORTLAND, 6, OREGON

April 24, 1944

Dear Selma,

I got your letter today and I'm answering it right now—the first chance I got. I spun one off to the folks before this but I'm following it up with one to you. This is the last chance I'll have to write at all until Friday. Boy have we got a schedule for the rest of this week. Tomorrow night we have a compass course at night. Wednesday and Thursday we spend out in the field. We have an all night problem and we sleep during the day out in the field. We get back to camp about 10:30 A.M. Friday morning. Great sport Honey—ha, ha.

That was certainly a swell letter you wrote. Golly, you certainly know how to do it—it hits me hard. About being serious Sweet— well here goes—I hope you agree with me. You and I are still both young—in our minds we are much older than we really are, but we are still pretty young. I want you to know Sel, that if it wasn't for this war and I was home for good I would surely start planning things. But planning such things is a serious thing. First of all I want to have a future and something to look forward to for all types of support. That is the most important thing, don't you think? I imagine everyone wants to be happy and comfortable after they are married and that's one thing I want to be sure of before I jump into anything. I'm sure you understand Sweetheart. If this damn war would only end soon. If I happen to go across, I'm sure I would change my mind about a lot of things. Sel you're a perfect girl and as you should know by now, I am very fond of you. I'll prove it too, if I ever get the chance and believe me, I'm looking forward to that chance.

I'm glad you took your picture. I know it will come out good. I'll be waiting Sweetheart.

I guess things are just fine at work. That 21 year old deal sounds like a nice girl. I didn't think school teachers are like that.

Nothing new in Texas Sweet. Next week is going to be another one of those rough weeks. We start our proficiency tests and one of the toughest physical strains is to march 5 miles in 55 minutes with full field equipment (40 lbs.) I'm not worried though. I figure if half of these old men around here can do it, I surely can. I'll write you all about them after we've finished.

Well Honey, I guess that's about the dope for now. Take care and write me.

All yours,
Bob

PVT. BERNARD D. BROWNE 39337016
CO. I 410TH INF. A.P.O. 470
CAMP HOWZE, TEXAS

MISS SELMA NEPOM
c/o LANE SCHOOL
7200 S.E. 60TH ST.
PORTLAND, 6, OREGON

April 25, 1944

Sweetheart,

I received another one of those wonderful letters today and I'm answering it now because I won't be able to write for the next two days.

Say Hon, I'm glad I'm so popular at school. You know how well I get along with all the little kiddies. I'm glad to know I'm so important though.

Selma I'm glad to know that you don't mind me telling you when I go out with other girls. Even if I didn't tell you, you would know it, because it's only natural. It's a proof of my fondness toward you. If I didn't care for you it would be silly for me to mention anything to you about other girls. See what I mean. The next time you mention anything about a "truer love" I'm going to spank you good. You shouldn't even think of anything like that. The only reason I go out with other girls (once or twice a month) is to get my mind away from the Army. I don't even think of loving or even liking the girl I take out. It would be different if I didn't have you to look forward to, but the Army gets me down so often that I just have to get away and try to forget it all. Please understand Honey. Don't ever say anything like that again Sel. There's no reason for it. Besides I think I'm the one that's going to have to watch out. There are an awful lot of fellas in Portland now and they'd give anything to get to know a swell girl like you. Please love me Sweetheart. I want you to know that whenever I go out with girls nothing goes on between us. It's just the same to me as going out with another fella in civy clothes. Please believe me Sel.

I think I understand you, all that I can. I only wish we could be together more. I think we're both being cheated by being so far apart. Just wait for this damn mess to end. If I know myself right, you won't have a minute to spare. Sel do you understand me. Our families have been very close all our lives, but if you're not sure you know what I'm like, let me know. As for you—well, let me take care of you.

I'm glad your Dad went to San Francisco. That sure is a rip-roaring city now.

Well Sweet, that's about it for now. Take care and I'll say good night—

Love,
Bob

Pvt. Bernard D. Browne 39337016
Co. I 410th Inf. A.P.O. 470
Camp Howze, Texas

Miss Selma Nepom
c/o Lane School
7200 S.E. 60th St.
Portland, 6, Oregon

April 28, 1944

Sweetheart,

Well we finally got back and it sure feels good. We got back about 4:00 P.M. today filthy as a pig, but I'm all cleaned up now and my thoughts are with you. We had quite a time out there in the woods. We hiked about 22 miles and captured (??) 14 objectives. Sure was rough. We slept out in the woods two nights and both nights were beautiful. The sky was full of stars and a great big moon. It sure is peaceful out there at night but it's a holy terror during the day.

Honey I'm sending you a snap that I just found mixed in with my stationery. It is one that was taken in front of the college hang-out while I was at school. How about some of you Sweetheart. Some Sunday when you aren't doing anything take some snaps. I sure would like to have some to keep in my billfold. I'm sure looking forward to your picture Honey.

Say that new outfit of yours sure sounds swell. Boy I'd give a million to see you in it. I'd give a million to see you.

I got a letter from Bobby today and I guess he got the same medicine that I got. He got taken out of Cadet training and is now in the Air Corp as a private. Sure are a lot of us in this army. I just hope he stays in the Air Corp and doesn't get shoved into some other branch of the service. As long as he's in the Air Corp he's pretty well out of danger and promotions are much better there than any other outfit. It sure is too bad though.

I imagine your father is really taking a trip. I'll bet he's sure going to get kidded about going to Reno. Tell your Mom not to worry about a divorce— she's always got me to fall back on.

Well Sweet, that's about the deal for now. Take care and write soon. Give my best to the family. I'll write again tomorrow if possible. Good night Sel.

Love ya lots,
Bob

Pvt. Bernard D. Browne 39337016
Co. I 410th Inf. A.P.O. 470
Camp Howze, Texas

Miss Selma Nepom
716 S.W. Harrison St.
Portland, 1, Oregon

.... *April 29, 1944*

Dear Selma,

Well here I am again. I hope you don't get tired of me. I'm writing you as much as possible over the weekend because next week I may not have much of a chance. I found out this morning that we have an eleven-day field problem coming up in about two weeks or so. That means we spend 11 days in the woods of Texas going through tactical problems. Our position is supposed to be about 70 miles from here. Sure hope I'll be able to write. I think we'll have enough time.

I'm glad to hear that you're going to the beach when school is out. Sure wish I could go with you Honey.

I'm also glad to hear that you also have that traveling blood in you. One thing I always wanted to do and that's drive all through the states and see everything. I accept your cordial invite and I sure hope it will be possible someday. Traveling, I think, is an education in itself. I sure do like it.

I came to the Service Club today with the fellas to get a good meal—well, anyhow it's good compared to the company meals. We come here every Sat. night for that purpose.

They have some wonderful classical record albums and all I do is play them in the record room. They got a new one last week, "Brahms concerto in B flat minor" and it sure is beautiful. My favorite is still Rimsky Korsakoff's "Scheherazade Suite." It's another beauty. These clubs are really nice, but they sure do make a fella homesick.

I got a letter from Hesh today Sweet, and he plans to be home soon. He seems to be getting along fine at school and likes New Jersey a lot. He's got a pretty good set-up I guess.

Well Sweetheart I guess that's about it for now. Please excuse the scribbling. I miss you and think of you always.

I love you,
Bob

PVT. BERNARD D. BROWNE 39337016
CO. I 410TH INF. A.P.O. 470
CAMP HOWZE, TEXAS

MISS SELMA NEPOM
c/o LANE SCHOOL
7200 S.E. 60TH ST.
PORTLAND, 6, OREGON

May 2, 1944

Dear Selma,

Well by the looks of things I guess you've already gathered that I'm in the field again. We came out last night and will stay until Thursday night. It rained pretty hard last night, and we got kind of wet in those tents, but we are all dried out now—thanks to the sun.

Boy this is sure a rugged life. It's just like boy-scouts only a little more discipline, ha ha!!

We are supposed to start a dawn attack tomorrow morning. Today we are digging in and getting prepared just in case the enemy should attack us first. Everything out here is tactical. No loud talking or anything. No smoking at night. We got up at 4:00 A.M. for breakfast. I still don't know what I was eating. We're out about 75 miles from camp somewhere in Oklahoma.

Well Sel how's the job and school? We're not allowed to receive any mail out here but I hope to have some from you when I get in.

I got a letter from Junne yesterday (Lew's wife) and she tells me that her girlfriend's husband is stationed here. He's a captain in the Tank Corp. I looked him up but he had left for overseas 3 days ago. Boy they sure do send em out fast here. We have a bunch leaving (old men) our company in a week or two. I guess one of these days my turn will come. I've got to see you though, before that time comes. They should give me a furlough. They'd better.

Well, Sweetheart, I don't have much more time, so I'd better kiss it off. Be good Honey and don't work too hard. Sounds like a wonderful job with all those kids.

Love,
Bob

Bernard D. Browne Co. I - 410th Inf. A. P. O. 470

Camp Howze, Texas

May 4, 1944

Sweetheart,

We just got off from the field about two hours ago and Honey I'm really dead tired. We sure had it rough out there. That's field work I guess. By the looks of things I think we're switching from night problems to field problems. We leave again next Monday for three days—return for one—and then go out once more for seven days. It's going to be tough Sweet, because I won't be able to write to you as much as I would want to. I'll write you though, as much as possible while in camp. If you don't hear from me every once in a while you'll know that I'm out with the natural life of Texas. It sure is awful.

I love you Selma. I hope everything is fine at home and that Portland is keeping up with her reputation. This may sound pretty silly for a guy like me to say, but whenever I'm in bed or just relaxing I'm always thinking of you. I sure wish we could be together more. I think I'm safe to say that we both seem to be a pair. We understand each other perfectly and that's half of it right there

Honey I'm awfully tired tonight so please excuse the awful penmanship. I'm doing my best to keep awake.

I'm scheduled to go on Guard Duty this Saturday. It's a 24 hour shift so I'll be on Saturday and Sunday. I'm hoping to be a prisoner guard over the German Prisoners of War. In any respect I'll write you from the Guard House and tell you all about it.

Well sweetheart I hate to cut this off now but I'd better get some shut-eye. I'll write again when possible.

Yours with love,
Bob

PVT. BERNARD D. BROWNE 39337016
CO. I 410TH INF. A.P.O. 470
CAMP HOWZE, TEXAS

MISS SELMA NEPOM
c/o LANE SCHOOL
6700 S.E. 60TH ST.
PORTLAND, 6, OREGON

May 4, 1944

Sweetheart,

We just got off from the field about two hours ago and Honey I'm really dead tired. We sure had it rough out there. That's field work, I guess. By the looks of things, I think we're switching from night problems to field problems. We leave again next Monday for three days—return for one—and then go out once more for seven days. It's going to be tough Sweet, because I won't be able to write to you as much as I would want to. I'll write you though, as much as possible while in camp. If you don't hear from me every once in a while you'll know that I'm out with the natural life of Texas. It sure is awful.

I love you Selma. I hope everything is fine at home and that Portland is keeping up with her reputation. This may sound pretty silly for a guy like me to say, but whenever I'm in bed or just relaxing I'm always thinking of you. I sure wish we could be together more. I think I'm safe to say that we both seem to be a pair. We understand each other perfectly and that's half of it right there.

Honey I'm awfully tired tonight so please excuse the awful penmanship. I'm doing my best to keep awake.

I'm scheduled to go on Guard Duty this Saturday. It's a 24-hour shift so I'll be on Saturday and Sunday. I'm hoping to be a prisoner guard over the German Prisoners of War. In any respect I'll write you from the Guard House and tell you all about it.

Well Sweetheart I hate to cut this off now but I'd better get some shut-eye. I'll write again when possible.

Yours with love,
Bob

Pvt. Bernard D. Browne 39337016
Co. I 410th Inf. A.P.O. 470
Camp Howze, Texas

Miss Selma Nepom
716 S.W. Harrison St.
Portland, 1, Oregon

May 5, 1944

Dearest Selma,

Honey I haven't received any mail from you for the past three days. What's up Sel? Your probably pretty busy. I miss your letters. I guess I know how you feel when you don't get any from me. I sure wish I could write you more, but I just don't have the time. The only time we have free for writing is at night and some nights we have details etc. I expect to be going out in the field again soon and that is worse than ever. I wrote you one letter from the outpost that I was posted at. I gave it to one of the cooks to mail when he got back to camp. It's really pretty tough to write while you're out like that. You know that I would if I could though.

Well Honey, there isn't much new around here. We had a Divisional Parade today and it sure was a beauty—they tell me. A sergeant was awarded the Silver Star for gallantry in action in Tunisia. A two-star general pinned it on him.

I sent you a bottle of cologne when I went to town the other night. I hope you get it alright. It's a little gift from me to you Sweetheart. I tried a lot of them but I seemed to like it best of all. I hope you do too. I got Mom four hand rolled linen handkerchiefs. I think she'll like them. One of them was red, white, and blue—had a spread eagle in one corner and two service stars in the other. It was really nice.

We got in a few air cadets yesterday and those poor guys sure are unhappy. We should have quite a few of them here soon. Sure feel sorry for em.

I'm on guard duty this weekend and I just finished cleaning my pistol for tomorrow's guard inspection. I hope it stays clean.

Honey, that's about it for now. Hope to hear from you soon. Regards to the family and my love to you.

Your own,
Bob

Pvt. Bernard D. Browne 39337016
Co. I 410th Inf. A.P.O. 470
Camp Howze, Texas

Miss Selma Nepom
c/o Lane School
7200 S.E. 60th St.
Portland, 6, Oregon

May 5, 1944

Dear Selma,

I wrote you a so called letter last night and to be truthful I don't know how I ever did it. I was so tired that I even forgot what I wrote to you.

I'm sorry I didn't write to you sooner Honey but I was out in the field and it's really hard to get any mail out or in. By the looks of things we're going to have a lot of field work in the future. Our cycle of training seemed to change from night work to field work. Next week we go out again for about three days, come back, and then go out again for a week. That's all of the schedule I've seen so far but that's enough.

There really isn't too much doing around here. Today we ran the Army Ground Force Physical Exams and they sure were rugged. We hiked four miles in 40 minutes which is really making fast time. We ran practically all the way. We had to wear full field equipment which didn't help matters at all.

I put in for a pass to town tonight so that I can buy something for Mom. I got her a beautiful card about a week ago and now I want to get something to go with it. Sure wish I was home for Mother's Day.

We got some Air Cadets in this morning who, like us, were taken out of school and put into the infantry. Golly, I sure feel sorry for those fellows. I know just how they feel. They sure are putting a lot of men into the infantry, why—I don't know. I guess they need them though. Those poor fellows walk around here like they're lost in the fog. Some of them haven't even seen a rifle before.

A bunch of old men took physical exams this morning for P.O.E. shipment, so I imagine they'll be overseas soon. The way the rumors go, all A.S.T.P.'s and Air Corp men will train and leave together. I sure hope so. You don't realize how ignorant some of these Doughboys are. Believe it or not, some of them can't even write their own names.

Well Sweetheart, I guess that's it for now. I hope everything is fine with you. I'll write again tomorrow if possible. Write Honey.

Love,
Bob

PVT. BERNARD D. BROWNE 39337016
CO. I 410TH INF. A.P.O. 470
CAMP HOWZE, TEXAS

MISS SELMA NEPOM
c/o LANE SCHOOL
7200 S.E. 60TH ST.
PORTLAND, 6, OREGON

May 7, 1944

Dear Selma,

I got your letters yesterday and was sure glad to get them. One of your letters was missent to Abilene, Tex., but it finally caught up with me. That's why I got two at the same time.

You're wonderful Honey—your letters are just the way I want them to be. I'm glad to hear that you are a great believer in fate because so am I. I figure what should happen is going to happen and no power on earth can stop it. I hope that's true because I think you and I will be together one of these days. It's hard to tell but that's the way I would want it. Let's hope fate is on our side. I think it is.

Well Honey I just finished Guard Duty about an hour ago and I just got through shaving so that I could go to the show with a couple of the fellows. "Between Two Worlds" is on and it's supposed to be pretty good.

Not much new at camp—same old stuff. Soldiers, soldiers everywhere.

I'm glad to hear that Hesh will be home soon. I'll bet he'll sure be glad to see you. Show him a good time Sel, but not too good. Oh, OK, there goes that green streak again. I'm sorry—I'm just jealous, I guess. I'll bet he'll sure be glad to get home. He's been a long way from home. I know how he feels. He's got a good radio deal out of it which should help him quite a bit when he's through with school.

Yes, Banny wrote me about Ben Cohn getting his discharge. I'm sure glad to both of them. They can both really settle down now and plan things. I wonder what he'll do.

Well Sel, I guess that's it for now. I'll write again when possible.

Love,
Bob

Pvt. Bernard D. Browne 39337016
Co. I 410th Inf. A.P.O. 470
Camp Howze, Texas

Miss Selma Nepom
c/o Lane School
7200 S.E. 60th St.
Portland, 6, Oregon

May 8, 1944

Sweetheart,

I got your letter today and you sure are wonderful. I seem to go for you more and more every day. See what you're doing to me?

I'm glad to hear of the success of the carnival. They really did alright. I'm proud of you all.

I'm also glad to hear that you had your fortune told. I sure hope it's true because if it is, I should be coming home sometime before Christmas. Boy, I would like nothing better. Keep praying Honey, we'll be together one of these days, you just wait and see.

Well, I found out that we leave for the field next Monday for sure. We are scheduled to stay out for 12 days. I'll manage to write to you somehow. They may not be the neatest letters, but I'll keep in touch with you anyhow.

We went through the gas chamber today and had quite a time. We had all the poisonous gases thrown at us but they didn't bother us if our gas masks were adjusted and I saw to it that mine was adjusted. Some of the fellows had a little trouble though and had to keep going through until the gas didn't bother them. Sure is tough stuff to take.

Selma—I agree with you when you say we had such a wonderful time that one night. I found out that you and I are very much alike. To be frank—that night sort of knocked me out. I seemed to fall for you like a ton of bricks. I had no idea that I would—but I did. You're a wonderful girl Sel and I love you more than you think. You're so thoughtful and unselfish and everything. I just hope nobody beats me to the punch. Sure wish I was closer to you so I wouldn't have to worry about invaders.

Well Sweet, I'd better go to bed now. I think of you a lot and love you more.

Your own,
Bob

Pvt. Bernard D. Browne 39337016
Co. I 410th Inf. A.P.O. 470
Camp Howze, Texas

Miss Selma Nepom
c/o Lane School
7200 S.E. 60th St.
Portland, 6, Oregon

May 10, 1944

Dear Selma,

Just a line to let you know that your Texan is still here thinking of you. We had quite a heat spell the last couple of days. I got a short haircut Honey and it's only about ½ an inch long on top. If you saw me, you would scream. It's much cooler that way though, and I guess that's all that counts. I sure hated to do it though.

We spent all day today out in the drill field going through gun drill and all that stuff. We didn't learn much—all we got out of it was getting tired. We had a couple of fellows pass-out because of the heat today so I guess they'll start feeding us salt tablets soon.

We lost 18 fellows today who were sent to Fort Dix, N.J. They'll probably be sent across from there. They sure are clearing out this regiment in a hurry. I guess they have to make way for the Air Cadets that are coming in regularly. We got three more in our company today. Those poor guys are really getting it in the neck. I sure hope Bobby doesn't have to come into the infantry. I don't think he will because he has had no ground force training.

Well Sweetheart—not much more to say except that you're always in my mind. I think of you constantly Sel, really I do. I miss you Honey and I'm looking forward to the day when we'll be able to get together again. Take care Sweet and write soon.

Yours to love,
Bob

Pvt. Bernard D. Browne 39337016
Co. I 410th Inf. A.P.O. 470
Camp Howze, Texas

Miss Selma Nepom
716 S.W. Harrison St.
Portland, 1, Oregon

May 11, 1944

Dearest Selma,

I came to town tonight because I had to mail a bunch of stuff to the folks. My father's birthday is the 29th of this month so I got him a swell after shave set. He loves Yardleys-so I got him a beautiful set. For a while I didn't know what to get.

As you can see, I'm writing you from the Soldiers Juke Joint "The U.S.O." A couple of the fellows came in with me and at present they're having a dashing game of ping pong. They can't figure out why I write you so often. They keep telling me I've got it bad. They're right too. I can hardly wait until I get your picture, so I can show them what I have to look forward to. One of the fellows is practically engaged himself. He keeps asking me—when? He says when I do he'll also do it. He's got his ring all ready and everything.

Not much new Honey. The boys at camp had a big beer party tonight so I imagine when we get back Co. I will be completely out. Oh, what a morning they'll have tomorrow.

Well Sweet—that's it for now. Those guys won't leave me at peace for a minute. Take care Sel and write.

Love you,
Bob

PVT. BERNARD D. BROWNE 39337016
CO. I 410TH INF. A.P.O. 470
CAMP HOWZE, TEXAS

MISS SELMA NEPOM
c/o LANE SCHOOL
7200 S.E. 60TH ST.
PORTLAND, 6, OREGON

May 14, 1944

Dearest Selma,

I started a letter to you last night but didn't have time to finish it, so I'm starting a new one today.

I got a swell letter from you yesterday and I was glad to hear that you got the cologne alright. For a while I had my doubts about it getting there in one piece.

I put in a call for home 5 hours ago, but the way things look I don't think I'll ever get through. The telephone system sure is the bank around here.

As far as going overseas, I am qualified. If and when well, you know just as much about that as I do. We really don't know what's going to happen from one day to the next. That's the Army though.

I got a letter from Bobby today and he is stationed at Sioux Falls, South Dakota. He starts radio school tomorrow. He doesn't like that part of the country at all. It's not much like Washington. You just can't beat the West Coast.

Well, we're still having this damn heat here. It struck 92° yesterday and it was really a scorcher. I can just imagine what it's going to be like in July and August. We had two problems last week and the heat really made work out of them. We feel much better though after we've come back and taken a shower. Just like new.

Well Honey that's about it for now. Take it easy and write again quick-like.

I love you,
Bob

PVT. BERNARD D. BROWNE 39337016
CO. I 410TH INF. A.P.O. 470
CAMP HOWZE, TEXAS

MISS SELMA NEPOM
716 S.W. HARRISON ST.
PORTLAND, 1, OREGON

May 15, 1944

Dearest Selma,

Just a line to let you know that all is well, and we didn't leave for the field today. The reason—because so many fellows are leaving for over-seas duty. More than half of our company are leaving and they are all privates. I was hoping some non-coms would leave so that I would have something to work for—but I guess I'll be a Pvt. for my entire military career. They sure did take a bunch out though.

Honey, I got a letter from Monte Chusid today and he is going home on furlough again. He was just home when I was. He's either awfully lucky or he's going over-seas soon. I hope it's the former. He's sort of worried about it though, but even if he does go over he'll have a nice office to work in and won't be fighting on the front lines. He'll be safe enough.

It got a little cooler today, thank goodness, but I don't think it will last long. We'll probably start taking salt tablets soon to replace the salt that we lose through perspiration.

Well Sweetheart, how's the job coming along? I hope everything is alright.

Selma, guess what I thought of last night? It's practically an impossibility but I'll tell you regardless. I thought how nice it would be if you could come down this Summer. It sure would be wonderful to see you and be with you. No fooling Sweet, I can hardly wait till my next furlough comes up. I'm constantly thinking of you Sel—I've really got it bad—no foolin. I'm hoping to get a furlough sometime in September, but you know how the Army is.

Well Sweet, I'd better get some sleep now. We should have a pretty big day tomorrow. Regards to the family.

Love,
Bob

PVT. BERNARD D. BROWNE 39337016
CO. I 410TH INF. A.P.O. 470
CAMP HOWZE, TEXAS

MISS SELMA NEPOM
c/o LANE SCHOOL
7200 S.E. 60TH ST.
PORTLAND, 6, OREGON

May 18, 1944
Somewhere in Texas—damned if I know where

Dear Selma,

Well here I am Honey, with the birds and the bees and all the trees. I'm as close to nature as I can get. So far it isn't too bad but the next few days should be pretty rough. I know we'll be moving around quite a bit. We've been loading ammunition all morning so I guess things will start popping soon.

We arrived here yesterday morning and will be here until about next Friday—all in all, about 10 days. I'll write you whenever I get the chance. I hope it will be every day.

Well Sweetheart, how's the job coming along. I imagine you'll be through soon for the summer vacation. Just think of the rest you'll be able to take. You'll probably get another job—if I know you. Selma, have you decided to go to college? I hope you have. You're still young and that's the best time to go to school. You'll have plenty of time to work later, if you want to.

Well Sweet, I'd better get back to work for a little while. I'll write to you tomorrow if I can. Regards from all the birds and the bees.

Yours with love,
Bob

Pvt. Bernard D. Browne 39337016
Co. I 410th Inf. A.P.O. 470
Camp Howze, Texas

Miss Selma Nepom
716 S.W. Harrison St.
Portland, 1, Oregon

May 19, 1944

Dear Selma,

I got two wonderful letters from you today and you sure are swell. You're so thoughtful and everything. I got that poem and it sure does help. A poem like that can almost fit in anyplace.

I was glad to hear that you are getting along O.K. I'm sure glad you got some more stationery. I love nothing better than a girl that watches small things like that, because in reality they really mean a lot. Also, I like the way you always watch your clothes—Honey you're tops and I want you to know that I think so. I mean it Sel.

Golly Oceanside sure does sound wonderful. We'll go there the first chance I get. Sure hope it won't be long.

I like the sound of their home. Just like I want someday.

Well Sell, we're still out here playing games. We got up at 2:00 in the morning this morning and hiked for 3 hrs. in order to get away from the enemy. We got to sleep about 10:00 A.M. after digging in and everything.

Sweetheart, that's it for now. Take care and I'll write tomorrow if possible.

Love,
Bob

Poem for today:

I love you dear with all my heart;

Once together we shall not part;

For parting only brings sweet sorrow;

And I'll love you far beyond tomorrow.

Hope you like poetry Sel—

PVT. BERNARD D. BROWNE 39337016
CO. I 410TH INF. A.P.O. 470
CAMP HOWZE, TEXAS

MISS SELMA NEPOM
716 S.W. HARRISON
PORTLAND, 1, OREGON

May 21, 1944

Dear Selma,

Well here I am back at camp again and it sure is swell to get all cleaned up. I just got up from a nap and I sure as h--- hate to go out again tomorrow. By-the-way Sel I doubt whether I'll be able to write to you next week, because it's going to be very tactical and we'll probably be on the go all day long. I'll write you though, as soon as I get back to camp.

Sel, I love your stationery. It's really sharp. I got your picture in today's mail—wow! what glamour. I like it a lot Honey. Thanks loads. I've got it in a position where I can see it all the time. You sure are swell.

Sweetheart, I don't mind at all if you showed my letter to Hesh. Remember though Hon, those letters are for you and no one else. If it cleared things up though, that's all that counts. I sure hope you didn't hurt him. He is a swell fellow—I've always thought so, but you belong to me and no one else. Aren't I selfish though? Sure wish I could be with you. That day will come though.

We're still getting more and more fellows in all the time who are replacing those who have left. I guess they're turning this place into a real replacement depot. With all the non-coms coming in I guess I'll never get a rating.

Well Sel, that's about it for now. Write to me and I'll answer as soon as I get back to camp. Thanks again for the picture Hon.

Yours to keep,
Bob

Poem for today (Sunday):

It isn't as often that a guy like me,
Finds himself in love, you see;
But to be in love with a girl like you,
Is the answer to a prayer of which God only knew.

(When they start getting corny, let me know)

Pvt. Bernard D. Browne 39337016
Co. I 410th Inf. A.P.O. 470
Camp Howze, Texas

Miss Selma Nepom
7200 S.E. 60th St.
Portland, 6, Oregon

May 24, 1944

Dearest Selma,

Well here we are back at camp again. Just like playing games. I got your letters Sel and I sure love to hear from you.

We'll be in until Friday, when we'll go out until Sunday afternoon. They sure do mangle our weekends. Oh well—who cares.

Say that walking business really sounds like fun. You'll have to try it on me when I get home. Gee Honey, I hope it's soon. I do want to be with you so bad.

The mercury is up again, believe me. Our clothes were just wringing wet when we got through today, and it's only May. Sure hope I get used to it soon.

We got in a big bunch of A.C. today and most of them left on furlough. One good thing about this camp and that is that they see to it that you get a furlough app. every six months. That means I'll be home in September.

Well Sweetheart, I'd better go to bed now. I'm thinking of you constantly, with all my love.

Yours to be,
Bob
P.S. See "Tender Comrade" when it comes. It's sad but very very good for you and I to see.

PVT. BERNARD D. BROWNE 39337016
CO. I 410TH INF. A.P.O. 470
CAMP HOWZE, TEXAS

MISS SELMA NEPOM
716 S.W. HARRISON ST.
PORTLAND, 1, OREGON

·· *May 26, 1944*

Dearest Sel,

Well Doll, we're here in the barracks waiting to move out for our problem. We'll probably leave in a couple of hours.

I received the box of candy you sent and it sure is wonderful. You sure are a peach. No foolin Sel, that candy is very good. You just can't buy good candy anywhere in the South. All they have is junk. Thanks an awful lot Honey, it's greatly appreciated.

It's been raining here for the past couple of days and it really got nice and cool. It seems that it gets so hot here that they just have to have a storm of some kind to break the heat. I love rain—I should, I was born and raised in it. It's pretty bad though when you have to go out in it. We always get soaked.

You should see this place. Everyone is practically asleep. They've got a tough problem ahead of us—they tell us. Next week we have a problem in which we follow tanks for an attack. It should be interesting. I'll write you and tell you all about it.

Selma, please stop worrying about your picture. I like it. It's of you and that's all that counts. I'm also looking forward to those snapshots so that I'll have something for my billfold.

Well Doll, that's about it for now. I want to get a little sleep before we leave so I'll say so-long for now. I'll write when I get back—Sunday or Monday.

Yours with love,
Bob

PVT. BERNARD D. BROWNE 39337016
CO. I 410TH INF. A.P.O. 470
CAMP HOWZE, TEXAS

MISS SELMA NEPOM
716 S.W. HARRISON ST.
PORTLAND, 1, OREGON

·· *May 27, 1944*

Sweetheart,

We got off of the field today about 4:30 P.M. and a bunch of us fellows came to the U.S.O. to spend some time. They're having a dance tonight, but I would much rather write to you.

I got a swell letter from you today Sel. I'm sure glad to hear that you're going to U. of W. It's a wonderful school. I sure wish I could be with you. I'm scared of all those wolves up there. Honey I don't want to keep you from going out with other fellows and having a good time, but I want you to remember that you belong to me and nobody else. We have to go out once in awhile or we'll go crazy but as long as we understand each other that's all that counts. You're mine and I'm not going to allow anyone else to take you from me. I sure am selfish, aren't I?

We had quite a time in the field. We got soaked by rain, but, as always, we dried out eventually.

Golly I sure am glad you'll be in a Sorority. It sounds like a much better deal up there.

Not much doing around here at present. Thanks to the rain it is a little cooler. It will probably get hot though, soon enough.

Well Doll, if everything goes well, I should get home sometime in September. That's the day I'm sure looking forward to.

I got a letter from Lew today and he's still flying everywhere. He ferries the new B-29 and he says they really are big boats. He sure loves it though.

I guess that's it for tonight Doll. Give my regards to all and I'm in love with you—sshh!!

Yours,
Bob

Pvt. Bernard D. Browne 39337016
Co. I 410th Inf. A.P.O. 470
Camp Howze, Texas

Miss Selma Nepom
716 S.W. Harrison St.
Portland, 1, Oregon
May 29, 1944

Dearest Doll,

I received two of your letters today and here I am right back at you.

Golly, I'm sure glad to hear that you're going to the beach. No fooling, I would give anything to be with you. Get a real good tan. Say hello to the old place for me.

Today we had it pretty easy for once. We got all our equipment and weapons cleaned up for a big inspection which will come off soon. That means we'll be in garrison for a while anyhow, thank goodness.

When I get home on my next furlough it would really be swell if we could go to the beach together. Maybe we could make a big party out of it. Something to look forward to anyhow.

Honey, Banny is feeling just fine. For a while she was pretty woozy but that's all over with now. She and I are both praying for a boy, Dave wants a girl. I think it will be sometime in August. I'm hoping it will be on my birthday. Just think Doll, I'll be an uncle. Sure sounds funny. Why don't you call her up sometimes Sel—she would like that.

Well Hon, not much new here—as for heat—well, it's hot as hell. I imagine they'll start giving us salt tablets soon. We're sure going to need them.

I tried to call the folks again last Sunday, but it's just impossible to get through within 8 hrs. I guess my letters will have to do the trick until furlough time.

Well Doll, I'll write again tomorrow if all goes well. Have fun and give my regards to all.

Love,
Bob

P.S. Excuse messy letter Honey.

Pvt. Bernard D. Browne 39337016
Co. I 410th Inf. A.P.O. 470
Camp Howze, Texas

Miss Selma Nepom
716 S.W. Harrison St.
Portland, 1, Oregon

May 30, 1944

Dear Selma,

Here I am again Honey, still at it and I like nothing better. I have hopes of not going out this week—sure would be swell.

We had a tank problem today and it sure was a Honey. We worked right along with the tanks on making an attack. On rough terrain we rode on them. What a thrill. Those babies sure are powerful. It sure gives you a funny feeling to be riding along and all of a sudden you hit a tree and down goes the tree. I sure wouldn't want to be in the tank corp though. You're always couped up in very little space and it sure does get hot in those things.

The tank that we had with our platoon was a General Sherman heavy tank. It weighs 30 tons and is really a massive thing. It is armed with one 3 inch, 57mm cannon and 4 30 cal. machine guns. It is armored with welded sheets of steel 3 inches thick on top and sides and 1-1/2 inches thick on the bottom. They sure can take a lot of beatings. The crew consists of 5 men, and they really are packed like sardines. Well Doll, enough of G.I. talk.

I'm sure sorry to hear that the weather was bad at Rockaway. I'll bet it was swell to be there though, regardless. Tell me all about the dance Sel, it sounds like a real deal, especially with good old "Rube." Sure wish I was there with you. Maybe that day will come soon. I'm wishing hard enough.

Well Doll, that's about it for now. Tell Normie about the tanks—he should like that.

Good night Sel—give my best to all.

Love,
Bob

PVT. BERNARD D. BROWNE 39337016
CO. I 410TH INF. A.P.O. 470
CAMP HOWZE, TEXAS

MISS SELMA NEPOM
716 S.W. HARRISON ST.
PORTLAND, 1, OREGON

June 2, 1944

Dear Selma,

Well Hon, what do you think of the new stationery. Besse sent it to me about a month ago but I was saving it until I ran out of the other.

Sweetheart, I got those so called "deals" today and they sure are the thing. Sel you sure are swell. Every letter I get from you makes me miss you more and more. Don't stop writing though Doll.

These last couple of days have really been swell. All we've done is get everything all cleaned up and ready for an inspection which comes off tomorrow. The way we've cleaned and scrubbed around here, everything should come off pretty smooth. I hope the Major is in a good mood.

Well Doll, we leave for the field again Monday and we stay out for a full week. We're going to take up amphibious training. Should be pretty interesting. I'll write you from there every day if possible.

Lewie has been shipped to Reno, Nevada for advanced ferrying training. It may be his jumping off point for England. I sure hope not. I got a letter from Junne and the poor kid is worried to death. They've been married such a short time. Sure wish the damn mess would end. Boy, the things I've got in mind. Nothing would stop me.

I've got K.P. again Sunday. Of all days to get it, it has to be on a Sunday. Oh well, that's the easiest day of the week in the kitchen. I'll probably wash dishes again. That and potato peeling seem to be my favorite jobs in there.

Well Doll, that's about it for now. I'm thinking of you constantly and I miss you an awful lot Sel. Thanks again for those cute "deals"—they'll really come in handy.

Regards to the family.

Your lover,
Bob

PVT. BERNARD D. BROWNE 39337016
CO. I 410TH INF. A.P.O. 470
CAMP HOWZE, TEXAS

MISS SELMA NEPOM
716 S.W. HARRISON ST.
PORTLAND, 1, OREGON

··· *June 3, 1944*

Dear Selma,

I got your letter today and am answering it while I have the time. I'll be busy pretty late tonight trying to peel about 500 potatoes. I love to do it—ha, ha. You should be proud of me.

I was glad to hear that you had such a good time at the beach. Golly, I'll bet it's just swell there. Sure would like to see your tan. I would be satisfied in just seeing you though. As for me, they just don't give us the chance to get tan around here. We always have to keep our shirts on while we're out on the fields. My hands are starting to get brown though. The sun is hot enough.

Sweetheart, I don't blame that fellow for liking Dallas. It sure is a beautiful city. It's a very wealthy city which accounts for a lot. All of the homes are really beautiful. It reminds me somewhat of L.A. except for the Palm trees. It sure is funny to see some of the big businessmen walking around with cowboy boots on. Typical of Texans.

Well Doll, I hope everything is alright on the home front. I miss you Sweet. I got a letter from the Folks today and they are both fine. Sure do miss all of their kids though.

I'll write again tomorrow if possible, Hon. Have a good time at the beach and write soon.

Love,
Bob

Pvt. Bernard D. Browne 39337016
Co. I 410th Inf. A.P.O. 470
Camp Howze, Texas

Miss Selma Nepom
716 S.W. Harrison St.
Portland, 1, Oregon

··· *June 5, 1944*

Dear Selma,

I got two of your letters today and was glad to get them. I sure did hit it lucky this week. I didn't have to go out in the field today because my turn came up for regimented Guard Duty. It really is a break for me because it's really pouring down and those poor guys must be soaking wet by now. Guard won't be a snap, but it will be better than playing cops and robbers out in the fields of Texas.

I want to talk to you about something important Sweetheart so brace yourself. I agree with you that Love is Blind. I'm nuts about you and you know that but as far as marriage goes, it's just got to wait until this war is over with. I'm very much against war marriages for the simple reason that I'm in a line combat outfit and as far as I know I may be overseas in a few weeks or maybe not at all. It all depends on what they need. I am qualified physically for overseas duty and will have my training qualifications in about a month. So darling I just can't depend on anything, as you can see. If I were limited service or station compliment, or something like that, it would be a different story. Please try to see what I'm trying to say, Doll. Sure wish I could talk to you. I'm sure I could make you see what I mean.

Selma, I want you to know that I am very, very fond of you. As far as I'm concerned, we've both got an awful lot to look forward to. As you say, it may be infatuation or even lonesomeness, but I doubt it very much. I sure hope it isn't. It's true that it is very possible—me being away and everything, but I doubt it very much. Let's not think of it Sweetheart.

I'm sure glad to hear that you're going to the beach again. I'll bet you'll have a beautiful time before the Summer is over with. I sure hope so.

By the way—thanks an awful lot for the snapshots, they sure are cute. You must have had a perfect time. Have fun Doll.

Well Sweet—I'd better get some sleep now. Regards to all and I'm always thinking of you.

Yours with love,
Bob

Pvt. Bernard D. Browne 39337016
Co. I 410th Inf. A.P.O. 470
Camp Howze, Texas

Miss Selma Nepom
716 S.W. Harrison St.
Portland, 1, Oregon

June 7, 1944

Dear Selma,

We came to town again tonight to get one of those halfway decent meals. We really had some beautiful steaks. Can't compare to Mom's cooking, but it was much better than garrison meals.

I got your letter today Hon. and was, as always will be, glad to hear from you.

I was glad to hear about the good news for Betty & Eric. That sure is swell. I hope he stays there for the duration. I doubt whether he will, but it's a good thought anyhow.

This U.S.O. is really packed tonight. They've having some kind of a show and it really drew the crowd. Place is full of G.I.'s.

It sure is hot this evening. It was hot all day. Yesterday it was pretty cool. I can't figure out this Texas weather. I'm not going to try either.

Well Sweetheart, I'd better head back for camp now so that I won't be late. I'll write again when possible.

Love,
Bob

PVT. BERNARD D. BROWNE 39337016
CO. I 410TH INF. A.P.O. 470
CAMP HOWZE, TEXAS

MISS SELMA NEPOM
716 S.W. HARRISON ST.
PORTLAND, 1, OREGON

June 9, 1944

𝒟ear Selma,

Got your letter today Doll and was sure glad to hear from you. I'm glad to hear that you are all caught up on your work. Just take it easy for a while. You must really be on the ball.

Honey so far here are my plans for after the war. They say it's foolish to plan anything when you're in the service, but I like to do it anyhow. Sweetheart, my father wants me to go in with him and work directly with him. I was planning to go to school and get a degree in optometry, but I hate to say it, but I think I lost all patience for school. Pop's been depending on me a lot. What do you think of it Sel? Tell me the truth because you'll have your say in it one of these days.

I was sure surprised to hear that Benny is in Italy. I didn't know he was in the Tank Corp either. I'll bet he's really doing O.K. He's probably a captain by now.

Yes Sel, Junne went with Lew to Reno. Poor kid really feels bad but they knew what they were getting into I guess.

Well Doll—I'd better get some sleep. I'll write again soon.

Love,
Bob

Pvt. Bernard D. Browne 39337016
Co. I 410th Inf. A.P.O. 470
Camp Howze, Texas

Miss Selma Nepom
716 S.W. Harrison St.
Portland, 1, Oregon

June 11, 1944

Dear Selma,

I received your two-in-one letter today and was sure glad to get it.

Sel I'm awfully sorry about what I said in one of my recent letters. I guess I just wasn't thinking while writing. I guess I just felt sorry for some of those poor wives that hang around day after day waiting for their husbands to get off. Sel, I hope you never see what some of these poor girls go through when their husbands go to P.O.R. (overseas). I've seen it happen to so many of them. It's really tough.

I'm sorry Sel, that I ever mentioned anything at all about it. I must have been half dazed or something. Just overlook the whole thing Doll.

So, you're going to have a figure like Betty Grable huh? Well, that's O.K. with me. Golly just think of the surprise I'll have when I get home on furlough again. I sure hope it's soon, but I don't think it will be for 3 or 4 months yet. I'm looking a lot forward to it Hon.

Well it's raining here again. All it does is get hot as h—— and then it has to rain in order to cool down to a mere 102°. As far as country goes, Texas really isn't too bad. It's plenty green, but no trees at all. It sure is funny to go to town and see men and women riding horses all over the streets. Gas rationing doesn't seem to bother them at all.

We sure did have a swell time last night. Mom sent down some salami and a rye bread yesterday and we (4 of us Jew Boys) went to town, went to a grocery store and bought some tomatoes, sandwich spread, and some pickles. We went to the city park and really had a picnic. We sure had a swell time. We went around talking to each other with a real Jewish accent and believe me, those boys from N.Y. can really do it. Sure had a swell time. Had a good old-time bull session along with it so we were civilians for a day.

Well Doll, that's about it for now. Take care and give my best to everybody at home.

Love,
Bob

PVT. BERNARD D. BROWNE 39337016
CO. I 410TH INF. A.P.O. 470
CAMP HOWZE, TEXAS

MISS SELMA NEPOM
716 S.W. HARRISON ST.
PORTLAND, 1, OREGON

June 13, 1944

Dearest Selma,

Just a line to let you know that I'm fine and pray that you are the same.

We leave for the field tomorrow and won't be back until Friday morning sometime, so I doubt whether I'll be able to write because it's supposed to be tactical. I'll write you Friday though for sure.

We're going to have a regimental problem which means that it will really be a big one. We'll probably have tanks and artillery all around us. Those problems sure get to be a pain, but I really have no complaints coming at all. I should feel very fortunate just being here in this country.

I got a card from Monty Chusid today telling me that he's on his way over. His address is in New York, N.Y. so I guess he's on his way to England. He's in a good outfit so he hasn't much to worry about.

Well Sweetheart, how have you been? I imagine your job of not doing anything at school is getting pretty boring. How are things at home and in that great city?

Not much doing around here Doll—it's the same as ever. I fired the pistol again today and did pretty well. That's our weapon that's really hard to master because of the short barrel. I think I did it though.

Well Sweetheart, that's about it for now. I'll write you again when possible. Take care Doll.

Yours with love,
Bob

Pvt. Bernard D. Browne 39337016
Co. I 410th Inf. A.P.O. 470
Camp Howze, Texas

Miss Selma Nepom
716 S.W. Harrison St.
Portland, 1, Oregon

June 16, 1944

Dearest Selma,

Well here we are back in camp again and it sure is a good feeling. We got back last night about 10:30. I got your letter this morning. Selma, I really don't mind whether you type or write a letter to me. Just so I hear from you, that's all that matters to me.

Say, they're really giving you a physical check-over. That's good though so you'll get it all over-with before you go to school. Golly Honey, I sure wish I was going with you. You're going to a wonderful school Sel, you probably know that though.

Well Doll, we had quite a time in the field—in fact it was pretty rough. We were allowed only one canteen (one qt.) of water a day and that really put us on a tough water discipline. In this heat, that's something that's very hard to get along without because we're constantly perspiring. I guess that's something I'll have to get used to also.

Sweetheart, I'm sorry about the short letters, but there's really nothing I can tell you that you don't know already.

Sel, I'm glad to hear you went on a date. Sounds like you had a swell time, and that's all I care about. Have plenty of fun Sweetheart with em all until I get home, and then let me take over. Gee Doll, I miss you a lot. Whether you know it or not (you should though), you've got a guy that really thinks you're tops. I miss you a lot Honey. I'll write again tomorrow if I get the chance.

Your lover,
Bob

Pvt. Bernard D. Browne 39337016
Co. I 410th Inf. A.P.O. 470
Camp Howze, Texas

Miss Selma Nepom
716 S.W. Harrison St.
Portland, 1, Oregon

.... *June 18, 1944*
4:45 P.M.

Dearest Selma,

I got your letter yesterday and this is the first chance I've had to write. Believe it or not, I'm writing you from the shore of beautiful Lake Dallas— about 50 miles from camp. Mel (the boy from Chicago) and I came out this morning and we have really had a swell day. I've been using the owners aquaplane and Mel has been pulling me all around the lake in a speed boat. It sure is fun Honey—hard to get used to but once you get it, it's a snap. I fell off of the d--- thing about 20 times but you just can't beat it.

Mel is sleeping at present and I'm trying to get caught up on my mail. I haven't written to the folks for the past 4 days—aren't I awful Honey. I'll write them today for sure though.

Well Doll, last week was really a hectic one. They really put us through the mill. For one thing, I've fired and qualified in every weapon that the infantry uses. We had a two-day problem that was really rough. We even ran through a practice alert shipment. I guess things will be popping again soon. I think the next shipment will be non-coms only so I can rest a little longer.

Well Doll, what's new at home? Anything at all? What are you planning to do when your job is over-with? Golly, I'll bet you're getting all ready for school. I sure do hope I get my furlough soon. I sure do miss you Sel.

I got a letter from Besse and she is spending a few days with the Folks in Salem. I imagine they're all in Portland today making a big fuss over Pop. I sent him a card the other day along with a sharp tie—straight from Texas.

Sweetheart, that's about it for now. Take care and write soon.

Yours,
Bob

PVT. BERNARD D. BROWNE 39337016
CO. I 410TH INF. A.P.O. 470
CAMP HOWZE, TEXAS

MISS SELMA NEPOM
716 S.W. HARRISON ST.
PORTLAND, 1, OREGON

June 19, 1944

Lover,

I got your swell letter today which you typed from work and here I am right back at you.

Guess what Sel, Irv Potter is stationed here, and I bumped into him a couple of nights ago. Golly I was sure glad to see him. He's really changed—looks like a wonderful soldier. One of these weekends we're both planning to go to Dallas and get together with Harry Glickman who is stationed about 40 miles the other side of Dallas (about 180 miles from here). He's in a different regiment than I am which means we'll see very little of each other but we're keeping in contact with each other with postal cards. Just think, I'm writing to somebody who lives in the same camp.

Well Sel, not much has been happening around here. We're getting up tomorrow morning at 4:00 o'clock to prepare for an inspection that we're going to have out in the field.

I'm glad to hear about Sol going to school. He's really doing O.K. for himself. That guy worries me Sweetheart. I don't like those 10 day leaves he's getting all the time. I'm glad you're going to be at Rockaway. Golly, I'm sure jealous, aren't I? It's a bad thing, but I like you <u>too</u> much.

Well Doll, I'd better call it for now. I'll write again when possible.

How do you like this poem that I'm enclosing? I got it from the fellows. What do you think of it—It sure surprised me. Night Sweetheart.

Love,
Bob

P.S. Regards to all

Her name was Gracie, one of the best,
That night I put her to the test,
She looked so sweet, so pretty, so slim;
The night was dark, the lights were dim.
I was so excited my heart missed a beat
For I knew I was in for a damned good treat.
I'd seen her stripped, I'd seen her bare,
I'd felt her over everywhere.
When I first tried her, she screamed with joy——
That was the first night. Boy! Oh, Boy!
I got up quickly, as quick as I could,
I handled her gently, I knew she was good;
I rolled her over, then on her side,
Then on her back I also tried.
She was one big thrill, the best in the land,
That P-38 of the Fighter Command!

BERNARD DAVID BROWNE
A.S.N. 39337016
CO. I, 410TH INFANTRY
A.P.O. 470, CAMP HOWZE, TEXAS

MISS SELMA NEPOM
c/o GENERAL DELIVERY
ROCKAWAY, OREGON

June 21, 1944
11:30 P.M.

𝒟*ear Selma,*

I just got off of work and believe it or not I feel swell. Reason? – here it is. All this week I'm working as Lifeguard at the Officers Swimming Pool in the main Post. What a break. The regular Lifeguard had to leave on an emergency furlough so they looked through our records—I guess—and found out I was certified so I got it. I still can't get over it. I go to the pool at 9:30 in the morning and stay on till 10:30 P.M.—an hour off for lunch. It's an outdoor pool and about one in the afternoon that place really gets packed with mostly wives of the officers. At night all the brass comes pouring in. I just sit around on a tall platform and look out for the elite of the Army. So far, I've had no trouble—I sure hope it keeps up. This job ends Saturday when the other boy returns. He's station compliment here so I doubt whether I'll ever get a good deal like that. It's nice to have a taste of it though.

Well Doll, I guess you and Charlotte are really having a time by now. Sure wish I was there with you all.

I saw "Bathing Beauties" last night and it sure is a swell picture. Be sure to see it Sel, it's really a panic.

I'm glad to hear that you went to hear Teagarden. He sure was good the last time I heard him.

I got another letter from Hesh today and he seems to be getting along fine. He's getting a lot of good schooling. He's got a good break. He seems to write to me more often lately. I wonder why?

Well Hon, I guess I'd better get to bed now because it's getting pretty late. Have a good time at the beach and give my best to Charlotte.

Love,
Bob

BERNARD DAVID BROWNE
A.S.N. 39337016
CO. I, 410TH INFANTRY
A.P.O. 470, CAMP HOWZE, TEXAS

MISS SELMA NEPOM
c/o GENERAL DELIVERY
ROCKAWAY, OREGON

June 25, 1944

Dear Selma,

Well Honey today is Sunday and is considered one of the worst days to spend in camp. I had to stay in though because I couldn't get a pass so here I am. I just got back from the Service Club where we spent a nice afternoon listening to records. I'm going to a show with the gang in an hour or so. I don't know what's playing but they say it's a good picture.

I'll bet the beach really has been swell, hasn't it? Write and tell me all about it. You and Charlotte take it easy with all those wolves floating around there.

Mom and Banny are planning to go to Seaside for a week or two in July. The doctor says it will be good for Banny and I'm sure the rest wouldn't hurt Mom any so I'm glad they're going.

Not much new around here Honey—same old stuff and the usual rumors. We get out in the field a week from Monday and stay out for about 4 days.

They took a bunch of S.C.U. men out of our company last week because they weren't fit for combat. Among them was one of my best friends here—the one from Chicago—a really swell Jewish fellow. He's blind in one eye so he got out. By looking at him, you'd think nothing was the matter with him, but that one eye is really shot.

Well Sweet, I guess that's about it for now. Write soon Doll and have a good time at the beach.

Love,
Bob

BERNARD DAVID BROWNE
A.S.N. 39337016
CO. I, 410TH INFANTRY
A.P.O. 470, CAMP HOWZE, TEXAS

MISS SELMA NEPOM
c/o GENERAL DELIVERY
ROCKAWAY, OREGON

June 26, 1944

Dearest Selma,

I got two swell from you today (I'm shot) letters from you today and my morale went up to the top, believe me. I'm sorry if you haven't gotten many letters from me, but no foolin Honey I've been busy as h---. They're really starting to run us ragged again. We got a new C.O. last week and he's really a G.I. boy. Strictly on the ball. It's every C.O.'s ambition to have his company on top and I guess you can hardly blame them.

Not much exciting around here. We had a U.S.O. show tonight and it was pretty good. They were from South America and were really O.K.

Honey I'm trying to get you a division magazine which just came out. They don't have any extras at present, but I think I know where I can get one. I've got a picture in it. It only shows me from the back, and you don't even know that it's me, but the company photographer says it is, so I'll take his word. It's really a nice magazine. It shows you just what we go through. I had one sent to the folks and I'll send you one Honey if I can get one.

Well Sweet, that's about it for now. Have a good time at the beach and write soon.

Love,
Bob

BERNARD DAVID BROWNE
A.S.N. 39337016
Co. I, 410TH INFANTRY
A.P.O. 470, CAMP HOWZE, TEXAS

MISS SELMA NEPOM
c/o GENERAL DELIVERY
ROCKAWAY, OREGON

June 28, 1944

Dear Selma,

I got your letter today which you mailed at Rockaway. Golly that place sure sounds wonderful. By the way give my regards to Miss Troy, she's a pretty good egg. I'd give anything to be there with you Sweet.

Guess what Sel—the mercury rose to 109° today in the shade. Golly, this heat is really terrific. I think I'm getting sort of used to it though—I just let myself go and quit trying to stay cool, because it's really impossible.

We spent the day today out in the field getting ready for the big problem next week. The way I understand it at present is that we leave Monday morning and return Thursday sometime. I'll write you from the field if it is at all possible.

I got a letter today from one of my boy friends from Salem. He got his appointment to Annapolis and he's been there for four days now and he really loves it. He's really a brain. He sure likes it there. It looks like I'll be saluting all the boys one of these days.

Well Sweetheart—that's about the dope for now. Take care Honey and have a good time, a real good time for both of us.

Love,
Bob

Bernard David Browne
A.S.N. 39337016
Co. I, 410th Infantry
A.P.O. 470, Camp Howze, Texas

Miss Selma Nepom
716 S.W. Harrison St.
Portland, 1, Oregon

July 1, 1944

Dear Selma,

Well here it is Saturday afternoon and we just finished a big regimental parade. They tell us that it was really sharp. I would sure like to see one once in a while rather than march in them all the time.

Not much new around here Sweetheart—same stuff day after day.

I'm taking it for granted that you're home from the beach by now. Boy I'll bet you had a wonderful time. I hope by next summer I'll be able to go with you.

I got a letter from Hesh today and he seems to be getting along fine. Sel Doll, I think Hesh sort of figures that I broke you and him up. He doesn't say it directly, but I sort of read between the lines. Personally, it doesn't bother me at all because when I want something, I try my best to get it regardless of what or who stands in my way, so prepare yourself Honey. Selma, please don't mention it to him. I would rather just keep it between you and I.

Well Honey, that's about it for now. Take care Honey and write again soon.

Love ya,
Bob

BERNARD DAVID BROWNE
A.S.N. 39337016
CO. I, 410TH INFANTRY
A.P.O. 470, CAMP HOWZE, TEXAS

MISS SELMA NEPOM
716 S.W. HARRISON ST.
PORTLAND, 1, OREGON

.... *July 3, 1944*

Sweetheart,

I got your letter today that you mailed from the beach. I'll bet you're surprised to find me still a garrison soldier after I told you we were going out in the field this week. I'll tell you what happened. We had to pull regimental guard this week so that means we will go out next Monday. I'll write you tomorrow from the Guard House—how romantic!!

Selma, I'm awfully glad to hear that you had such a wonderful time at the beach. Golly I'll bet it was wonderful there. So, my dear little hitch hiker—you're hitting the road these days, huh? I would have given a million to have seen that. I'll bet you two were really cute.

Golly Honey, I miss you an awful lot too—really, I do. I can hardly wait for that furlough to come around. I'm supposed to get my next furlough six months from the day I returned from the previous one which was April 8. Regardless of that, I'm going to ask for one in August. I would like to get home for my birthday. Sel, you can expect to see a lot of me when I get home—even if I have to import you to Salem. Sure will be swell to be with you Doll. You're a wonderful girl Selma, I learned that in the very short time that I spent with you. It was also so wonderful talking to you over the phone from my grandmother's house—and still better was when you saw me off at the station. Honey, you really looked sharp. All I did on the way back was to brag about you to Bob. He kept agreeing with me too.

The main reason Mom and Banny are going to Seaside is that they both need a rest (especially Banny) so they figured that they would stay at the Hotel there and really take it easy.

I'm glad to hear about Eric's transfer. I sure hope he stays on the coast for the duration. That would really be a break for both of them.

Well Sweet—that's about it for now. I'll write you again tomorrow.

Love,
Bob

Bernard David Browne
A.S.N. 39337016
Co. I, 410th Infantry
A.P.O. 470, Camp Howze, Texas

Miss Selma Nepom
716 S.W. Harrison St.
Portland, 1, Oregon

July 4, 1944

Darling,

Well here I am spending the 4th of July in the Guard House. I'm a prisoner guard so all I do is take out the German P.W.'s and keep them mowing the lawn all day. It sure is funny to hear them talk German all the time. They really rattle that stuff off. All of them that are here are, or rather were, part of Rommel's Afrika Corp.

Well Honey I suppose you're home by now. I'll bet you're ready to go to the beach again. I don't blame you Sweetheart. I hope by this time next Summer I'll be able to go with you. It's a lot to ask for, but I'm hoping.

Not much happening around camp lately. We had a big U.S.O. show here last night—pretty good too.

I got a letter from Besse today and she's still in California and hopes to stay there. They both like it there a lot. They're located at Ft. Ord which is really a beautiful post. They have a little place in Carmel, California which is right on the beach. Sounds wonderful doesn't it. As for the south—they can have it. Texas isn't too bad though except for the terrific heat.

Honey, that's about it for now. I'm thinking of <u>you</u> always and miss you an awful lot. Take care Doll and write soon. Regards to the family.

Love as always,
Bob

Bernard David Browne
A.S.N. 39337016
Co. I, 410th Infantry
A.P.O. 470, Camp Howze, Texas

Miss Selma Nepom
716 S.W. Harrison St.
Portland, 1, Oregon

July 5, 1944

Dearest Selma,

Well Honey, I'm through with Guard Duty and I've got some free time so I'm trying to catch up on my letter writing. When I got back to the company from the Guard House, I found out that I had been made a Pf.c. Boy, was I surprised. Great promotion isn't it Honey. Anyhow I'm out of the rut. I sure wish you were here to sew my chevrons on for me. I don't do such a sharp job. Guess I'll have to take them to town.

We had a little rain last night and it really cooled off for a while, but it is slowly getting hot and sultry again.

Well Honey, tomorrow the pleasure has been bestowed on me to serve on K.P. It will probably be my luck to get pots and pans (the worst of them all). I'll write you the first chance I get and tell you all about it.

Well Sweetheart not much more around here. How are things at home? Anything new happening in town? I'll bet you've got a beautiful tan by now.

Well Doll, I guess I'll say good night for now. Regards to all Sel.

Loads of Love,
Bob

Bernard David Browne
A.S.N. 39337016
Co. I, 410th Infantry
A.P.O. 470, Camp Howze, Texas

Miss Selma Nepom
716 S.W. Harrison St.
Portland, 1, Oregon

July 7, 1944

Dear Selma,

I got your letter today that you sent from the beach. I was glad to hear that Isy was home. Boy I'll bet he's solid stuff in the lieutenant uniform. I'll bet he really looks good.

Well Honey, we just finished an 18-mile hike about an hour ago and it really was rough, especially after having K.P. the previous day. No fooling Honey, I'll bet I peeled about 250 potatoes and washed twice as many dishes. My favorite job—ha, ha.

Tomorrow I take two booster shots for typhoid and tetanus, so you can see that my morale is really up.

I was glad to hear that you're going to help your father out for a while. I'll bet he really needs you bad.

Well Sweetheart I just can't think of anything else to say except that I miss you a lot—an awful lot.

Honey, I think I'd better get some sleep now. Take care Doll and write soon.

Love,
Bob

Bernard David Browne
A.S.N. 39337016
Co. I, 410th Infantry
A.P.O. 470, Camp Howze, Texas

Miss Selma Nepom
716 S.W. Harrison St.
Portland, 1, Oregon

July 9, 1944

Dearest Selma,

I got a wonderful letter from you yesterday and being that today is Sunday I've got plenty of time to write letters. I didn't get a pass today because I had one last weekend and there are a lot of others who didn't—so they got passes this weekend. They sure are rough on passes around here.

Well Honey—Sunday on the post is just like spending a day in the morgue. It's so dead and all you see are G.I.'s running all over the place.

I went to a show this afternoon with a couple of the fellows and then we went to the Service Club and fooled around there for a while. They had a dance then which wasn't bad at all. Otherwise nothing exciting. Same ole stuff.

Honey as for my furlough I don't know just when I'll get it, but it should be sometime in early September. A bunch of new men got in and they've got to get furloughs before we'll get ours. I sure hope the time passes fast. No fooling Doll, I can hardly wait to get back again.

Well Sweetheart, it's getting pretty late now so I think I'd better get some sleep. Good night Sel—I'll write again tomorrow if possible.

Love,
Bob

BERNARD DAVID BROWNE
A.S.N. 39337016
CO. I, 410TH INFANTRY
A.P.O. 470, CAMP HOWZE, TEXAS

MISS SELMA NEPOM
716 S.W. HARRISON ST.
PORTLAND, 1, OREGON

July 10, 1944

Dearest Selma,

I just got off of a detail which lasted all day. Boy they sure do lay it on at times. It wasn't too bad though, just took a lot of time.

Honey, I shall now tell you what I can about the German P.W.'s. I can understand them quite a little, because they speak high German which is very similar to the Jewish language. They seem to be determined that Germany is going to win the war, but that is only natural. They always say that the American Soldiers are so young. Most of them seem to be old men. They like to talk about their families and girlfriends.

They really have it very soft here. They can either work or not work. They make 86¢ a day if they don't work and $1.94 a day if they do work. Most of them work. They run around all day in short pants and really live a life of leisure. When marching to and from work they always sing German songs.

As for violence—they cause very little because they seem to have it easier here than they ever had it before in their lives. They really live a good life here and eat the best of food.

How's that Doll—did I answer all your questions? If not let me know.

Well Sweetheart nothing much new around here. I received a letter from the folks today and they tell me that Lewie flew over Salem and stopped at the Salem Air Base for refueling. He couldn't leave the field and being there such a short time, he called the folks—but as luck had it the folks were visiting some friends. They sure were disappointed when he wrote and told them what happened. He is now ferrying B-29's and he says they really are powerful.

Well Doll, that's about it for now. Tell your father to take it easy and wait till I come home—then we'll be able to hit it together—you just wait till this is over. You and I are going to get so stinko nothing will be able to save us. I hope to make it a beach party. A whole gang of us. Start making plans now Sweetheart.

Well Sweetheart—I'll write again tomorrow if possible. Give my best to the family and tell Mom (I'm taking things for granted) she's still my favorite girl.

Love,
Bob

BERNARD DAVID BROWNE
A.S.N. 39337016
CO. I, 410TH INFANTRY
A.P.O. 470, CAMP HOWZE, TEXAS

MISS SELMA NEPOM
716 S.W. HARRISON ST.
PORTLAND, 1, OREGON

July 12, 1944

Dear Selma,

Sweetheart, those snaps you sent me sure were swell. I was so glad to get them that you can now consider yourself a girl friend of 47 other fellows. They sure were swell Honey. I put two of them in my billfold and the other two are in my writing kit. That one with you and your Mom can't be beat. Thanks an awful lot Sel.

We're not allowed to keep cameras on the post, so I sent mine home when I first got here. Maybe if I can get hold of one in town someplace, I'll take some snaps and send them to you. Don't worry about sending me too many. I have a place for all of them. They serve as my moral support. Your big one is located so that I can see it all the time while in my bunk. Sure wish you were here with me Sweetheart.

I sent you a little gift tonight. It really isn't much, but I thought you might like it. I want it to mean a lot to you because I send it with all my love. I sure would like to give it to you in person. It means the same regardless though.

Well Doll, as you can tell by the stationery, I came to town tonight just to get away from that hole. Three of us came in and we got a good meal and stuffed ourselves with watermelon. The South is full of that stuff and in the hot weather it really helps keep you cool.

Well Honey, that's about it for now. Regards to all—I'll write again when possible.

Love,
Bob

BERNARD DAVID BROWNE
A.S.N. 39337016
Co. I, 410TH INFANTRY
A.P.O. 470, CAMP HOWZE, TEXAS

MISS SELMA NEPOM
716 S.W. HARRISON ST.
PORTLAND, 1, OREGON

July 13, 1944

Dearest Selma,

Well Honey, here I am again. I got a letter from you today. Golly your letters are wonderful. You don't realize what they do to me. It's just like a future to look forward to, you're included too.

Honey I'm awfully sorry if my last letter seemed depressing, I must have been feeling pretty bad. I'm sorry Doll—I just get that way every once in a while because this war is so damned foolish. It's ruining so many things. Oh well, here's hoping it will be over with soon.

Sel, we are scheduled to go out into the field Monday and return Saturday evening. We do all individual cooking so if you don't hear from me, you'll know that I couldn't cook very well. By the way, how do raw eggs taste?

Honey I'd better sign off now because my pass is up in an hour. I'll write again tomorrow.

Yours,
Bob

Bernard David Browne
A.S.N. 39337016
Co. I, 410th Infantry
A.P.O. 470, Camp Howze, Texas

Miss Selma Nepom
716 S.W. Harrison St.
Portland, 1, Oregon

July 14, 1944

Dearest Selma,

I just got back from a show and really saw a good picture, "Since You Went Away" with Shirley Temple. It's really a swell picture Sel, you'll have to see it.

I sure was surprised to hear that Norma is going to have a baby. That's really news. I'll bet Dave is strutting around like a proud papa already. That's sure swell.

Say I didn't know you were such a gambler. You'd better take it easy, 8¢ is a pretty large amount to win all at once. You should see us at times—really rough.

About 4 of us are planning to go to Dallas over the week-end—that is if we ever get away from here. We have a regimental parade tomorrow and they usually last till about 3 or 4 in the afternoon. They sure are a mess in this heat.

We leave for the field Monday for sure. I'll write you from the hills of Texas and tell you just how it is out there.

Well Honey, I'd better go to bed now. I'll write again soon. I miss you always and do love you. I only hope we can get together again soon. Regards to all.

Yours only,
Bob

BERNARD DAVID BROWNE
A.S.N. 39337016
CO. I, 410TH INFANTRY
A.P.O. 470, CAMP HOWZE, TEXAS

MISS SELMA NEPOM
716 S.W. HARRISON ST.
PORTLAND, 1, OREGON

July 16, 1944

Dearest Selma,

Well Honey, it's now Sunday evening and I just finished packing my stuff for the field tomorrow. We leave at 3 o'clock in the morning. I sure hope I can cook. Time will tell, I guess.

Well Sel, what's been doing lately? Anything new happening? Sure do miss you Honey.

I didn't have much of a weekend. We went to town and painted that place as red as possible. We couldn't go to Dallas because we didn't have enough time. We're planning on next weekend though. I hope we get in Saturday morning from the field. I'll write you from the field as much as possible. I'm taking along that cute stationery you sent me so here's hoping I'll get a chance to use it.

I got a letter from Mom and Banny and they're really having a nice time at Seaside. They sent me a pound box of Saltwater Taffy. Boy it really hit the spot. It sure did remind me of those wonderful days.

Well Sweetheart I think I'd better get some sleep now so that I can meet the birds and the bees with a bang tomorrow. I'll write tomorrow if possible. Give my regards to all.

Love ya,
Bob

P.S. Check the Army humor.

BERNARD DAVID BROWNE
A.S.N. 39337016
Co. I, 410TH INFANTRY
A.P.O. 470, CAMP HOWZE, TEXAS

MISS SELMA NEPOM
716 S.W. HARRISON ST.
PORTLAND, 1, OREGON

July 17, 1944

Dear Selma,

Well Honey, here I am with the birds and bees on our first break. We walk on an average of 9 miles a day and supposedly do all our fighting at night.

I cooked my first meal today and it was really O.K. I hope the rest turn out that good. I'll have to cook you a meal when I get home Sel—don't think I can do it do you? I'll show you someday.

I'm sitting under a sycamore tree and they sure are wonderful for shade. They have these trees all over the South. They sure are funny looking things though.

Well Sweetheart I really don't have much more to say except that this stationery sure does come in handy.

I'll write you again tomorrow Honey if possible. Regards to all.

Love,
Bob

BERNARD DAVID BROWNE
A.S.N. 39337016
CO. I, 410TH INFANTRY
A.P.O. 470, CAMP HOWZE, TEXAS

MISS SELMA NEPOM
716 S.W. HARRISON ST.
PORTLAND, 1, OREGON

July 18, 1944

Dear Selma,

I got your letter today Honey and it sure came in handy out here.

Well it got daylight about thirty minutes ago. I just finished cooking a wonderful breakfast. I guess anything will taste good out here.

Last night when we decided to stop for the night, I took off for a farmhouse and brought back a gallon of milk. It sure was good. Straight from the cow.

Selma I really don't know just what I need for my birthday. I've really got everything that the Army allows. It sure is swell of you though. You're really a Doll. Just so I know that I've got you to come home to, well that's the only gift I ask for.

Well Honey I'd better call it for today because I think we'll be moving out soon. Regards to all Sel and will write again when possible.

Love,
Bob

BERNARD DAVID BROWNE
A.S.N. 39337016
CO. I, 410TH INFANTRY
A.P.O. 470, CAMP HOWZE, TEXAS

MISS SELMA NEPOM
716 S.W. HARRISON ST.
PORTLAND, 1, OREGON

July 19, 1944

Dearest Selma,

Well Honey here it is Wednesday afternoon and only 3 more days to go. We've got two more big problems which should bring us up to Friday night or Saturday morning. This field work isn't bad, but this heat makes it awfully uncomfortable. Last night we went swimming in a lake close by and it really felt good with the layers of dirt we had on us. We weren't supposed to go in but we did anyhow.

How are things with you Honey? What have you been doing lately? – Anything exciting?

I got a letter from Lew today and he thinks he'll be going overseas soon. At present he's training with an overseas unit so I guess time will tell. I sure hope he doesn't go over though.

Well Doll, I have to go on a patrol soon, so I guess I'd better quit for today. I'll write again tomorrow. Regards to all.

Love you,
Bob

Bernard David Browne
A.S.N. 39337016
Co. I, 410th Infantry
A.P.O. 470, Camp Howze, Texas

Miss Selma Nepom
716 S.W. Harrison St.
Portland, 1, Oregon

July 21, 1944

Dearest Selma,

Here I am back at camp and it sure felt wonderful to take a good shower and put on some clean clothes. The first thing we heard when we got back was that we're going out again next week to run company problems so don't be surprised if my next letter comes from the field. I sure hope it's not true though.

We had quite a time out in the field Honey. We worked together with tanks and the engineers. We went across pontoon bridges under fire and it sure does give a guy a funny feeling to hear everything popping around him.

I think I did a pretty good job of cooking because I'm still alive. You would have been proud of me Hon, no fooling.

I got a letter from you today and I'm glad to hear that you like the pin. It really isn't much Sweetheart, but I want it to mean a lot. I hope you wear it wherever you go. Whether you know it or not, I've got high hopes in the back of my head, but it takes two to make a deal. You had better prepare yourself when I get home on furlough. Just listen to me—I sound like a lovesick pup or something—I'm sorry Sel.

Well Doll, there isn't too much more to say and I'm pretty tired, so I think I'll go to bed now. Regards to the Folks.

Love,
Bob

Bernard David Browne
A.S.N. 39337016
Co. I, 410th Infantry
A.P.O. 470, Camp Howze, Texas

Miss Selma Nepom
716 S.W. Harrison St.
Portland, 1, Oregon

July 23, 1944

Dear Selma,

Well Honey we leave again for the field tomorrow and don't get back until Saturday sometime. I doubt whether I'll be able to write or not because everything is going to be tactical. I'll write though if it is at all possible. I think I've spent more days in the field than I've spent in garrison. I guess we need it though.

I got your letter today Honey and it sure was good to hear from you. I think you're right about working for your father. I imagine he really needs you pretty bad. This war business sure is playing hell with help. My Pop is having the same trouble with his help. Sure is rough.

I came to the Service Club today and got caught up on my letter writing. By the way Sel, Dave Gold is stationed here. He got here about a couple of weeks ago.

Bob is still in South Dakota—he doesn't seem to like it up there very much. He should get home on furlough soon, but I don't know just when.

Well Sweetheart after I finish your letter I'm going back and get all my stuff ready to take out tomorrow. If you don't hear from me for a while you'll know why. I'll write as soon as I get back. Take care Honey. Regards to all and my love to you.

Yours,
Bob

BERNARD DAVID BROWNE
A.S.N. 39337016
CO. I, 410TH INFANTRY
A.P.O. 470, CAMP HOWZE, TEXAS

MISS SELMA NEPOM
716 S.W. HARRISON ST.
PORTLAND, 1, OREGON

July 26, 1944

Dearest Selma,

Well here I am back from the woods again. We got in this afternoon and we're supposed to go out again tomorrow, but there is rumor that the problem has been called off. I sure hope that's true. Those problems are really rough in this heat.

I got a letter from Monte Chusid today and he is in England. He claims to have a nice set-up over there. He likes it there very much. He's already anxious to get back though.

Golly Honey, it sure has been hot here lately. I don't think it will ever cool down this time. It doesn't seem to bother the Southerners at all so I guess I'll eventually get used to it.

Well Sweet, how have things been going at home? How's that sweet, luscious girl friend of mine? Tell her that I miss her a lot, an awful lot.

That's about it Doll, regards from all the fellows. Regards to all—

Love to you,
Bob

Bernard David Browne
A.S.N. 39337016
Co. I, 410th Infantry
A.P.O. 470, Camp Howze, Texas

Miss Selma Nepom
716 S.W. Harrison St.
Portland, 1, Oregon

July 27, 1944

Dearest Selma,

Honey, we leave for the wilderness once again in exactly 1-1/2 hours. I guess those rumors were really rumors after all. We leave tonight and get back Saturday afternoon sometime. All we seem to do is go out and come in and go out again. What a wonderful life. It's the infantry though and I'm supposed to be an infantry man, so I don't mind—ha, ha.

I'm sorry to hear that Charlotte isn't going to school with you. I know that you and she are very close to each other.

Sweetheart I <u>really</u> don't know what I want for my birthday. You just get me anything you can think of, anything at all, and I'll love it just because it's from you. I wish I could tell you Sweet, but I really don't know of anything. I sure wish I could have you, but I guess that's quite a bit to ask for right now Honey.

Well Sel, I certainly hope you get a chance to see "Naughty Marietta." It's supposed to be wonderful. I sure do miss all that stuff. Hope to make up for it someday.

Well Sweet, I'd better get all my stuff ready to take out. I'll write when I get back.

I love you,
Bob

BERNARD DAVID BROWNE
A.S.N. 39337016
CO. I, 410TH INFANTRY
A.P.O. 470, CAMP HOWZE, TEXAS

MISS SELMA NEPOM
716 S.W. HARRISON ST.
PORTLAND, 1, OREGON

.... *July 30, 1944*

Dearest Selma,

Well Honey, here it is Sunday and still plugging it out. I just got back from swimming. I went in the officer's pool here on the post and nobody ever knew the difference. I know the Lifeguard there—so that's how I got in. Boy it sure feels good in this heat. This afternoon it was 108° and no foolin, it was hot. I used to think it was hot when it hit 90° at home but never again. I still don't see how these Texans get used to it. It doesn't seem to bother them at all. Maybe I'll get that way.

I got a letter from Besse today and Dave was shipped to Fort Meade, Md. so they will probably be there in a couple of days. Besse will go with him, of course. He thinks that he'll be used there in the cadre but if not, I guess he'll be shipped over. I don't think he will though.

Well Honey, how are you. Working hard? I sure do wish I were home. Today you and I would be at Oswego or some lake swimming. Wouldn't that be swell.

I guess that's it for now Doll. Take it easy and I'll write again when possible.

Love,
Bob

BERNARD DAVID BROWNE
A.S.N. 39337016
CO. I, 410TH INFANTRY
A.P.O. 470, CAMP HOWZE, TEXAS

MISS SELMA NEPOM
716 S.W. HARRISON ST.
PORTLAND, 1, OREGON

July 31, 1944

Dearest Selma,

I received two wonderful letters from you today Honey and I still can't figure out how you write such long and beautiful letters. I try but I just can't think of enough stuff to say.

I was glad to hear that you like your job. It's really a pretty good deal working for your own parents. They really need the help too.

Well Sweet, tomorrow we take a 25-mile hike. We start tomorrow evening after dinner and should finish in about 6 hours. We carry about a 22 lb. pack along with our pistols which weigh about 4 pounds. I sure am glad that we get to make it at night instead of during the day.

Today I was on supply detail which really was a snap. All I did was count and mark about 200 mortar tubes. I finished about 2:30 in the afternoon. I wish I could get a detail like that every day.

I got a letter from Besse today and she is visiting Dave's folks in N.Y. She will then go to Ft. Meade.

Mom has been pretty busy lately because we are having our house remodeled. I imagine it really keeps Mom tied down.

Well Sweetheart—I'll write you again tomorrow—until then I remain yours—

With love,
Bob

P.S. Regards to all.

BERNARD DAVID BROWNE
A.S.N. 39337016
CO. I, 410TH INFANTRY
A.P.O. 470, CAMP HOWZE, TEXAS

MISS SELMA NEPOM
716 S.W. HARRISON ST.
PORTLAND, 1, OREGON

August 1, 1944

My Sweetheart,

Honey, we leave again for the field tomorrow, and don't get back until Friday afternoon. I guess the General got ants in his pants again. It seems like we go out every other day. It's rough stuff in this heat—no foolin.

I got your wonderful letter and as long as I've got you, there's no need to worry about my morale. I only wish I had you with me.

Glad to hear that you got your admittance slip to school. Don't worry about your grades Sweet, you'll do alright. Sure wish I was going there with you.

I pulled K.P. again today and believe me I'm going to make a wonderful wife for some gal. So help me—I'll break every dish I get hold of. I'll swear I washed 500 dishes today. I love that job—no foolin.

Well Doll—how are you? Remember that I'm always thinking of you and always wishing I was closer to you. Sure do wish this damn war would end. Sel—give my best to the folks and I'll write when I get back.

Love,
Bob

Bernard David Browne
A.S.N. 39337016
Co. I, 410th Infantry
A.P.O. 470, Camp Howze, Texas

Miss Selma Nepom
716 S.W. Harrison St.
Portland, 1, Oregon

August 3, 1944

Dearest,

Honey I just got in from the field a short time ago and we leave again tomorrow afternoon and return late Sunday nite. Sweetheart, please excuse the brevity of this letter but I just have a short time until lights go out. I love you Sel and miss you. I got your letter today and I seem to love you more with every letter I get.

I saw Dave Gold in the field and he, I, & Irv Potter plan to go to Dallas the first weekend we have free. When that will be, I don't know.

Honey I'd better run now if I want to mail this in time. I'll write you again Monday if not sooner. I love you Honey and hope to prove it to you some day.

Regards to all.

Your lover,
Bob

G.I. Talk ??

WE WAC'S DON'T CARE TO TALK ABOUT OUR EXPERIENCES IN THE ARMY — AND ANYWAY I REALLY PREFER DANCING.

→ But ↴

THIS IS WHAT HAPPENED

August 9, 1944

Dearest Selma,

Just a line Honey to let you know that I'm still here and kicking. I try to write you everyday while in garrison so that it will make up for the times I didn't write while out in the field.

We really didn't do too much around here today except the usual routine of G.I. work. We're getting ready to put on a demonstration for some 3 star General that's coming to visit us Friday. Those guys sure got to be a pain in the neck. I guess they know what they're doing though.

Honey, we've got a 4 day problem scheduled for next Monday through Thursday. If possible, I'll write you from there. It's a divisional problem so we should be kept pretty busy.

Golly that weather sure does sound wonderful at home. Now that all furloughs have been cancelled I

G.I.? GOSH!
OH MY YES THE
C.O. SAID — BLA
THIS K.P. IS
THE O.D.
BLA!
BLA!
ETC.

SNAFU!

126

2.

don't know what to expect.

Sweetheart, we've been alerted. That is the reason for the cancelation of farloughs - I guess. Our moving date is _rumored_ to be sometime around September 15. As to where we go - well, it may be across or it may be just to some other camp. I don't know anything about that. Honey please don't let it scare you because it may not be nothing at all. I only hope I'll be able to see you before that time. I haven't told the folks yet, and I don't expect to so please keep it quiet Honey.

Well Doll, that's about it for now. Take care Sweet. I love you —

Forever,
Bob

BERNARD DAVID BROWNE
A.S.N. 39337016
CO. I, 410TH INFANTRY
A.P.O. 470, CAMP HOWZE, TEXAS

MISS SELMA NEPOM
716 S.W. HARRISON ST.
PORTLAND, 1, OREGON

August 8, 1944

Dearest Selma,

Honey here I am back in civilization again. We returned from the field this afternoon about 2:00. I came to town tonight to get a white man's meal and write to you, the folks, and Lewie. It sure does feel swell to be back.

I got your letter while out in the field and was as always more than glad to get it.

We sure did have a rough time out there, Honey. It's really rough to work in this heat. About ¼ of our company passed out before the problem was finished. Here's hoping we'll get to stay in garrison for the rest of the week anyhow.

By the way Sel, how did the Ice Capades turn out. I'll bet they were really good. They usually are.

Honey I met some nice fellows from Tillamook, and they were sure happy to talk to another Oregonian. I didn't mind it too much myself. They just got here about two weeks ago and are taking special training with the engineers here. They hate the South, almost as much as I do.

Well Sweetheart, that's about all I have time for now. Take care and give my regards to the family. I love you Sweet.

Yours,
Bob

Bernard David Browne
A.S.N. 39337016
Co. I, 410th Infantry
A.P.O. 470, Camp Howze, Texas

Miss Selma Nepom
716 S.W. Harrison St.
Portland, 1, Oregon

August 9, 1944

Dearest Selma,

Just a line Honey to let you know that I'm still here and kicking. I try to write you every day while in garrison so that it will make up for the times I didn't write while out in the field.

We really didn't do too much around here today except the usual routine of G.I. work. We're getting ready to put on a demonstration for some 3-star General that's coming to visit us Friday. Those guys sure get to be a pain in the neck. I guess they know what they're doing though.

Honey, we've got a 4-day problem scheduled for next Monday through Thursday. If possible, I'll write you from there. It's a divisional problem so we should be kept pretty busy.

Golly that weather sure does sound wonderful at home. Now that all furloughs have been cancelled, I don't know what to expect.

Sweetheart, we've been alerted. That is the reason for the cancellation of furloughs—I guess. Our moving date is <u>rumored</u> to be sometime around September 15. As to where we go—well, it may be across, or it may be just to some other camp. I don't know anything about that. Honey please don't let it scare you because it may be nothing at all. I only hope I'll be able to see you before that time. I haven't told the folks yet and I don't expect to so please keep it quiet Honey.

Well Doll, that's about it for now. Take care Sweet. I love you—

Forever,
Bob

Bernard David Browne
A.S.N. 39337016
Co. I, 410th Infantry
A.P.O. 470, Camp Howze, Texas

Miss Selma Nepom
716 S.W. Harrison St.
Portland, 1, Oregon

August 10, 1944

Dear Selma,

Honey, I got your letter today and you must have been feeling pretty badly about something. I'm awfully sorry if I seemed a little too mushy wushy in my last letter—maybe I was and I'm sorry Sel. After all, I only spent one night with you and I write you letters that seem to sound like I've been going with you for years or something. Please excuse it Sel—it won't happen again. From now on I'll be just another one of the guys. Maybe it is better that way. You are right when you say that what's to be will be. I believe in that also.

As for my emotions running away with me, well I don't think that will ever happen to me with anyone that I am fond of. I hope and think you understand me.

Well Sel, today we put on a demonstration problem for the general. Those guys sure do like the attention and when you come right down to it, all they are, are a bunch of politicians in uniform. Anyhow, we put on a good demonstration for him and he seemed well pleased so that's all that counts, I guess.

Not much new around here. We are scheduled to take glider training in a week or so. It should be pretty interesting. I'll write you all about it.

I'd better turn in now and get some sleep. I'll write again tomorrow if possible.

Bob

BERNARD DAVID BROWNE
A.S.N. 39337016
CO. I, 410TH INFANTRY
A.P.O. 470, CAMP HOWZE, TEXAS

MISS SELMA NEPOM
716 S.W. HARRISON ST.
PORTLAND, 1, OREGON

August 11, 1944

Dear Selma,

Well here I am again still pounding it off. I came to town tonight with some of the Jew boys to attend services and go to a U.S.O. party put on by the Jewish people of Dallas. It was really pretty nice—we ended up eating corned beef sandwiches and dill pickles. We really had quite a time. It does a fella good to get out like that every once in a while.

Not much new around here Sel except the same old stuff. This weekend we're planning to go to Ft. Worth for the weekend. I hope we don't get stuck on detail or anything.

I'll write you and tell you all about it. Ft. Worth is supposed to be quite a place. It represents Texas quite well. Dallas is really a beautiful place. I went to Southern Methodist University and stayed overnight at the Phi Delt House. That sure is a beautiful college. Not many men left there though. I saw the famous Cotton Bowl there and it really is nice.

Well Sel, I guess that's about it for now. Take care and write me when you get the time.

Love,
Bob

BERNARD DAVID BROWNE
A.S.N. 39337016
CO. I, 410TH INFANTRY
A.P.O. 470, CAMP HOWZE, TEXAS

MISS SELMA NEPOM
716 S.W. HARRISON ST.
PORTLAND, 1, OREGON

August 14, 1944

Dear Selma,

I received two of your letters today and was sure glad to get them. They seem to do a lot for me, especially on Monday Mornings.

We went on Guard this afternoon and I was chosen Colonels Orderly so that accounts for the typewriter. It's really a swell job. All I do is sit in the Colonels office and take phone calls all day. The trouble is that it only lasts for twenty-four hours. It's more fun sitting in his office and watching his staff run all over the place for him.

We went to Ft. Worth this weekend and really had a good time. Irv poured out his heart and soul over K.P., so only Dave Gold and I went, and we met Irv there Sunday morning. Sel we really had a perfect time there. That city is wide open, no foolin. Saturday night Dave and I got a little tight and he told me all about his past love life. At one time he seemed to like Elaine Rosenstein an awful lot. He sure was disappointed when she got married. He's really a swell kid Sel. He seems to know you well, so you were in our conversation most of the time. We're planning to go there again the first time we get another chance, because it's really a good city to have a good time in. Something similar to Portland.

Well Sel, how have things been going in Portland? Is Jantzen still off limits to service men? It better not be when I get home. How are the Folks Honey? Be sure to give them my best. Tell my best gal that I'm not forgetting that drunk she promised us.

I guess that's about it for now Sel. Take care Hon and write soon. I'll write again tomorrow if I get the time. Dave told me to give you his regards.

Love,
Bob

BERNARD DAVID BROWNE
A.S.N. 39337016
Co. I, 410TH INFANTRY
A.P.O. 470, CAMP HOWZE, TEXAS

MISS SELMA NEPOM
716 S.W. HARRISON ST.
PORTLAND, 1, OREGON

.... *August 17, 1944*

Dear Selma,

Well Sel, this is your doughboy again still trying like h--- to get a furlough. I hate to say it, but I don't think I'll get one from this post. I'll probably get one when I get to our next post. I hope it's closer to home than this one is.

Last night, Dave, Irv, and I went to the show here on the post. We saw the "Seventh Cross" with Spencer Tracy. Very good picture, see if it you haven't already.

We took a nine-mile march today and had to make it in two hours. No foolin Sel, it was really a rat race. There wasn't a dry spot on us when we crossed the finish line. Boy this Texas sunshine is really the stuff. It's so hot here that the trees have to chase the dogs around. BIG JOKE!!

Selma you just can't beat the west coast for climate and country. It's really better there than any other places I've ever been. Texas is really a nice state, but the climate here kills it off. It sure is funny though, to look out across a field and all you see is cacti growing all over the place, no trees at all. Also, no hills. You can look out for miles and miles and all you can see is flat country with the distant horizon in the background. They have beautiful sunsets here Sel, just like out on the Pacific. Really very pretty.

Well, I should be an uncle about the 12th of September, maybe a little sooner. Banny seems to be getting along fine. She sends her regards to you as well as the rest of the family does. You seem to be a very popular girl in our family—especially since my last furlough—don't let it worry you Sel—a lot of big buildings often fall down. I don't want you to think that I'm trying to tie you into something. I'm leaving that up to you. After all, what's to be, will be.

I guess that's about it for now Sel. Take care and write soon.

Bob

133

Bernard David Browne
A.S.N. 39337016
Co. I, 410th Infantry
A.P.O. 470, Camp Howze, Texas

Miss Selma Nepom
716 S.W. Harrison St.
Portland, 1, Oregon

August 18, 1944

Dearest Selma,

I got your [letter] today and I seem to understand you more and more with every letter I get from you. Selma you are perfectly right about this writing business. It may seem to be a big thing and then when we come right down to it it's really nothing at all. I guess what I'll have to do is wait till I get home and try to prove it to you in my own way. Just give me a fair chance Honey and I'll give any of those other fellows all the competition they want.

I got a letter from Besse and Dave today and they don't like it up there at all. They say it's terribly hot in Maryland. I know just what they mean. They went to Washington D.C. last weekend and visited with Dave and Oscar Gass. By the way, Dave and Bette also have a beautiful child. That Gass family of ours are really on the ball aren't they Honey?

Well Sel, tomorrow we spend the entire day out in the field firing our machine gun. We have about 2500 rounds to fire for about 8 of us so you can see that we should get quite a bit of practice in before the day is over with.

I saw Dave tonight and he was pretty mad because they've been using him in the kitchen for the past couple of days. He took some snapshots last weekend and as soon as we get a chance to get them developed, I'll send them to you.

Well, I guess that's about it for now. Give my regards to all. I'm not going to say I love you and I'm not going to say I don't love you—I'm just going to let you figure it out. Aren't I mean though Honey?

Love,
Bob

BERNARD DAVID BROWNE
A.S.N. 39337016
CO. I, 410TH INFANTRY
A.P.O. 470, CAMP HOWZE, TEXAS

MISS SELMA NEPOM
716 S.W. HARRISON ST.
PORTLAND, 1, OREGON

August 19, 1944

Dear Selma,

Hello Doll, how are you? Dave, Irv, & I came to town tonight to go to services. We are now at the U.S.O. and are planning to go back to camp as soon as I finish this letter to you. They both say hello to you— They sure would like to be home again. Not me though—I love it here!! Crazy, aren't I?

Well Hon. we spent all day today firing the machine gun and the flame thrower. Really had a hot day—no fooling. I fired about 800 rounds on the machine gun and it was more fun chopping the targets off of the stands. No fooling we just ripped those targets to shreds.

We are planning to go to Dallas this weekend. I sure hope we didn't get detailed or anything. I'll write and tell you the result.

How are things at home Sel? I got a letter from the folks today and Pop is planning to go to Brietenbush for a week. He likes those hot mineral baths they have there.

Well Hon., I guess I'd better go back to camp now. Take care and write soon.

Love,
Bob

BERNARD DAVID BROWNE
A.S.N. 39337016
CO. I, 410TH INFANTRY
A.P.O. 470, CAMP HOWZE, TEXAS

MISS SELMA NEPOM
716 S.W. HARRISON ST.
PORTLAND, 1, OREGON

August 20, 1944

Dearest Selma,

I got your letter today Honey and was glad to hear from you.

We just got back from swimming and it sure was wonderful. It keeps you cool for a while. They have a nice lake about 15 miles from here so about 8 of us had a swimming party all day today. A typical G.I. Sunday.

We start our glider training Wednesday and it lasts for four days. They give us Airborne training just in case we'll need it someday. Ever since the invasion they're giving this training to all infantry outfits. Honey, we start in at 6:30 in the morning and get off at 9:30 at night so if you don't get many letters for those four days, you'll know why.

Sel I got a tip about furloughs today from our company clerk and he doesn't think I'll get a furlough until we move from this post. I don't know how soon that will be, but whenever we do you can count on me coming home. I sure hope you'll be at the train to see me. I'll give you plenty of notice Honey. Golly, just think pretty soon you'll be going to school. I sure hope I get home before you leave.

Well Sel, that's about it for now. Take care Sweet and I <u>think</u> I love you—fooled you didn't I Doll?

Love,
Bob

Regards to all—

Bernard David Browne
A.S.N. 39337016
Co. I, 410th Infantry
A.P.O. 470, Camp Howze, Texas

Miss Selma Nepom
716 S.W. Harrison St.
Portland, 1, Oregon

August 21, 1944

Dearest Selma,

I got your swell birthday present today Honey and thanks an awful lot. That card was a cute one. The fellows sort of went for your candy but I got most of it anyhow. They found out about my birthday, so I imagine I'll be taking an ice-cold shower with my clothes on about Thursday night. That's the usual routine anyhow. Maybe they'll think of something new this time. Dear boys, I love them all.

Glad to hear that Hesh got home again. That guy sure does get a lot of time off. I wish I had half of his leave time. I imagine he's still taking you out Sel. He's a swell guy and all that, but just give me half the chance he's had. There I go raving again—just ignore me when I talk like that.

We're making another 9-mile hike tomorrow in two hours. It will probably end up being a rat race like most of them do. We're making it the first thing in the morning so it shouldn't be too bad. That's the infantry for you Sweetheart. It's a rough outfit, but it's a good one. To tell you the truth—I think I'm getting used to it. I still wouldn't want to be an infantry officer though. It's glorious while in this country but in combat they get knocked off like flies. Lewie promises to teach me to fly after the war. That's something I always wanted to do. How about you Honey? Wouldn't you love to fly?

Well Sweet, that's about it for now. Here's looking at you (your picture is looking right at me and vice versa) You have beautiful eyes Sel. Write soon.

Love,
Bob

BERNARD DAVID BROWNE
A.S.N. 39337016
CO. I, 410TH INFANTRY
A.P.O. 470, CAMP HOWZE, TEXAS

MISS SELMA NEPOM
716 S.W. HARRISON ST.
PORTLAND, 1, OREGON

··· *August 22, 1944*

Dearest Sel,

Honey I got your gift today and it sure is beautiful stuff. Golly it's wonderful. I got a gift from you yesterday and another today. Those cards are the cutest things. Thanks an awful lot Selma. You'd better be careful now or I might start falling for you. You certainly are a swell girl. I guess I'm not the first guy that told you that, but I really mean it.

Well Sel, we finished our nine-mile hike today and it wasn't bad at all. It's those long ones that really get a guy—feet first. That one today was really a snap though.

We start our glider training tomorrow and here's hoping it will be interesting. The stuff we've been having around here is boring as hell. We have the same stuff day after day.

We had a baseball game tonight and beat our attached Field Artillery Co. 8 to 3. We really played a good game too. Your one and only plays first base—I imagine sport talk is dry

to you Honey but give me enough time and you'll love it. Golly if it wasn't for the sports we get around here a guy would go AWOL every other day. We had our last swimming meet last Tuesday night. We lost Honey. We had a lot of points for free-style swimming, but we lost out on our dives. It was lots of fun though.

Well Sel, that's about it for now. Take care of yourself Honey and I'm thinking of you—

Love,
Bob

P.S. Thanks again for the swell birthday gift. Regards to the family.

BERNARD DAVID BROWNE
A.S.N. 39337016
CO. I, 410TH INFANTRY
A.P.O. 470, CAMP HOWZE, TEXAS

MISS SELMA NEPOM
716 S.W. HARRISON ST.
PORTLAND, 1, OREGON

August 23, 1944

Dear Selma,

We came to town tonight just for a change. Some of the boys got a little surprise for me. I think it's a quart of White Horse Scotch just between you and me.

The folks sent me a cake and I got it today, so the entire company got the cake. I managed to get a little piece though.

I sent you our divisional magazine today. I hope you get it alright. It shows you just what we go through here.

Well we had our first day today with gliders. They really are interesting. We spent the day playing with parachutes and safety belts. More fun. I think tomorrow we get it in a little more detail. We work from 1:30 tomorrow afternoon until 10:30 tomorrow night so I guess we'll really get a lot done. We finish our training and have our time test Saturday afternoon.

Otherwise not much new. Please excuse the messy letter—I want to write a letter to the folks before this place closes up. Take care Honey and I like you.

Love,
Bob

BERNARD DAVID BROWNE
A.S.N. 39337016
CO. I, 410TH INFANTRY
A.P.O. 470, CAMP HOWZE, TEXAS

MISS SELMA NEPOM
c/o GEN. DEL.
ROCKAWAY, OREGON

August 24, 1944

𝒟ear Selma,

I'm writing this letter during our 30-minute training break so excuse it Honey if it's a short one. I got your birthday letter today and you timed it perfectly. You sure are a sweet girl. Don't get swell head now.

We've been running around all day and we don't get through until 10:30 tonight. It's very interesting training though, so the time passes pretty quickly.

I'm sure glad to hear that you're going to Rockaway again. You'll probably be there by the time this letter arrives. Have a real good time Sel—good enough for both of us. We'll be there together one of these days—I hope.

Well Hon. I'd better run now because we'll be leaving soon. Take care Honey and regards to all at the beach. Have fun.

Love,
Bob

Bernard David Browne
A.S.N. 39337016
Co. I, 410th Infantry
A.P.O. 470, Camp Howze, Texas

Miss Selma Nepom
c/o Gen. Del.
Rockaway, Oregon

··· *August 25, 1944*

Dearest Selma,

Hi Honey. Well I'll bet by now you're having a wonderful time at the beach. Golly, I'd give anything to be with you. Who are you there with Sel? Are the Folks with you? I'll bet it's wonderful there this time of the year. I sure do like that place. Remember those good ole days a long time ago. I sure hope history repeats itself. I'll be going back there one of these days.

Sel, about those pictures. Out of the eight, Dave said only two came out and I'm enclosing them. You can see that one of them isn't too good either. He said that the film was too old or something like that. The pictures were taken at a lake about 15 miles from here. We had just gotten out of the lake about an hour before we took them. Irv wasn't with us because he was on detail that day. The short fellow is a Jewish fellow from Chicago. Really a good kid. Plenty of fun. Honey we're trying to get some more film and if and when we do, I'll send you some more pictures.

Well Sel, we finish our glider training tomorrow and we go up for a two-hour time test. All it is, is another way of transporting troops. I guess they're doing away with the boat these days. The gliders hold 20 men and 500 lbs. of equipment, including ammunition etc. They are towed by C-47's and are let loose just before they reach their destination. The gliders are 43 feet long and have a wingspan of 83-5 feet. In our glider we have a six-man crew and a jeep. More fun to load those things on. They just fit in the sides.

Well Honey, I'd better get some sleep now. Take care Hon. and have fun. Write and tell me all about it.

Love,
Bob

BERNARD DAVID BROWNE
A.S.N. 39337016
CO. I, 410TH INFANTRY
A.P.O. 470, CAMP HOWZE, TEXAS

MISS SELMA NEPOM
c/o GENERAL DELIVERY
ROCKAWAY, OREGON

Dear Selma,

Believe it or not, but it's raining in Texas. It's been raining for about three hours now. It sure cooled it down nice though. As long as I've been here, it's the first time it's rained so hard and long. Usually it rains for not more than 15 or 20 minutes. I guess fall will be here soon. That's what the Texans say anyhow.

We finished our glider training today and we are now qualified to be transported by air. It spoils you for any other type of transportation because it's so fast. It really gets you there in a hurry.

I got a letter from Lew and Junne today and he flew to Portland again last week. He didn't have more than just a few minutes there so all he could do was call Banny and Dave. They sure were surprised to hear from him. It only takes him a little over two hours to fly from Reno to Portland. No fooling Sel, you just can't beat flying.

Well Honey, how's the beach? Golly I'll bet it's wonderful there. Sure wish I was there—maybe someday.

Well Hon., I guess that's about it for now. Have lots of fun and say hello to everybody I know there.

Love,
Bob

BERNARD DAVID BROWNE
A.S.N. 39337016
CO. I, 410TH INFANTRY
A.P.O. 470, CAMP HOWZE, TEXAS

MISS SELMA NEPOM
C/O GENERAL DELIVERY
ROCKAWAY, OREGON

August 28, 1944

Dearest Selma,

Honey I came to the U.S.O. tonight so that accounts for the typewriter. I sure do need the practice. so I use it whenever it is not being used by someone else.

I got your letter today Honey and it sure was a corker. You'd better watch out or I might start calling you all mine. By the way, that trip you mentioned into Canada sure did sound wonderful (I'm tongue-tied). One thing about you and I and that is that we both love to travel. Isn't it exciting though? Someday we'll prove it to ourselves, O.K.?

Sel, I got a letter from Besse today and Dave is on his way over she thinks, because the last time they were together he told her that he wouldn't be able to see her anymore while he was at Dix, so she thinks that he is on his way. It looks that way to me too. On her way home she's stopping to see me for a week or so. She'll probably take the car home from here, unless she decides to ship it. It sure will be swell to see her. It looks like both Betty and her hit it together. This damn war sure is a pain in the neck, especially when two people are married. Here's hoping it will be over with soon. The news sure does look good.

Well Honey, how is the beach treating you? Golly I'll bet it's sure nice there. I sure hope it isn't raining. Tell my girlfriend that I'm looking very much forward to those cookies. Golly Honey, you're a wonderful girl. I guess a guy always has to go away before he realizes what he has at home. Just goes to show you that roses always grow in your own back yard. That's a compliment Honey.

Believe it or not but it's been raining here for the past two days. This Texas weather is crazy as hell, no fooling. I think and hope that the heat spell is overwith. It sure was a rough one.

Well Sweet, I guess that's about it for now. Take care Doll and have fun.

Love,
Bob

Bernard David Browne
A.S.N. 39337016
Co. I, 410th Infantry
A.P.O. 470, Camp Howze, Texas

Miss Selma Nepom
c/o Gen. Del.
Rockaway, Oregon

August 30, 1944

Dear Selma,

Just a line to let you know that I received your letter from Rockaway today and was sure glad to hear that you are having such a good time. That place just can't be beat. I'd give anything to be there. Believe it or not, but that is one place that I really miss. I seem to miss the entire beach that we have. I've been to the Gulf of Mexico a couple of times, but you can't compare it to the Pacific.

I got a letter from Besse today and she plans to leave New York the 5th of Sept. and will arrive here the 7th. Sure will be swell to have her down here. I only wish that you were with her. I've got a funny feeling that tells me that I should see you soon. Golly, I'd give anything to get home again soon. It seems like there's something I'm going to have to prove to you. Just give me the chance. Something else Honey, I'm far from being lonesome, because there are plenty girls down here. Remind me to tell you about some of them when I get home. It's really funny. I still think your tops so there. Maybe it's your mother. She seems to be what I'm after. You're just an alibi for me to come to the house. Aren't I mean Honey? I really don't mean it though, you know that.

It stopped raining today Sel, so I imagine from now on we'll be having some more heat off and on.

Well Doll, that's about it for now. Regards to the entire gang and my love to you Honey.

Love,
Bob

Bernard David Browne
A.S.N. 39337016
Co. I, 410th Infantry
A.P.O. 470, Camp Howze, Texas

Miss Selma Nepom
c/o General Delivery
Rockaway, Oregon

August 31, 1944

𝒟earest,

I got your letter today and you sure do have a swell crowd at the beach. Boy, what I wouldn't give to be there. Honey, if I do get a furlough it won't be until the end of Sept. Honey, I've just got to see you soon. Things are really beginning to pop around here. We should be out of here and at another camp by the middle of the month. I don't know just where we're going, but if it's within 400 miles of home expect to see me, because I'll get home one way or another. Sure wish I knew where we were going.

If we expect to be stationed at some camp for awhile, Mom will probably come down if I don't get a furlough, and I won't let her come unless she brings you with her. Would you come Honey? That would sure be wonderful. To tell you the truth though Sel, I don't think we'll be at our next camp very long. It's hard to tell though.

I got another letter from Besse today and she plans to arrive here at 10:45 A.M. Thursday morning. I'm trying to get a pass for that day so that I'll be able to meet her at the train. I'm keeping my fingers crossed anyhow.

Don't worry about Marv Sel. I think the end will be in view by then. I'm sure glad to hear that he's going to school at Washington. Great school.

Well Hon., not much new happening around here. We haven't been on any field problems for three weeks now. We're slowly getting ready to move, I think. All we do is have classes all day.

We started football practice last night and our first game is the 6th of Sept. We play the Engineers. We'll really take em for a ride, because we've got a very good team. Listen to me brag. I'll write and tell you how it turns out.

Well Sweet, I'd better say goodnight for now. I love you just a little bit—how's that?

Love,
Bob

BERNARD DAVID BROWNE
A.S.N. 39337016
CO. I, 410TH INFANTRY
A.P.O. 470, CAMP HOWZE, TEXAS

MISS SELMA NEPOM
716 S.W. HARRISON ST.
PORTLAND, 1, OREGON

September 1, 1944

Dear Selma,

Well Hon., I imagine by now you are home again. I'll bet you hated to leave, didn't you? Was it very crowded there over Labor Day? I'll bet you had a lot of fun there.

Well Sel, I think the heat spell has left Texas. Ever since that rain it seemed to cool down quite a bit. I sure hope it stays that way. The nights are really cool and nice. One thing about this state and that is they have beautiful nights here. The sky is always packed with stars. Sure wish you were here to see them.

I saw Dave tonight and he's in hopes of becoming a P.F.C. soon. He's sure trying hard. I think he'll get it too. He had to run a night problem tonight so he couldn't come to town with me and Mel. We're planning to go to Dallas this weekend if everything goes well. It will probably be our last or next to last free weekend. Our outfit will probably be restricted about a week or two before we leave here. I'm trying to get a three-day pass when Besse gets down here so that I'll be able to show her some of Texas. It sure is different than any other state I've ever been in.

Well Sweet, how are things at home? Are you planning to work for your father until you go to school? Golly, I'd sure like to see you before you left for school. Maybe my prayers will come true.

That's about it for now Honey, I'd better type a letter to the folks. Take care Sel and I'll write again the next chance I get. Sweetheart, what size clothes do you wear? I want to know.

Love,
Bob

BERNARD DAVID BROWNE
A.S.N. 39337016
CO. I, 410TH INFANTRY
A.P.O. 470, CAMP HOWZE, TEXAS

MISS SELMA NEPOM
716 S.W. HARRISON ST.
PORTLAND, 1, OREGON

.... *September 5, 1944*

Dear Selma,

Well Hon., it looks like the heat is once again in Texas. It went up to 112°
this afternoon and it was really hot. I'm hoping it won't keep up long.
They say that the cool weather starts in around the middle of October.
I'm ready for it right now.

I got a letter from you today from Rockaway. I was glad to hear that
the rain lifted and you finally got some sun. Isn't it wonderful to lie in
the sun and just let it beat down on you? I'd be scared to try that in this
state—it would bake me in short order. They don't seem to lie in the sun
around here in order to get tan.

Besse will be here Thursday morning and I'm hoping to get some
time off so that I'll be able to pick her up at the depot. She may stay here
for the holidays, but we're not sure yet. She may want to go home. She
probably wants to, because she feels pretty bad about Dave being shipped
out. I guess it's really rough on married people.

Dave and Mel went to Dallas over the weekend, but your man was
on detail so he couldn't go. They had me on K.P. over the weekend. We
hit it about once every eight weeks. Anyhow they had a wonderful time,
as usual. That place is really a G.I.'s paradise. People treat you wonderful
there. When Besse gets here we'll probably go there for a weekend.

Well Hon., that's about it for now. Take care Sweet and regards to all.

Love,
Bob

BERNARD DAVID BROWNE
A.S.N. 39337016
CO. I, 410TH INFANTRY
A.P.O. 470, CAMP HOWZE, TEXAS

MISS SELMA NEPOM
716 S.W. HARRISON ST.
PORTLAND, 1, OREGON

September 8, 1944

Dear Selma,

Well Hon., Besse got here yesterday and I met her at the train. She got a very nice place to stay at—it's a private home and the people are really wonderful. The hotels in this town are all full and will be that way for a long time. I knew these people and they offered to let her stay there. They really are swell people. They too, are in the oil business. Everyone in Oklahoma and Texas seem to be in one way or another connected with the oil game. They call it "Black Gold".

I'm sorry to hear about the heat at home Sel, it sure is awful stuff isn't it? Just take it as easy as you can Hon. Don't do any more than you have to. That's about the only way to beat the heat. I've tried everything.

About Dave and Irv. Yes, they do have girlfriends. Irv is pretty well set with a girl in New York, he claims. He met her while he was stationed there. Dave has or rather had a girl

in Waco, Texas. For awhile they were pretty thick, but I think its sort of died down since he left there. How's that Honey, does it answer em all? I would much rather talk about you and me. It interests me more.

Now Sel, about the size of your clothes. Thanks very much for the tip on sizes—I should have known. Honey, I saw something that I wanted to buy you. I guess it would be wisest to try them on though first. I'll wait till I get home. It was a pair of black lounging pajamas. Really beautiful. The inside was red, and the jacket was quilted and fitted tight around the waist and bloused out on the hips. They were really nice. I think you would have looked wonderful in them. I guess the only wise way to buy though is to try them on. You're right.

I tried all day today to think of some good poetry—nothing clicked though. I guess I'll have to wait until I go out into the field again. All

I can get out of this atmosphere around here is corn. Not much of a poet, am I?

Besse sends her best to you and the folks. She'll probably visit you as soon as she gets home. As soon as she gets settled anyhow.

Well Sweet, that's about it for now. Golly isn't this a long letter though? I went to Dallas last weekend with the gang and really had a swell time. Got a lot to tell you when I get home.

Take it easy in the heat, Sweet—I'll write again when possible.

Love ya,
Bob

BERNARD DAVID BROWNE
A.S.N. 39337016
CO. I, 410TH INFANTRY
A.P.O. 470, CAMP HOWZE, TEXAS

MISS SELMA NEPOM
716 S.W. HARRISON ST.
PORTLAND, 1, OREGON

September 10, 1944

Honey,

It's now Sunday morning and I thought I'd write you a letter before I go to town to pick up Besse. Golly Sel, it's actually getting cold here at night. Last night I almost froze. I guess my blood is still pretty thin from the heat we've had. It looks as if the Texas heat is going up your way.

There are about 47 G.I.'s here just snoring their heads off. They sure do learn to take advantage of these Sunday mornings. They sleep till about noon and then get up and sleep some more.

Honey, don't worry about your wisdom teeth. They really don't hurt when you have them pulled—just so you have a good dentist. Don't let it bother you because it's not half bad. It's over in a second.

Well Sel, not much new around here. I think Besse is going to stay for the holidays and then drive home. She's trying to get another girl to drive with, because she doesn't want to drive all that way alone. If she can't get anyone I imagine we'll ship the car home. Write soon Honey and say hello to everybody for me.

Love,
Bob

Bernard David Browne
A.S.N. 39337016
Co. I, 410th Infantry
A.P.O. 470, Camp Howze, Texas

Miss Selma Nepom
716 S.W. Harrison St.
Portland, 1, Oregon

·· *September 11, 1944*

Dear Selma,

Just a line Honey to let you know that I'm still here trying my best to make what they call, a good soldier. Do you think I ever will? Sort of doubt it myself. I want to be a civilian too bad. That day sure will be wonderful won't it? Besse and I went to dinner tonight and then went to see Arsenic and Old Lace. It sure is a wonderful picture. Be sure to see it if you haven't already. It's really a scream.

I got a letter from Banny today and she said that Lew flew into Portland Friday morning and only had time to call them. He flies from Reno to Seattle via Portland, but all he stops in Portland for is to refuel, which takes a short time. He's trying to fix it so that he'll be able to spend a few hours there so that he could spend some time with them and the folks. He flies over Salem on his way and the folks always know it's him because he dips low over the house and circles a few times. Mom gets mad because she can't see why he can't stop for a few minutes. We've both explained it to her many times, but she still can't see why. Aren't they wonderful though Honey?

Well Sel, how are things at home? Anything new in Portland? Most important of all, I want to know all about you. What have you been doing lately? I'll bet you're starting to get all ready for school. Golly, I'll bet you'll have fun there. If you meet any nice fellows, go out with them, but inform them that you are private property. If they ask you whose, you tell them that you belong to some soldier that will be home one of these days to make sure. I'm not taking too much for granted there, am I Honey? If I am let me know. You know it's a funny thing about you and I. I've taken you out so little and I've learned more about you in that little time than I've learned about many girls in months.

Maybe it's because I've known you all my life. Golly, I've just got to get a furlough soon.

Well Sweet, I'd better say goodnight for now. Lights will go out in just a few minutes. Regards to all Hon.

LOVE YA,
Bob

Bernard David Browne
A.S.N. 39337016
Co. I, 410th Infantry
A.P.O. 470, Camp Howze, Texas

Miss Selma Nepom
716 S.W. Harrison St.
Portland, 1, Oregon

September 16, 1944

Dear Selma,

I just got back from Dallas last night and I found two letters waiting for me at camp today. I got a two-day pass so Besse and I spent them in Dallas—we really had a swell time too.

Sel, I sent you a little gift for New Years—I hope you like it. I looked all over Gainesville for the stuff, but personally, I don't think they ever heard of it.

Say, I'll bet you, Betty and Ruth really had a good time at the Village—no Honey, I've never been there. Is it nice?

As you probably know already, I am an Uncle. Banny had a baby girl September 14. We got a wire that same night. My folks spent the whole day at the hospital. I sort of wanted a boy, but I guess a girl will do. Banny wanted a girl anyhow and so did my father.

Well not much new around here. We've been running around like wild the past week getting ready to move. We should go on restriction sometime soon. Whenever we do, Besse will probably leave for home. She's going to stay for the holidays though regardless.

I got a letter from Lew today and he's still knocking himself out flying all over the country. He's got a birthday coming up the 20th of next month and I don't know what to buy him. How about some suggestions Honey?

I saw Dave and Irv this afternoon and they're both looking swell. Yes Honey, they go out whenever they get the chance. Irv seems to be pretty serious but still he has to get out and get away from it all. You understand.

Well Sweetheart, that's about it for now. Regards to the family and my love to you.

Yours in time,
Bob

BERNARD DAVID BROWNE
A.S.N. 39337016
CO. I, 410TH INFANTRY
A.P.O. 470, CAMP HOWZE, TEXAS

MISS SELMA NEPOM
716 S.W. HARRISON ST.
PORTLAND, 1, OREGON

September 17, 1944

Dear Selma,

Hello Sweetheart. Sel, I'm awfully sorry about those short letters but I just don't seem to be able to write long letters. I admire you for it though. I can't seem to think of enough to say. I should improve with practice though, shouldn't I Sel? Another thing, lots of times I'm pretty well rushed for time, especially now that we're getting ready to move. I don't know when and where we're going, but I think it will be soon. We were ordered to take off our patches and I'm keeping my fingers crossed. It may be P.O.E. but nothing is certain yet. Honey, I'm sending you the last patch I took off. I hope you like it—It represents the great 103rd Division as well as myself.

Besse is leaving after the holidays for home and we're shipping my car home. It's better that way with the tire situation like it is. I sure hated to send it home but we were ordered to, so home it goes. Besse sends her best to you along with a very Happy New Year to you and the rest of the family.

Glad to hear your tooth is out. It's best to get rid of those bad ones right away. Glad it's out anyhow.

I got a letter from Lew today and he expects to be stationed at Sacramento this winter. He sure hopes so. He likes California a lot. I don't think Sacramento is as nice as L.A. though. He expects to fly to Portland again in a week or so.

Well Honey, there's not much more around here. Everything is practically all packed up. The officers mess is closed so all the officers are eating with their companies. I guess it won't be long. I'm still hoping to get home though. I've just got to see you before I go across.

Well Sweet, I guess that's all for now. Take care Honey and write soon.

Yours with love,
Bob

BERNARD DAVID BROWNE
A.S.N. 39337016
CO. I, 410TH INFANTRY
A.P.O. 470, CAMP HOWZE, TEXAS

MISS SELMA NEPOM
716 S.W. HARRISON ST.
PORTLAND, 1, OREGON

September 18, 1944

Dearest Selma,

Honey, I just got back from chapel and Irv, Dave, and about 3 others came over to the Service Club. We're all sitting here sleeping and writing letters. Happy New Year Sel, from the gang.

I haven't seen Besse for a couple of days. We're restricted now and we're so busy that I don't have time to do much of anything. We're getting ready to move somewhere soon. I sure wish I knew where. Keep your fingers crossed.

Besse already got a V-mail letter from Dave and he's in France. He just left New York three weeks ago. He said he didn't even see England so he must have gone directly to the French Coast. I sure hope he doesn't hit combat right away.

How have you been Sel? I'll bet the holidays were nice at home. Plenty of servicemen I'll bet. Here's hoping that next year I'll be able to spend them at home with you.

Well Doll, I'd better say good-bye for now. I'll write again when possible. Regards to the family.

Love,
Bob

BERNARD DAVID BROWNE
A.S.N. 39337016
CO. I, 410TH INFANTRY
A.P.O. 470, CAMP HOWZE, TEXAS

MISS SELMA NEPOM
716 S.W. HARRISON ST.
PORTLAND, 1, OREGON

September 21, 1944

Dear Selma,

It's now 1:45 P.M. and I'm sitting on a bunk that has just been stripped of linen. We turned in practically everything. All we are taking with us is just what we were recently issued. We'll probably be living out of duffel bags for a couple of days. I think we'll be out of here by Sunday though. Sure would like to know where we're going.

I got your letter today Honey and was glad to hear that you received the gift O.K. Also, glad to hear that you liked it.

I doubt very much whether Mom will come visit me unless we're stationed at our next post for quite awhile. Sel if you don't get any letters from me for a little while it will mean that we're P.O.E. Most times they let you write, but lots of times they don't. It all depends on the C.O.'s. I'll write you though the first chance I get.

Glad to hear about Sid and Aaron getting furloughs. They've both got a pretty good set- up.

Golly this place is really a mess. It's just like a mad house. Everything is being moved.

I think Besse will be leaving soon because the division is on battalion restriction which means that I can't see Besse and she can't see me. All I can do is talk to her on the phone.

Well sweetheart I'd better help these guys out. I'll write you again tomorrow if possible. Regards to all.

Love,
Bob

BERNARD DAVID BROWNE
A.S.N. 39337016
CO. I, 410TH INFANTRY
A.P.O. 470, CAMP HOWZE, TEXAS

MISS SELMA NEPOM
716 S.W. HARRISON ST.
PORTLAND, 1, OREGON

September 22, 1944

Honey,

I've just got a very few minutes to tell you that this will be my last letter for a little while. Maybe a week or so. I'll write to you though Sel as soon and whenever possible. When you get this letter, we'll be on our way to someplace.

Take care of yourself Sweetheart and don't worry if you don't get any mail for awhile.

I love you,
Bob

European Theater

FRANCE, GERMANY, ITALY, AUSTRIA

(The Cactus Route)

Pfc. B. D. Browne 39337016
Co. I, 410 Inf. A.P.O. 470
c/o Postmaster
New York, N.Y.

Miss Selma Nepom
716 S.W. Harrison St.
Portland, 1, Oregon

September 26, 1944

Dearest,

Honey, as you can see our mail is being censored so I guess it looks like
the real thing this time. I can safely say though, that I am someplace on
the east coast. I feel fine, the food is wonderful, and I miss you very very
much. I wanted to see you very much before I left but I guess it will have
to wait awhile. I don't know how long we'll be here, and I won't know until
we leave here. Don't worry about a thing Sweetheart, just keep writing
as much as possible.

Besse should be home by now. You'll probably be seeing her soon.
We sure had a wonderful time together.

We are allowed no visitors here and besides we're restricted so I doubt
very much whether Mom will visit me. It wouldn't do any good.

Honey, I've got to go now. I'll write you whenever possible. I miss you
always and think of you all the time. Regards to the family Sel.

Love,
Bob

Pfc. B. D. Browne 39337016
Co. I, 410 Inf. A.P.O. 470
c/o Postmaster
New York, N.Y.

Miss Selma Nepom
716 S.W. Harrison St.
Portland, 1, Oregon

·· *September 27, 1944*

Dear Selma,

Just a short time Honey to let you know that I'm getting along O.K. and everything is fine. I miss you a lot.

I got two of your letters today which were forwarded to me and it sure was swell hearing from you. Sweetheart you're so right about leaving everything up to fate. I wanted to take care of a lot of things before I left though, but I'm praying that it will all wait. It had better. Just remember one thing Honey, one of these days I'll be coming home again, and I want you to be there when I do.

Sel about the car—I got it a few months ago. I bought it from a Colonels wife who was selling it cheap because she was going to Cuba where her husband was stationed. It was really a very good buy. It's a 1941 convertible Mercury coupe with red leather upholstery. It has four pre-war white side wall tires and has about 18,000 miles on it. It's in top condition. You'll probably see it when it gets home. I'm sorry about not telling you—I just thought you wouldn't be interested. I hope you are though Sweet—I want you to be in everything I do. Well Doll, that's about it for now. Regards to the family.

I love you,
Bob

Pfc. B. D. Browne 39337016
Co. I, 410 Inf. A.P.O. 470
c/o Postmaster
New York, N.Y.

Miss Selma Nepom
716 S.W. Harrison St.
Portland, 1, Oregon

September 30, 1944

Dearest Selma,

I received two letters from you yesterday which were forwarded to me here. Your letters are wonderful Honey and so are you.

Sel I think it's alright to tell you that I visited New York City last night and really had a time in the big city. I saw everything there was to see. Honey it's exactly like Portland only on a much larger scale. I'm sending you a check that they give you when you enter the Stage Door Canteen. It's exactly like the movie showed it. It's in back of all the movie theatres where the Stage Door entrances are. Betty Grable was there also Linda Darnell, Jean Parker, Ann Shirley, Betty Davis and many others. Charlie Lewis and his orchestra. They were supposed to be good but weren't too sharp.

It's quite a city for Service Men but I'll still take the West Coast any day. The people here seem to be so unrefined. They don't seem to give a damn about anything. They never seem to settle down but I guess that's just their way of living.

Well Honey how are things at home? When do you plan to leave for school? I'd give anything to be with you now. I've got so much to tell you.

I'd better leave now Sel. I'll write again when possible. Regards to all.

Love you,
Bob

FC. B. D. BROWNE 39337016
Co. I, 410 INF. A.P.O. 470
C/O POSTMASTER
NEW YORK, N.Y.

MISS SELMA NEPOM
716 S.W. HARRISON ST.
PORTLAND, 1, OREGON

October 15, 1944
– Somewhere at Sea

Dearest Selma,

Here it is Sunday and it really is a beautiful day. The ocean is very blue and the sun is shining bright. I'm sitting here on the main deck listening to a European news report so I imagine we're getting close to land. It will be a few days though.

Honey, I got the box of cookies yesterday on the boat. They gave out packages but we'll get no mail until we reach land. I want to thank you a lot Sel—they were really swell. There are also about 20 others that want to thank you. Those cookies really got around in a short time. I also have quite a few envious friends. Thanks again Sel.

I slept on deck last night with a sailor friend of mine. He's from Salem and we both went to high school together. I sure was surprised to find him on a tank ship. He's been on tank ships ever since he joined the navy and likes it a lot. He's really teaching me what the Navy is like.

Sel, I've got another poem for you—I'll write it on another page.

Love,
Bob

No. _____

PASSED BY
U · S
ARMY EXAMINER
(CENSOR'S STAMP)

To
MISS SELMA NEPOM
716 S.W. MORRISON ST.
PORTLAND, 1, ORE.

From
Pvt. Bernard D. Nepom, 39227016
(Sender's name)
Co. I 440 Inf. A.P.O. 1172
(Sender's address)
℅ Postmaster — New York, N.Y.
Oct. 15, 1944
(Date)

Dear Selma,   — Somewhere at Sea —

Just For You!

I do believe that God above,
Created you for me to love,
He picked you out of all the rest,
Because He knew I'd love you best;
I once had a heart of my own, its true,
But it now its gone from me to you,
Take care of it as I have done,
For you have two and I have none;
If I go to heaven and you're not there,
I'll paint your name on the golden stairs,
For all the angels to know and see,
Just what you really mean to me;
If you have not come by Judgment Day,
I'll know you have gone the other way;
So I'll give the angels back their wings,
Their golden harps and everything;
And just to show you what I'd do
I'd go to hell, dear, just for you. —

With Love,
Love,
Bob

POST OFFICE DEPARTMENT PERMIT NO. 115

Pfc. B. D. Browne 39337016
Co. I, 410 Inf. A.P.O. 470
c/o Postmaster
New York, N.Y.

Miss Selma Nepom
716 S.W. Harrison St.
Portland, 1, Oregon

October 17, 1944
Somewhere at Sea

𝒟*earest* 𝒮*elma,*

Well Honey, this looks like it, doesn't it? At the present time we're quite a distance out at sea. We're on a beautiful boat and the food is wonderful. So far, I have not gotten seasick, but plenty of them have. I'm keeping my fingers crossed just in case though. Sel there isn't too very much that we're allowed to say as yet. I miss you more than ever and am looking very much forward to my return. I have alot planned Honey, and I'm hoping it will all come true someday.

I called the folks from New York and talked to them for quite awhile. You were included in the conversation too. Curious Honey? Sel, I'll write you again when possible. Write real soon. I miss you alot.

Love,
Bob

Pfc. B. D. Browne 39337016
Co. I, 410 Inf. A.P.O. 470
c/o Postmaster
New York, N.Y.

Miss Selma Nepom
4540 17th N.E.
Seattle, 5, Wa.

·· *October 22, 1944*
Somewhere in France

Dearest Selma,

Honey, this is the first chance I've had to write since we've hit port. At present all I can tell you is that we're somewhere in Southern France right on the coast. We're located in a mountainous section and it's rained at least once a day since we've landed, but when the sun shines it's really beautiful. The French farmers seem to think it's God's Country and I see why. It's really beautiful here. The French seem to be a very friendly people.

On landing we had to walk through the city on our way to our area. It was sure interesting, because as we went through, all the French people would stand along the narrow cobble-stone streets and would greet us with BONJOUR. The boys and girls would walk along with us and ask us for cigarettes and chewing gum. One little French boy gave us a bottle of wine for a pack of chewing gum. It was supposed to be good wine too.

The city looked just like they all do in history books. The streets are very narrow and houses large and tall. They're built close together and have their yards in the back patio style. Nice place to visit but I'm already dying to get back.

I miss you a lot Honey and sure do look forward to your letters. I wrote the folks today also. Sel, I'll write you every time I get a chance. I don't know how long we'll be here but just remember that I hope to return someday and I want you to be there. I've got to go now Sweetheart. I'll send you some French money the first chance I get. Regards to the family.

I love you,
Bob

P.S. Sel, we weren't allowed to take large photographs along with us so I had to send it home. Send me a smaller one Honey, 3" by 4" so that it will fit in my writing kit. So far, the snapshots are doing the trick.

Pfc. B. D. Browne 39337016
Co. I, 410 Inf. A.P.O. 470
c/o Postmaster
New York, N.Y.

Miss Selma Nepom
716 S.W. Harrison St.
Portland, 1, Oregon

.... *October 24, 1944*
Still in France

Dear Selma,

Just a line to let you know that it's raining once again, and I think this time it might last quite awhile. It really rains here once it gets started. Sort of reminds me of Oregon.

Sel I haven't received any mail for quite awhile. I imagine you're been pretty busy. I really miss your letters more and more. What's new at home and how are the folks getting along? I got a letter from Besse today and she still thinks I'm in New York. I wrote to them a couple of days ago so they should know what's what by now.

Dave Gold and I got together last night and talked over old times. It's the first time I've seen him since we got here. We both agree that France is nice but we'll take the states anytime.

Well Honey, that's about it for now. There's really very little that I can say except that I miss you a lot. Take care of yourself Sel and write soon. Regards to all.

Love,
Bob

Pfc. B. D. Browne 39337016
Co. I, 410 Inf. A.P.O. 470
c/o Postmaster
New York, N.Y.

Miss Selma Nepom
716 S.W. Harrison St.
Portland, 1, Oregon

·· *October 30, 1944*

Dearest Darling,

I received your first letter today since I've been here and it was almost as good as being with you again. Honey, every letter I get from you I seem to love you more and more. If you only knew how much I want to come back so that you and I can start living our lives together. I imagine this letter sounds pretty foolish, but it's not lonesomeness, I really mean it.

I got a letter from Banny and the folks today and they told me all about the baby. She sounds wonderful, dimples and all.

I imagine you're at school now working hard. Selma, have a good time, but remember you belong to me. Sel, there's a Jewish fellow here with me from Chicago and he used to be stationed near Seattle. Tell me what house you're in, because he claims he knows a lot of girls in the Jewish Sororities.

Enclosed in this letter you'll find some French franc notes. One franc here is worth about 2¢ at home. If you want anymore Honey, let me know. Everything is in paper except for one francs—they're copper coins.

The weather has been pretty nice lately except for the rain we had last night. Sleeping on the ground isn't very comfortable in the rain—too damn muddy. That's how an infantryman lives though—makes the best of everything.

Saturday night we visited the city nearby and take it from me Honey, the Germans really ruined France. All the people are so poor and shabby looking. The restaurants have very little food left. They all have plenty of money, but it's almost worthless, because there is so little to buy. I looked for some souvenirs for you, but I couldn't find anything worth sending. All the streets are cobblestone and they have small automobiles similar to Austins. Believe it or not most of them are made by Ford. They also have Shell and Standard gasoline here. A lot of the French automobiles run by burning charcoal. It's really funny to see a car go down the street with a burner on the rear end. It looks just like a water boiler.

Being that we're on the Riviera Coast most of the cars are convertibles. Practically all of the wealthy homes are built on the hill behind the city. It reminds me a lot of Astoria.

Well Honey, I guess that's about all for now. I miss you all the time and I'll write Honey, whenever I get the chance. Write soon.

With all my love,
Bob

Pfc. B. D. Browne 39337016
Co. I, 410 Inf. A.P.O. 470
c/o Postmaster
New York, N.Y.

Miss Selma Nepom
716 S.W. Harrison St.
Portland, 1, Oregon

October 31, 1944

Dearest,

Just a note to let you know that I'm alright and love you. I received two more of your letters and they sure were good to see. If it wasn't for those letters I don't know what I would do. Young lady, do you know that you have a beautiful handwriting? Your letters were dated the 5th and 6th of October so they must have come in on the boat. I hope by the time you get this letter you'll know where I'm at.

Golly those clothes you bought sound wonderful. I can see that you found out my weak point. I love beautiful clothes and those you bought fill the bill. I'll bet that fur coat is beautiful. I'll see it when I get back.

Honey, I was glad to hear that Hesh got to see all the fellows. I'll bet he had a good time there.

My congratulations to your father on his birthday. I'll bet you had a party for him. Lewie also had his birthday the 20th of Oct. Couldn't send him anything except a letter. I've got a lot to make up for when I get home and you're going to help me Sweetheart.

I visited a Shul last night and it was really beautiful. Part of it was bombed but the most beautiful parts were untouched. When the Germans came through they killed all the Jews except for the girls. They burned all of the torahs (sp.) except for those which were hidden. A lady who was in the Shul told us all this. I couldn't understand her in French but I could the Jewish. It was really pitiful. She had 2 sons and husband killed and her daughter was taken. That's what the Jews went through in France.

Well Honey, I guess that's about it for today. Don't worry about me Sweet and take good care of yourself. I'll write again tomorrow if possible.

I love you,
Bob

PFC. B. D. BROWNE 39337016
CO. I, 410 INF. A.P.O. 470
c/o POSTMASTER
NEW YORK N.Y.

MISS SELMA NEPOM
4540 17TH N.E.
SEATTLE, WASH.

··· *November 2, 1944*

Dearest Selma,

At the present time Honey it's raining pretty hard out and I'm hoping the tent won't leak.

We leave for a night problem in about an hour and a half. We'll finish about one or two in the morning, so here's hoping it will stop raining by then.

I got a letter from the folks today and they told me that Lew was visiting them for the weekend. It will do the folks a lot of good just seeing him. I guess it's sort of up to him to take over now that I'm here.

We took a 10-mile hike today and we got to see quite a bit of France. We went through about 3 or 4 villages which were really quaint. I'm trying to get hold of some picture postal cards to send you, but they seem to be pretty hard to find. Well Sweetheart, I'd better close for now. I'll write again as soon as possible. Write soon Sweet.

I love you,
Bob

Pfc. B. D. Browne 39337016
Co. I, 410 Inf. A.P.O. 470
c/o Postmaster
New York N.Y.

Miss Selma Nepom
4540 17th N.E.
Seattle, Wash.

November 4, 1944

Dear Selma,

Honey we are now allowed to tell that we visited the city of Marseille, France. It is the largest port in France and the French scuttled many of their ships there when the Germans came in. It's very similar to Toulon.

I got a pass a couple of days ago to visit the city. It's far from modern but it's very historic and beautiful, regardless of those buildings which were bombed. All the streets are cobblestone and very rough.

There is very little that you can buy there. No food at all. All food is rationed to the French people. They have no sugar at all, very few dairy products. One egg is worth $4.00 to them. They do have plenty of wine and liquors. They seem to live on that stuff.

Dave Gold and I went in together. By the way Honey—Irv Potter is now engaged to that girl I told you about in New York. He gave her the ring when we were at P.O.E. in New York. Anyhow, Dave and I went to a French barber shop (COIFFEUR in French) and they really give you the works. They pay more attention to a man's hair than they do a woman's.

Well Sweetheart, that's about all I have time for now. Take care of yourself Honey and write often.

Yours with love,
Bob

P.S. Hope you like the pictures.

Pfc. B. D. Browne 39337016
Co. I, 410 Inf. A.P.O. 470
c/o Postmaster
New York N.Y.

Miss Selma Nepom
Phi Sigma Sigma
4540 – 17th N.E.
Seattle, 5, Wash.

November 17, 1944

Dearest Selma,

Honey, I'm sorry I couldn't write sooner but under the circumstances it was impossible. Sel I'm now in the thick of battle in France not too far from the German border. I'm living in a fox hole and haven't shaved or washed for 7 days. It's really rough stuff Honey. The Germans are rough boys to fight but I think we're a little more rougher.

I miss you more than ever Sweetheart and sure as hell wish this damn war would end so we could finish what we started, even though it wasn't much of a start.

I got a letter from the folks today, and also one from Lew and Junne. I suppose you know by now that Lew will also be a father in a few months.

How is school getting along Doll? I'll bet Seattle is the same as ever. Have fun Honey and when I get back we'll start all over again. Not much more to say Sel except I miss all those wonderful things about you. Write as often as possible.

Yours with love,
Bob

Pfc. B. D. Browne 39337016
Co. I, 410 Inf. A.P.O. 470
c/o Postmaster
New York N.Y.

Miss Selma Nepom
Phi Sigma Sigma
4540 – 17th N.E.
Seattle, 5, Wash.

November 19, 1944
(I'm with the 7th Army in France)

Dearest Darling,

I received your first letter from Seattle yesterday and I was sure glad to know all the good news. So you're now a sorority girl— Golly if you only knew the kidding that I was getting over that. The fellas are really laying it on. It sure is wonderful though. I'm glad you joined a house, you'll have much more fun that way. (I love you Honey)

I'll write to you as often as possible Honey, but you know how it is in a fox hole. So far today the shelling hasn't been too bad. The weather is still pretty wet and muddy.

Be sure to write Doll, and tell me all about school. Are you in with a good bunch of kids? Sel, send me a small picture of yourself that I can keep with me, about 3" x 4": Take care Honey and have fun. I love you and miss you as always.

Write soon and study hard.

Love,
Bob

Pfc. B. D. Browne 39337016
Co. I, 410 Inf. A.P.O. 470
c/o Postmaster
New York N.Y.

Miss Selma Nepom
Phi Sigma Sigma
4540 – 17th N.E.
Seattle, 5, Wash.

November 28, 1944
Closer to Germany

Dearest Selma,

Honey this has been the first chance I've had to write for quite awhile. It's impossible to write while we're on the move. That's why I'm unable to write Air Mail Honey. It's impossible to carry stationery. We get V-mail with our rations.

I received your letters and I'm sure glad to hear that you're getting along O.K. in school. It sure does sound wonderful. Have lots of fun Sweetheart. The first rest area we get to I'll write you longer letters.

We're still fighting it out in France and we've been moving quite rapidly. At present we're pretty close to the German border. I'm hoping this damn war will be overwith before we have to go through Germany. That would really be rough.

Well Doll, that's about it for now. I love you so take care of yourself and write often. Don't worry about the war situation—I hope it will be over in a few months.

Love,
Bob

Pfc. B. D. Browne 39337016
Co. I, 410 Inf. A.P.O. 470
c/o Postmaster
New York N.Y.

Miss Selma Nepom
Phi Sigma Sigma
4540 – 17th N.E.
Seattle, 5, Wash.

November 29, 1944

Dearest Darling,

Well Honey, this is the first chance I've had to write you a regular letter since we've been on the go. We were pretty lucky to take over a village so I confiscated this stationery. Sel, if you don't hear from me for a week or two at a time you'll know that we're moving again. We took this village last night and we'll probably be moving in a couple of hours. We're right in the thick of fighting and we've been having quite a few casualties. Pray for me Doll, those Germans are pretty rough fighters. We're giving them hell though.

Sel, I'm sending you some stuff that I got from Germans we captured. I'm sending you some Mark notes. One mark is worth about 40¢. Also I'm sending a German postage stamp. I'll send you whatever I can in a letter.

Honey, there's a fellow here in my outfit who spent quite awhile in Seattle. He was stationed near there and spent quite a time at U. of W. His name is Wally Schneider. He knows a few girls in Phi Sig by the names of June Shapero (now married), Mae Nelson, and another known as Betty. He was stationed with Balloon Barrage. Maybe you know them also.

Well Doll Baby I sure do miss you and pray god that someday soon we'll be able to start our lives all over. I want you to be one of the happiest in the world—just let me try Sweet.

Well Sel, I've got to get ready now. I love you and miss you always. Regards to all.

Love,
Bob

Pfc. B. D. Browne 39337016
Co. I, 410 Inf. A.P.O. 470
c/o Postmaster
New York N.Y.

Miss Selma Nepom
716 S.W. Harrison
Portland, Ore.

November 30, 1944

𝒟earest 𝒟arling,

Hello again Honey. We still are located in this little village so I'm able to write you a letter.

I got your letter today and you sure are a wonderful girl. I know that for sure. I was certainly glad to hear that you were able to visit your folks. Just can't beat em can you Sel.

Golly I would give anything to have this damn mess overwith. I want to do so many things and you're going to be with me. We're going to do a lot of traveling and really enjoy living. I've seen how terrible this world can be, but you and I will experience only the best. You deserve that and I'm going to see that you get it. Golly listen to me rave. I'm taking an awful lot for granted aren't I?

Sel you keep writing. Airmail. I also don't like V-mail, but it's the only means that I have. We're unable to carry stationery with us and we get V-Mail forms with our rations so that's the only reason I use it.

Well Honey, glad to hear that school is O.K. I'll bet Seattle is as good as ever.

Sel, I'd better close now because things are starting to pop again. Write soon—regards to all.

Yours with love,
Bob

P.S. I love you.

Pfc. B. D. Browne 39337016
Co. I, 410 Inf. A.P.O. 470
c/o Postmaster
New York N.Y.

Miss Selma Nepom
716 S.W. Harrison
Portland, Ore.

December 1, 1944

Dearest Selma,

Well Honey here we are in another village. We took it early this morning and I hate to say that one of my best friends was shot in the leg. The German that did it will not shoot anyone again. We had quite a few casualties but they had many, many more.

Honey this will probably be the last letter you'll receive for a few days because I think we'll be out in the field for awhile. Honey I haven't shaved for 10 days—you should see me—you'd die laughing. I even scare myself when I look in the mirror.

I got a letter yesterday from Besse. She and Mom are spending a few days at St. Martins Springs. It will do them both a lot of good.

Well Sweet, how's school coming along? Have you gone to any big affairs yet? Tell me all about your dates. Lets see now—the last date I had was in a little French village about 2 weeks ago, and believe it or not I slept in the same room all night. She was beautiful. Honey, she was a cow. It's the only place they had empty so Brown and 3 others sleep in the barn. The hay was really soft though. Golly it will be wonderful to get home. You just can't realize how wonderful and clean the United States are.

Well Sel, that's about it for now. I love you—take care of yourself and write often. Regards to all.

I love you,
Bob

Dearest Doll,

Just a line to let you know that I still love you, miss you and always will. I got this card from a prisoner. Take care of yourself and have fun. Regards to all. I'm getting your letters regularly. I'll write when possible.

Love, Bob

Miss Selma Nepom
4540 17th N.E
Seattle, 5,
Washington

Pfc. B. D. Browne 39337016
Co. I, 410 Inf. A.P.O. 470
c/o Postmaster
New York, N.Y.

Miss Selma Nepom
716 S.W. Harrison
Portland, Ore.

··· *December 5, 1944*

Dearest Selma,

Honey, I'm writing you from a French house which is really quite nice. We got a 24 hour relief after spending 4 nights and 3 days in the mud— sleeping, eating, & trying to fight. Sweetheart when I do get back I'll really appreciate living like a human being. A French outfit relieved us so I imagine it won't be long until the jump off will come. Our goal is the Rhine river and we're only about 15 miles from there now. Already the people are starting to look, talk, & act German.

When we take over a village we also take over anything we need. If we want a house we just take it. I guess that's how the Army works. It's an awful thing to do, but the men have to get rest and warmth, especially in weather like this. The weather has been against us. It's really been miserable. Plenty of rain and cold wind. Just like at home. But at home I enjoyed it sometimes.

Well Doll, how's school? I'll bet it's really wonderful there. Honey don't worry about not getting your letters off to me in time. I understand how it is when you first start school. They really keep you going don't they?

Well Honey, that's about all I can think of for now. Take care of yourself and give my regards to the gang. I'll write again whenever possible.

I love you,
Bob

P.S. I'm enclosing a couple of German coins, Nazi & anti-nazi.

Pfc. B. D. Browne 39337016
Co. I, 410 Inf. A.P.O. 470
c/o Postmaster
New York N.Y.

Miss Selma Nepom
716 S.W. Harrison
Portland, Ore.

December 6, 1944

Dearest Selma,

Well we moved into another village last night so thank goodness we got to sleep under a roof. Even a hard floor feels good.

The way things look Honey we'll be moving out for an attack in about 2 or 3 hours so I'm taking advantage of the time I've got. Believe it or not Sel I milked a cow last night. I practically had to tie the damn thing down to get it to stand still. I finally got a whole bucket full. Pretty good huh Sel? I even think the farmer was proud of me. Seems to be that all these people have their cows & chickens in the same house with them. The people live upstairs and the livestock downstairs. That's Europe for you Honey. They can have it.

I got a letter from the other doughboy in the family, Dave, who is with the 1st Army in Germany. He's going through hell like all the others but the thought of returning home seems to keep us all going. He's also very excited about Besse. Golly Sweetheart there's so much to live for that it actually hurts to think that this damn war won't end too soon. The Germans are very well fortified and will be from here on because they've had six years to prepare for us and they really did a good job. We'll break it though Sel, you just watch.

We had our first attack yesterday by the Luftwaffe and they did little damage. There were only about 12 planes and we got 3 of them. I don't think they have much left though.

Honey, I'm sending you some clippings from a German newspaper. If there's a good German student in the house—she'll come in handy. The paper was printed in Strassburg.

That's about it for now Sweet. Take care of yourself and write soon.

I love you,
Bob

War & Navy Departments
V-Mail Service

Pfc. B. D. Browne 39337016
Co. I 410 Inf. A.P.O. 470
c/o Postmaster New York, NY

Mrs. Dora Johnson
c/o Millers Dept. Store
Salem, Oregon

7 December 1944

Dear Mrs. Johnson,*

I received your very welcome letter today and it was sure good hearing from you.

My situation is and has been for the past month strictly front line duty. I've been right in the thick of battle and it's really been rough. German defenses are very strong but we'll get thru this alright. I'm with the U.S. 7th Army in France but now hope to be in Germany soon.

I haven't heard from Henry in quite sometime. I imagine he's pretty busy with school and all. He's very happy there and it looks like his future is planned for him. Don't forget—when graduation comes you and I are going to visit him. Golly that sure will be a wonderful day. Write whenever you get time and I'll do the same.

As ever,
Bob

**Mrs. Johnson was the widowed mother of Henry Johnson, one of my closest friends in high school when I moved to Salem. Miller's Dept. store, where she worked and Henry visited, was across the street from my Dad's jewelry store and optometry practice in Salem. When I went into the army, Henry joined the Navy.* —Bernard

PFC. B. D. BROWNE 39337016
Co. I 410 INF. A.P.O. 470
c/o POSTMASTER NEW YORK, NY

MISS SELMA NEPOM
PHI SIGMA SIGMA
4540 17TH ST. N.E.
SEATTLE 5, WASHINGTON

.... *8 December 1944*
— *Still Closer to Germany* —

Dearest Darling,

Well Honey we're on the move again and have a feeling we take another village soon so that we'll have a halfway decent place to stay. I doubt whether we'll hit another place for awhile though. The Germans are getting a little stiffer all the time. I hope we soon hit the Reich so that we can get this damn mess over with. You and I have a lot of unfinished business to take care of and the sooner we get started the better off we'll be—don't you agree Honey?

I got a letter from Banny and she keeps raving all about the baby. Besse nicknamed her "Eeny" being that her name is Alene. She really sounds wonderful. Golly I'm sure going to have a lot to come home to in a few months with Besse and Junne on the ball. Isn't life wonderful though Sweetheart.

Well Doll I guess that's about it for now. Take care of yourself, have fun, and write soon.

Love,
Bob

Pfc. B. D. Browne 39337016
Co. I, 410 Inf. A.P.O. 470
c/o Postmaster
New York, N.Y.

Miss Selma Nepom
Phi Sigma Sigma
4540 – 17th N.E.
Seattle, 5, Wash.

December 9, 1944

Dearest Selma,

Hello Honey. Once again I got a chance to write and I only wish I had more time. We start our new phase tomorrow so I imagine I won't have much time to write. With this rain and wind, fox holes won't be as nice as we expect them to. Golly I give anything if the weather would clear up for a little while. We've really been having terrible weather. Just like at home Sel, blue and rainy.

We haven't gotten any mail for the past couple of days, but I'm looking forward to some before we leave tomorrow. I'm sure anxious to hear about school and how you like it. I sort of feel responsible, because do you remember the way I talked you into going to school. I'll bet it's really swell Honey. I hope to get a taste of it someday—that is if I don't have too many grey hairs.

We got our P.X. supplies in this morning so we now have plenty of cigarettes, toilet articles, and believe it or not Hersheys chocolate. They really do give a lot of that out over here. Everyone seems to get plenty of everything. Whenever possible they give us all they can, which is really O.K. The last phase we were on we lived on canned rations for 8 days and every second day we got P.X. rations. They brought them directly to us, which would put them under enemy fire so you see that the famous Quartermaster corp is really on the ball. We call it the Jewish Man's business club.

Well Honey, I guess that's about it for now. Take care of yourself and write soon.

I love you,
Bob

Pfc. B. D. Browne 39337016
Co. I, 410 Inf. A.P.O. 470
c/o Postmaster
New York, N.Y.

Miss Selma Nepom
Phi Sigma Sigma
4540 – 17th N.E.
Seattle, 5, Wash.

December 14, 1944

Dearest Selma,

Honey, General Patch is really on the ball because we once again took what you might call a village (population 100). It sure did come in handy, because we were soaked through from the rain. Golly this weather has really been terrible—rain and mud that's all we have. We also have no Air support which means an awful lot to us.

Golly Sweet it sure would be swell if we could stay here for a couple of days, but they keep us moving right along. I guess being that we have the damn Krauts on the run, it's best to keep driving after them. At times though they really put up a resistance with both infantry and artillery.

Well Honey, how have things been going at school? It's sure wonderful to get your letters. Golly you have no idea how wonderful those United States of ours are. What I've seen of Europe isn't worth thinking about. People just live on what they can get out of the ground and from the few animals that they keep with them in their homes. They haven't seen white bread for the past four years. Same goes for coffee. All their other staple foods are (were) rationed to them by the Nazis. Practically everything they wear was rationed to them. Thank the lord you don't have to live like these people do. It's really hard to explain how awful it is. These people are used to it though so they don't mind it too much.

Well Sweetheart, that's about it for now. Take good care of yourself and remember that I'm thinking of you always. Till the day I come home which pray will be soon. Write often Honey.

I love you,
Bob

Pfc. B. D. Browne 39337016
Co. I, 410 Inf. A.P.O. 470
c/o Postmaster
New York, N.Y.

Miss Selma Nepom
Phi Sigma Sigma
4540 – 17th N.E.
Seattle, 5, Wash.

December 16, 1944

Dearest Selma,

Just a line Honey to let you know that I'm O.K. and miss you a lot.

I sent you a pair of hand carved wooden shoes yesterday. I couldn't send any larger ones because they wouldn't allow us to mail them. They're a small pair and were hand carved by a Frenchman. All the people who live in these small villages wear them. I'll bet they would sure ruin a person's feet in short order.

Well Honey, at present we are very close to Germany and maybe soon we will be there, unless we move to another sector. We've been moving right along.

We stopped in this village for a short time and will be moving out for an attack in about ½ an hour so I wanted to write to you before I moved out.

I haven't gotten any mail for the past couple of days but we hope to get some soon.

Well Doll I've got to run now so I'd better say good bye for now. Take care of yourself & write soon.

I love you,
Bob

Pfc. B. D. Browne 39337016
Co. I 410 Inf. A.P.O. 470
c/o Postmaster New York, NY

Miss Selma Nepom
Phi Sigma Sigma
4570 17th N.E.
Seattle, 5, Washington

·· *December 18, 1944*

Dearest Selma,

Here I am again Honey, letting you know that I'm fine, getting along O.K., and sure wish this damn mess would end so that I could get home again. If and when I do Sel, plan to take a little vacation from school.

Well Sweet, I can now say that we are now in Germany. We're just a little way over the border, but we are in Germany. The Siegfried Line is yet in front of us. I'll be happier once we get through that. As you probably know that is one of Germany's strongest points. They have large artillery pieces with 360° turntable so I imagine we'll really have a hot time. I don't know for sure but I think we're headed straight for the Black Forest in Germany. I sure as heck hope I'm wrong.

I got a letter from Lew today and I think he'll be going overseas soon. He took Junne home and he's spending a few days at home with the Folks before he goes to his P.O.E. I sure hope they keep him in the states. It's true that the Ferry Command isn't too rough, but it's bad enough just being overseas. Honey, it's really the bank no fooling. I guess those wonderful United States spoiled me. I'll really know how to appreciate them once I get back.

Well Sel, how's school getting along? I'll bet you're really getting into the run of things by now. Any good basketball games yet?

Honey, I'd better go now because I think we'll be moving soon. Take care of yourself and write soon.

Lovingly yours,
Bob

Pfc. B. D. Browne 39337016
Co. I, 410 Inf. A.P.O. 470
c/o Postmaster
New York N.Y.

Miss Selma Nepom
Phi Sigma Sigma
4540 – 17th N.E.
Seattle, 5, Wash.

December 23, 1944

Dear Selma,

I got a couple of your letters Sel and it sure was good hearing from you. Sel, I don't want you to worry about not being able to write. Sel, I realize you're awfully busy with school so don't feel bad if you can't write often. I think you and I understand one another well enough so that letters won't have to keep us tied. BUT <u>do</u> write whenever possible. Your letters mean an awful lot to me—you know that.

Well Sel, I can safely tell you now that I spent 3 days and 3 nights on German soil. We are now 100 miles north of where we were and will be here for a day or so before we move to the front. One good thing about moving and that is that we get a day or two to rest before moving to the front lines. We are once again in France though. We are in the Lorraine section of Alsace-Lorraine. Honey, it's really cold here too. Last night it went down to 2° below zero so you can imagin what the fox hole life will be like. Sort of wish you were here with me Sel. Golly I sure wish this damn mess would end.

I was glad to hear that school is getting along fine. Golly I'll bet it's really keeping you busy. You're in a good sorority though Honey so I imagine they really keep you on the ball.

I got a letter from the folks today and things seem to be fine at home. Besse will be a mother soon and also Junne. Golly things sure do happen as life goes on.

Well Darling, that's about it for now. Take good care of yourself, have fun, and write whenever possible. Have a good time at home and give my regards to all.

I love you,
Bob

Pfc. B. D. Browne 39337016
Co. I, 410 Inf. A.P.O. 470
c/o Postmaster, New York, N.Y.

Miss Selma Nepom
Phi Sigma Sigma
4540 – 17th N.E.
Seattle, 5, Wash.

December 24, 1944

Dearest Selma,

Well Sweetheart it will soon be Christmas Eve and I wanted to get this letter off to you right away because we leave for the front in about 2 hours so this may be the last letter for a little while. Honey, consider this a Christmas letter. I hope next year at this time you and I will be able to celebrate together. Golly once I get home we'll really do things. Just pray that it ends soon.

Sel, I'm sending you a bit of G.I. humor. One of the fellows got it from his boy-friend and I'm sending it to you. I thought it was pretty clever. Also I'm sending you a piece of distribution that came down. It's practically nothing but it's the thought behind it more than anything else.

We're still here in France and here's hoping than in a short time we'll be in Germany. All the people here have been under German control for the past 4 years. Here's some new dope Sel. When the Germans left here they took all girls over 14 years old and under 30 years old with them to Germany. They took only those who could have children so you can see what the Germans are like. This was told to us by French civilians so I imagine it is the truth. I guess that's the way the Germans operate Sweetheart. Thank goodness you're in the states Sel.

Well Doll, that's about it for now. Take care of yourself and if you <u>ever</u> get a spare moment drop a line to the folks. They would certainly appreciate hearing from you. Regards to all.

Love,
Bob

Pfc. B. D. Browne 39337016
Co. I, 410 Inf. A.P.O. 470
c/o Postmaster New York, N.Y.

Miss Selma Nepom
Phi Sigma Sigma
4540 – 17th N.E.
Seattle, 5, Wash.

·········· *December 26, 1944*

Dearest Selma,

Just a line to let you know that I received one of your letters today and also spent a lovely Christmas in a fox hole. They brought us a wonderful Christmas dinner though. It's very unusual that they bring it up directly to the front lines. It's the first hot meal we've had in 5 days. It consisted of roast turkey, corn, peas, cranberry sauce, bread and butter, mince meat pie, and hot coffee. It sure was wonderful to taste real food. We get 2 hot meals on the average of every ten days, that's only while in combat line duty though. Ever since we've been here though we've had very few rest periods. Usually a day or two at a time.

Golly Sel, that formal sure does sound wonderful. Here's hoping I'll be able to see it soon. We'll sure have a wonderful time Honey.

We're still here in France slugging it out. At the present time I'm the father of a 4 day old beard. You should see me, just like a bear. I'll shave though Honey, the first chance I get which may not be for four more days.

Sel, I'd better close now because things are starting to pop. Dave and Irv are still with the division, but I haven't seen them since Marseilles. Take care of yourself Doll and write soon.

I love you,
Bob

Pfc. B. D. Browne 39337016
Co. I, 410 Inf. A.P.O. 470
c/o Postmaster New York, N.Y.

Miss Selma Nepom
Phi Sigma Sigma
4540 – 17th N.E.
Seattle, 5, Wash.

December 27, 1944

Dearest Selma,

Well Honey this time I'm writing you from the cellar of a small house in a small French village that we took from the Germans just a short time ago. We're here to check for a counter attack just in case one comes. It's much better than a fox-hole so I consider myself quite fortunate. We might be here for a couple of days—I hope.

We haven't been moving too fast Honey because we've had an awful lot of resistance which really slows us up a lot. We are moving forward though which is much much better than moving backwards.

I got a letter from the Folks yesterday and also one from Banny. I suppose you know by now that Frieda is living in Salem. Ben seems to be managing a shoe store in Salem. They're supposed to have a fairly nice place.

Well Honey, that's about it for now. Take good care of yourself Sel and have fun. Write whenever possible.

Love,
Bob

Pfc. B. D. Browne 39337016
Co. I, 410 Inf. A.P.O. 470
c/o Postmaster New York, N.Y.

Miss Selma Nepom
Phi Sigma Sigma
4540 – 17th N.E.
Seattle, 5, Wash.

.... *December 29, 1944*

Dearest Selma,

Just a line to let you know that I'm fine and getting along O.K. I haven't heard from you for the past couple of days but I've always got tomorrow. I imagine you're kept pretty busy though.

We're still in this defensive position and it's really a pleasure just so we don't get a counter attack. I would really like to stay here for awhile but I only think it will be a couple of more days or so.

I got a couple of boxes today from the folks and they really went in a hurry. All the packages we get are emptied and then everybody digs in. Mom made me a scarf. Boy it was really a honey. Also a pair of gloves lined with rabbit fur.

How have things been going Honey? Anything new been happening at school? I was glad to hear about your good grades in English Comp. Keep it up Sel.

We took showers again today and it really felt wonderful to be clean again. They come up every chance they get. All they are, are big truck vans and they have shower units in back of the truck. They park and set up next to a stream where they get their water supply. The water is heated through a small unit in the motor. They really are alright though. Since we left Marseille we only had 2 chances to take showers so you can imagine how much they were welcomed.

Well Honey, it's been about a week now since we've heard rifle or small arms fire and it really is a wonderful feeling. We do have plenty of artillery coming in though, but there's twice as much going out. Resistance has been plentiful though. I imagine our poor General is knocking himself out somewhere in a beautiful suite trying to figure out where to move us next. Such is war Sel, I sure wish it was over—damn it.

Well Honey, that's about it for now. I'll write you again tomorrow if possible. Take care and write when possible.

Bob

DEAR Darling

Happy New Year

from the
Doughboys
of the
Cactus Division

FRANCE, 1944

FROM Bob
With love

Pfc. B. D. Browne 39337016
Co. I 410 Inf. A.P.O. 470
c/o Postmaster New York, N.Y.

Miss Selma Nepom
Phi Sigma Phi
4540 17th St. N.E.
Seattle 5, Washington

.... *1 January 1945*
France

Dearest Selma,

Hello again Honey. We just got notice that we're on the alert again for movement so I wanted to get this letter written to you before we leave. I think we'll be leaving tonight sometime.

I got your letter yesterday Sel telling me about seeing Bobby at the Phi Sig Formal. I'll bet that guy really looks good. I'd give anything to get a letter from him. I haven't heard from him for an awful long time. When I came over I lost his address with the hopes that he would keep writing, but no dice. I guess he's kept pretty busy though. How far is he stationed from home Hon? He must be pretty close.

It snowed here last night and it was really beautiful this morning. Snow, about 3 inches, all over the place. It was extremely cold though, but still beautiful. We had a little break in the routine this morning so believe it or not Yours Truly went sled riding. We got a big bobsled from one of the families here and we really had a time. We spent about two hours sliding down the hills. Sure was fun. Has it snowed around Seattle yet or is it still wet and cold? The folks say that it snowed a couple of days at home but it hasn't stuck at all. I guess it's good that it didn't stick though.

Not much new around here Sel except the same stuff and that's the artillery coming in. Every once in awhile the whole damn town shakes. I only hope they don't improve their aim.

Well Sel, that's about it for now. Don't study hard and write often. Keep up the good grades and have fun Honey.

Love,
Bob

Pfc. B. D. Browne 39337016
Co. I 410 Inf. A.P.O. 470
c/o Postmaster New York, N.Y.

Miss Selma Nepom
Phi Sigma Phi
4540 17th St. N.E.
Seattle 5, Washington

3 January 1945

France

Dearest Selma,

Honey, I received your letter today dated the 19th of December and as usual it was good to hear from you. Say those sorority rules sound pretty strict. I guess they sort of have to be, don't they?

The weather here has been bad but beautiful for the past week or so. It's all snow and ice and it really is rough. At night we get so cold we have no feeling at all. We sure have hit the good weather. While in the mountains we had rain and mud and now that we're on flat ground Winter hits us with snow and ice. Great country France, but only for a visit. You're in the Garden Spot of the world, take my word for it.

Glad to hear that you're having such a wonderful time in school. I'll bet it's really wonderful. Tell that roommate of yours to take good care of you for me.

I got a letter from one of my boyfriends from Salem, who is now going to the Naval Academy at Annapolis and he told me all about the Navy-Notre Dame football game. They really went wild because Navy won and nobody thought they ever would. They really had quite a celebration—champagne and everything.

Well Honey, that's about it for now. We go on patrol soon so I'd better say good-nite for now. Take good care of yourself and have fun.

Love,
Bob

Pfc. B. D. Browne 39337016
Co. I 410 Inf. A.P.O. 470
c/o Postmaster New York, N.Y.

Miss Selma Nepom
Phi Sigma Phi
4540 17th St. N.E.
Seattle 5, Washington

5 January 1945

Dearest Selma,

We made another move and we're now halfway settled so I'm taking advantage of the time by writing letters. I haven't heard from you for about 4 days now. You must be kept pretty busy with school and everything.

I got a letter from Banny last night and she sent me a picture of the baby. She sure is cute. The pictures were taken at 2 months and she really had some beautiful dimples. Sure is a doll.

Honey, I've got another poem for you—tell me what you think of it.

To You, Our Star —

I miss you more as weeks go by
And hope you miss me too,
Your letters mean so much to me
Do mine mean much to you?

That star you see high in the sky
Was meant for you and me
To a wish our luck and love
Will always, always be.

Day after day, thinking of you
Wondering how you are,
Makes me wish I were near you
Like that heavenly star.

May it shine bright all through the night,
And guide you through the day,
To everlasting happiness while you are
miles away.

I keep from thinking of lonely nights
But of the days to be,
When once again we'll laugh and love
And you are here with me. —

I think it's quite appropriate don't you Sel?

We're still experiencing plenty of snow and ice and I imagine it will be like that, if not worse, for a couple of months or more. Really is cold too.

Well Honey, we go on a raid soon so I'd better close. Keep writing and take care of yourself.

Love you,
Bob

PFC. B. D. BROWNE 39337016
CO. I 410 INF. A.P.O. 470
c/o POSTMASTER NEW YORK, NY

MISS SELMA NEPOM
PHI SIGMA PHI
4540 17TH ST. N.E.
SEATTLE 5, WASHINGTON

12 January 1945

Dearest Selma,

Honey I got one of your long-awaited letters yesterday and this is the first chance I've gotten to answer it. You sure can write wonderful letters Sel. They always give me that little spirit that a G.I. needs every once in awhile. I'm glad to know you're following our Army. We've been catching hell lately, but so far I've been very lucky—I guess. It could be much worse though Sel. We have lost some land but I guess that's to be expected at times.

At the present time we're in houses but have outposts out where we can see all German movement. It sure is strange to sit on a hill and watch German vehicles as well as men move around. The way things look they'll probably be making an attack around here soon. Hope I'm wrong though.

The way things sound Sel, you've been pretty busy at school. I hope you came out good on your midterms. I'll bet you've really seen some good football games this season. We get hold of newspapers every once in awhile and we really go through them.

Sel, I had my first fresh eggs (from the states) yesterday and they were really delicious. I got them for breakfast, both sunnyside up. Most of our food has been rations, but while in houses our kitchen cooks hot meals and sends them up to the lines. Even though most of it is dehydrated (eggs, milk, potatoes, apples, and many others) it really is good stuff. It's the best the government can get and that's good enough for me.

I'm looking forward for some of your mail tomorrow—that is if the mail truck gets here.

Well Sel, that's about it for now. Lets keep our chins up and just pray that the <u>Day</u> will come soon. I'd better say goodbye for now. Take care of yourself, have fun, and don't forget—I pray for you always.

Love,
Bob

PFC. B. D. BROWNE 39337016
CO. I 410 INF. A.P.O. 470
c/o POSTMASTER NEW YORK, N.Y.

MISS SELMA NEPOM
PHI SIGMA PHI
4540 17TH ST. N.E.
SEATTLE 5, WASHINGTON

15 January 1945

Dear Selma,

Got some free time now so I'm taking advantage of it by writing letters. Sort of think we'll be moving soon so this may be the last chance I get for a little while.

Today is another one of those beautiful days. Plenty of snow and sunshine. Yesterday I went skiing, believe it or not. I got the skis from some civilian and he was more than glad to let me use them. I sure had a swell time, it's a wonder I didn't break my neck.

One of the fellows did sort of sprain his ankle a little. He's alright though.

I got a package yesterday from the Folks and in it was included a box of cigars. We really had a time. Surprising the way they keep you warm when it's cold out.

We witnessed quite a bombing last night. It seemed to be about 20 miles away which would be the heart of the Saar valley. It might have been the city of Saarbrucken. Anyhow we really bombed the h— out of em. The flashes were so bright that it was just like daylight here. There was also plenty of flak in the sky. They did a good job of bombing wherever it was.

How's school getting along Sel? Anything exciting happening?

I got a letter from the Folks yesterday and they say that Frieda and Ben are very happy. They're supposed to have a beautiful little house.

Well Honey, that's about it for now. Take care of yourself and write soon.

Love,
Bob

Pfc. B. D. Browne 39337016
Co. I 410 Inf. A.P.O. 470
c/o Postmaster New York, NY

Miss Selma Nepom
Phi Sigma Phi
4540 17th St. N.E.
Seattle 5, Washington

17 January 1945
France — Letter #1

Dearest Selma,

I got your letter number one today dated the 5th of January. I was glad to hear that you received the stamps, money, and postcard. I hope they help you pass your course, but I'm sure you'd make it alright on your own. Glad to know they helped though. Every chance I get, I'll send you stuff like that. Haven't had the chance lately though.

Yes Sel, the mail system is certainly funny. I think this number system is alright. In fact lots of the fellows use it already.

Thanks for the regards to Wally. He mentioned something about June getting married, but I imagine he'll be pretty surprised about the others. He had no mutual agreements so if they found the <u>right</u> man I can hardly blame them.

Honey, it's true about feeling "up in the air" about one another and I'm sure once I get home we'll settle everything one way or the other and I think it will be my way. Taking a lot for granted, aren't I Sel? It's also true that we spent such a short time together that it doesn't seem possible. I think and know that the short time I spent with you, I learned more about you than I know about myself. Maybe it's because we've been so close (but yet so far) all our lives. Regardless though Sel, once we get together I'm sure we'll straighten things out. I think the best thing for us to do is have one big time together when I get home. Maybe a weekend at the beach or something like that. If you're at school at the time you'd better plan to leave for a few days because if you don't I'll come steal you away.

Well Honey, that's about it for now. Take care of yourself and have fun.

I think I love you, <-how's that
Bob

P.S. I'm still waiting for that head picture of you. 3"x4".

Pfc. B. D. Browne 39337016
Co. I 410 Inf. A.P.O. 470
c/o Postmaster New York, NY

Miss Selma Nepom
Phi Sigma Phi
4540 17th St. N.E.
Seattle 5, Washington

19 January 1945
France — Letter #2

Dearest Selma,

Well Honey we moved twice since my last letter and I'm now about 95 miles from where I was yesterday. We moved to a different sector which puts us right back in the mountains with plenty of snow and ice. Really do move us around don't they? I guess they must need us here for something??

Not much news otherwise Sel except that it is snowing and it looks as though it may last for awhile. I sure wish we didn't have it because it really makes things rough. I don't think it will start thawing though until late February or early March. I sure hope it comes soon though so that maybe we can end this damn war.

Honey, just before leaving yesterday Dave Gold and I got together. It's the first time we've seen each other since we got into combat. Sure was good to see him. We cried on each others shoulders for awhile and then one conversation led to [another] and about home. He seems to be quite serious about some gal in Vancouver B.C. I imagine you know more about her than I do. She seems to be a very nice looking girl. We're both more than anxious to get home.

Well Honey, how have things been going at school? Hope you're having a lot of fun as well as working hard. How do you like college life by now? I'd better sign off for now Sel. Take good care of yourself and have fun. Write often.

Love,
Bob

Letter #2

Pfc. B. D. Browne 39337016
Co. I 410 Inf. A.P.O. 470
c/o Postmaster New York, N.Y.

Miss Selma Nepom
Phi Sigma Phi
4540 17th St. N.E.
Seattle 5, Washington

21 January 1945

Letter #3

Dear Selma,

I received your long and wonderful letter today and it sure was wonderful hearing from you again. You write a wonderful letter Sel. Wish I could do the same.

Sel, the way you talk you really have plenty cigarettes. I guess the boys are really keeping you well taken care of. We seem to get plenty over here but I don't smoke so I never seem to be hunting for them. I'm glad to know that you have plenty though Sel.

Glad to hear about all the Sorority activities, they sure do sound good. It's good to know that there's somebody keeping watch for me. I'd much rather be watching you myself. School sounds good though Sel. I was sorry to hear that you had to go to school on New Year's Day. We had quite a time ourselves. We were expecting a counter- attack but it didn't come thank goodness. Well the situation is not much different at present. We had a new snow this morning and it's continued snowing all day. It's about 8" deep at the present time and it's still going strong.

Honey, I've got to say good night now because it's getting too dark to write. Take care, have fun, and write again soon.

Love,
Bob

Pfc. B. D. Browne 39337016
Co. I 410 Inf. A.P.O. 470
c/o Postmaster New York, NY

Miss Selma Nepom
Phi Sigma Phi
4540 17th St. N.E.
Seattle 5, Washington

24 January 1945
Letter #4

Dear Selma,

Just a line to let you know that we moved once again only to a more active spot. Things will really be getting hot here soon. I can't tell you just where I'm at, but you can probably tell by the papers. I imagine they really need us where we're at now.

They are still having quite a bit of trouble around Haguenau and Bitche. It's really plenty hot there.

Sel, I got a chance to get hold of some more German coins. If I were home I would make a bracelet for you, but all I can do at present is send them to you. I hope you like them. They were taken from a prisoner. He seemed so happy to be captured (truthfully he gave up) that he gave out everything he had. If you want any more, let me know and I'll get them for you if possible. They have 100 pfennigs to one mark and one mark is worth about 40¢ in our money.

Well Honey, that's about it for now. I hate to write such short letters but I just don't have the time—please understand Sel. Take care Sel, have fun, and write often.

Love,
Bob

Pfc. B. D. Browne 39337016
Co. I 410 Inf. A.P.O. 470
c/o Postmaster New York, N.Y.

Miss Selma Nepom
Phi Sigma Phi
4540 17th St. N.E.
Seattle 5, Washington

January 25, 1945
France — Letter #4

Dearest Selma,

I received your letter today dated the 8th of January. It was good to hear from you Honey and you made a big mistake by asking me to suggest something, because from now on I'm going to make a request in every letter. 1st Please send me one (1) Selma Nepom—hair – dark, eyes – dark, weight – 120, height – 5'7", looks – wonderful, body – still better, personality – superb. Well Honey—how did I do? Please send yourself special delivery so that I can sign for you. Seriously though Sel, send me a picture of yourself about 3" x 4". Also send candy (licorice—my favorite), and anything else good to eat.

The reason I didn't ask you before is because I didn't think you had the time to monkey with such stuff. You're a Doll, Sel.

Tell Shirley that I certainly appreciate her letting you use her room all the time. Sounds like the—house writing room. Glad to hear that she writes to Stan a lot. You have no idea what a letter means from the girl friend.

I got a couple of letters from the folks today and everything seems to be going along fine. Besse claims she's getting as big around as she is tall. Dave wants some snapshots so that he can see what she looks like. He's already starting to sweat it out. I think he sort of wants a boy. It sure would be nice to have a boy to go with Banny's girl and then Junne could have twins. Boy oh Boy what a mess.

Frieda & Ben come over to the house practically every morning. They seem to be doing alright there. Ben really got a break when he got out of the Army.

Glad to hear that you're following the 7th Army close, I think things will start popping soon. Where or when I don't know. Keep up with me though Honey.

Well Sel, how have things been going at school? Having fun? I'll bet those basketball games are really the stuff. By the way, I read where U. of H. didn't do too bad in football. Glad to hear it.

Well Honey, I'd better run along now. Take good care of yourself, have fun and write often. I'll write again as soon as possible.

I love you,
Bob

Pfc. B. D. Browne 39337016
Co. I 410 Inf. A.P.O. 470
c/o Postmaster New York, N.Y.

Miss Selma Nepom
716 S.W. Harrison
Portland, Oregon

28 January 1945
Front Line France — Letter #5

Dearest Selma,

Just a line Honey to let you know that I'm alright and getting along fine. I haven't heard from you for the past couple of days, but I expect a letter today or tomorrow. Sel, have my letters been coming in according to number? We've been having quite a fight for the past 3 days with some damn SS troops trying to break through our lines. It's been rough Sel and casualties are heavy, but thank goodness your one and only is still alright—knock on wood— We also haven't given any ground yet and we don't intend to. This snow plays hell on us but it can't be helped. We run around in white snow suits so that we can't be seen.

I ran into Dave again yesterday and we seem to be fighting right along side each other. His battalion is along side of ours so I get to see him about once every two days when we come back to thaw out. He's doing fine. He's up for Sgt. but I think he's like me and will refuse it. He may take it though. Honey, in combat the less you have the better off you are. It's hard enough watching out for your own life as well as others. Follow me?

Hope everything is alright at school. Dave mentioned some girl in Vancouver B.C. He's been writing to her for quite awhile. I'll send her name the next chance I see him. The girls there may know her.

Well Doll, that's about it for now. Take care, study hard, and write often.

Yours with love,
Bob

Letter #5

206

Pfc. B. D. Browne 39337016
Co. I 410 Inf. A.P.O. 470
c/o Postmaster New York, N.Y.

Miss Selma Nepom
Phi Sigma Phi
4540 17th St. N.E.
Seattle 5, Washington

.... *29 January 1945*

Dear Sel,

Just a note to let you know that I received your letter dated January 10th and it was sure good hearing from you and all about school. Sounds like you have quite a time playing cards. Sounds like fun.

Not much new on this side of the pond except that it's still snowing and it's cold as hell. We're still holding ground in fact we're starting to push a little every once in awhile. Sort of this reminds me of the game you play at school. Just a little different.

Got a letter from Junne today and she seems to think that Lew is on his way over. I sure hope she's wrong, but I haven't heard from him for quite awhile so it might be so.

Well Honey, I've got to take off right now. I'll write again when possible.

Love,
Bob

Letter #6

Pfc. B. D. Browne 39337016
Co. I 410 Inf. A.P.O. 470
c/o Postmaster New York, N.Y.

Miss Selma Nepom
Phi Sigma Phi
4540 17th St. N.E.
Seattle 5, Washington

30 January 1945
Front Lines

Dearest Selma,

I received two of your letters today, one dated the 23rd Dec. (from Portland) and the other dated January 16. Sure was good to hear from you Honey. You must have had quite a time in that airplane. That same thing has happened to Pop quite a bit. You're right though Sel, it is the best way to travel. Maybe someday you'll have your own plane Sel.

Glad to hear that you saw Sol and Hesh while in Portland. Looks like I'm going to have competition right along. Sure wish I was home to give a little resistance. Honey, you'll just have to go by my letters until I get home. Sorry to hear about Hesh cracking up. Sounds almost as rough as the infantry. Glad to hear he got what he wanted though.

I got a letter from Lew today with his A.P.O. #, but he couldn't tell me where he's going. I sort of think it will be England though.

Sel if you ever get a spare moment I would sure appreciate it if you would drop a line to the folks. They think you're a wonderful girl and would really enjoy hearing from you. The address is 1710 So. Winter St. They always thought a lot of you and the family, but as for me, I've just got one favorite in the family and that's my gal Tillie. Give her a big kiss for me the next time you go home Sel.

Well Doll, it's getting pretty dark so I'd better say good night. I'll write again when possible.

Have fun Sel and write often.

Love,
Bob

Letter #7

Pfc. B. D. Browne 39337016
Co. I 410 Inf. A.P.O. 470
c/o Postmaster New York, NY

Miss Selma Nepom
Phi Sigma Phi
4540 17th St. N.E.
Seattle 5, Washington

31 January 1945
Frontlines in Alsace

Dearest Selma,

I received another of your letters today dated the 17th of January. Really on the ball Honey. I was glad to hear that my letters are coming through.

About growing a beard, our commanding General says that we should shave every 2 days, but he never gets up to the front so we shave only when we want to. Great stuff—these beards.

I got a letter from Bobby today and he's getting along fine and expects to be a corporal soon. He's got something to do with B-27's just what I don't know. Sure was good to hear from him. Yes I heard about Celia and Irwin. That family of ours is really going to town in a hurry. That's life though Honey.

Sorry to hear about the rain at home, but it sure does sound wonderful. Pacific Coast rain seems to smell different than any other rain I've been in. Maybe it's me.

Sure is swell that Eric's parents are coming to the U.S. Are they going to live there permanently or just for a visit. Sure will be swell for Eric.

Sel, as for my job, I'm with a front line rifle company. I am what is known as I & R man for the company, which means, intelligence and reconnaissance. Due to my small knowledge of German (3 yrs in high school), I do all prisoner interrogation as well as go out on reconnaissance patrols which is going out into enemy territory and finding out information about the enemy. I travel with the rifle company and assist in all attacks and frontline activity. A company is made up of 5 platoons. 1, 2 & 3 are rifle platoons (30 men in each), 4th platoon is weapons platoon (mortars & machine guns) app 25 men and then there is hdq't platoon which consists of supply, communications, I & R, finance, and all clerical

209

work. We have about 24 men. We are with the front part of the 7th Army in Alsace. Just what town I can't say but we are in the Hagenau area.

The Germans have been trying to push through us, but we haven't given at all and we don't expect to.

Well Honey, that's about it for now. Take care of yourself and write often.

I love you,
Bob

Letter #8

Pfc. B. D. Browne 39337016
Co. I 410 Inf. A.P.O. 470
c/o Postmaster New York, N.Y.

Miss Selma Nepom
Phi Sigma Phi
4540 17th St. N.E.
Seattle 5, Washington

1 February 1945

Dearest Selma,

Just a line Honey to let you know that things are pretty well under control. The snow has finally started to thaw out and all there is now is water and slush. Sure is a mess. Those damn foxholes are half full of water. The way the civilians talk they think it might freeze over again soon. I sure hope not. The weather never seems to be with us. First it's all snow and ice and we practically freeze and then it thaws and you have mud to wallow around in. That's how it goes Sel, never satisfied.

I saw Dave again last night and he seems to be doing alright. He still plans on a big time once we get back to civilization. Both of us have tried to contact Irv, but no luck. We never seem to get close enough to him. Pretty sure he's getting along alright though. Sure is funny, the three of us were put in all different regiments 409, 410, & 411 infantries. Guess we were pretty fortunate to get in the same division though.

Well Honey, how have things been going in school. Anything exciting happen recently?

Selma, have you been getting my letters according to number or are they all mixed up. I got a letter today from the Folks which was post-marked the 21st of January. Pretty good time.

Well Honey, that's about it for now. Take care of yourself and write soon.

Love,
Bob

Letter #9

Pfc. B. D. Browne 39337016
Co. I 410 Inf. A.P.O. 470
c/o Postmaster New York, N.Y.

Miss Selma Nepom
Phi Sigma Phi
4540 17th St. N.E.
Seattle 5, Washington

4 February 1945

Dearest Selma,

Well Honey, just another note to let you know that I'm still fine, miss you an awful lot, and all that goes with it. I got a letter from you yesterday dated back in December. It's when you were sick in bed and were enjoying all the attention the girls were giving you. Take care of yourself Honey. Get that roommate of yours on the ball. Tell her that I want her to take special care of you for me. I'll pay her in German money if she'll take it.

I sent Normie a German Postal Card tonight. I'm sure he'll enjoy it being that he's taking German. Glad to know that he's taking it, it's a good language.

Well Honey, I go on patrol in a few minutes so I'll sign off for now. Take good care of yourself and write soon. I'll write again tomorrow if possible.

With love,
Bob

Pfc. B. D. Browne 39337016
Co. I 410 Inf. A.P.O. 470
c/o Postmaster New York, N.Y.

Miss Selma Nepom
Phi Sigma Phi
4540 17th St. N.E.
Seattle 5, Washington

7 February 1945

Dearest Selma,

I received your type-written letter today dated the 27th of January which is good time. It was good to hear from you Sel.

I haven't been able to write for the past couple of days because I've been so busy. We've also moved to one side of our sector, but it wasn't too far away.

The weather has made quite a change. All of the ice and snow has melted so now we have plenty of mud. I don't know which one is worse. The civilians say that for the next couple of months all they have is plenty of wind and rain. This damp weather sort of reminds me of home.

Glad to hear that you went to an operetta. Sure will be good to see one again. So you're ushering these days, eh kid? How do you rate, or was that one of your freshman pledge duties? How are your grades coming Sel? If I know you, as I'm pretty sure I do, you're getting close to straight "A's." Am I right?

Well Honey, I'm on call soon so I'd better say (gute nacht) good night for now.

Give my best to all and write again. Soon.
Ich liebe dich or

I love you,
Bob

Letter #10

213

Pfc. B. D. Browne 39337016
Co. I 410 Inf. A.P.O. 470
c/o Postmaster New York, N.Y.

Miss Selma Nepom
716 S.W. Harrison
Portland, Oregon

11 February 1945
Alsace

Dearest Selma,

Just a line Honey to let you know that I'm fine and miss you and every-thing at home an awful lot. Honey, I feel bad because of the fact that I didn't spend more time with you while I had the chance. I mean even when I was a civilian. I hope to make up for it one of these days.

Well, we're still here resting and it really is a break for us. It sure did come in time. We go to a show every day and sleep while not doing any-thing else. We start a training schedule tomorrow and I think it will last for about 3 days. I don't think we will be here too much longer. Today we got a lot of new clothes, equipment etc. We also had our weapons repaired and checked. I got a feeling that when we leave here we'll be part of a big offensive. Just a thought Sweetheart.

How have things been going at school? Did you ever receive those wooden shoes I sent to you? Let me know because they might have gotten lost in the mail.

Well Honey, that's about it for now. Write soon and take care of yourself. Send me candy, cookies, cake, etc.

I love you,
Bob

Letter #12 or 11?

Pfc. B. D. Browne 39337016
Co. I, 410 Inf. A.P.O. 470
c/o Postmaster New York, N.Y.

Miss Selma Nepom
716 S.W. Harrison
Portland, Ore.

February 13, 1945
Alsace

Dearest Selma,

I received your letter yesterday and it was sure good to hear from you. It only took your letter 10 days to get here which is very good time. I was glad to hear that you finally received those wooden shoes. They were given to me by a wooden shoemaker who lives in a little town east of Strassbourg. He was a very nice fellow and wanted me to send them home as a souvenir. All the people in France and Alsace-Lorraine wear them, how, I don't know. They have a little pair of slippers that they wear inside of them. The shoes are always left outside on the doorstep. All they wear in the house are their slippers. Sure is funny to look at some of their houses and see all the shoes lined up, from the grandfathers down to the youngest child. They are not worn in the larger towns though.

We're still here resting and will probably remain here for a few more days. We're having all of our weapons and equipment checked and replaced if need be. I got the chance to send cable grams home and I also sent you one. It may not make too much sense because there are form phrases that you pick to use. You can't say what you want like in a telegram. Hope you get it alright Sel.

The weather is still rainy. All it seems to do now is rain which makes for more mud. Hope it quits raining by the time we leave.

Well Honey, that's about all I've got time for now. Take care of yourself, have fun and write soon. Regards to the roommate, she'd better take good care of you.

With love,
Bob

P.S. Send plenty of candy, cookies, cake, etc.

Letter #13

Pfc. B. D. Browne 39337016
Co. I, 410 Inf. A.P.O. 470
c/o Postmaster New York, N.Y.

Miss Selma Nepom
716 S.W. Harrison
Portland, Ore.

.... *February 14, 1945*

TO MY VALENTINE –

Dearest Selma,

I received your letter today dated the 24th of January so you can see how mixed up the mail system is. It's good to hear from you though, even if you just say

"Dear Bob,

I'm fine.

Sel"

I received my first letters from Lew today since he left for overseas. He's stationed in London and claims they're really keeping him busy. He makes emergency flights for wounded soldiers etc. He doesn't think much of London. Claims it's awfully dirty throughout the country. He likes it though in a way for the fact that Pop was born there. He visited with my aunt Bessie and will probably spend most of his free time with them. He sure feels bad about leaving Junne but I guess it just can't be helped.

Sorry to hear that you haven't been receiving my letters. I write to you almost every chance I get, which sometimes isn't too often. I think it's this damn mail system Honey, sometimes it all comes in at once and other times it takes weeks.

Glad to hear about Eric's father. That sure will be swell. One of these days soon we'll have to have a big get together.

Well Doll, that's about it for now. Write soon and regards to the folks. Send cookies, candy, cake, etc. (How's that?)

I love you,
Bob

Letter #14

Pfc. B. D. Browne 39337016
Co. I, 410 Inf. A.P.O. 470
c/o Postmaster New York, N.Y.

Miss Selma Nepom
716 S.W. Harrison
Portland, Ore.

.... *15 February 1945*

Letter #15

My Darling,

> *Although we may be far apart,*
> *My thoughts are always with you.*
> *I miss you more each day Sweetheart,*
> *Until the day my dreams come true.*
> *Lovely memories of days gone by*
> *Keep lingering with your kisses.*
> *I'm longing for the day when I*
> *Can change "My Darling's" name to* <u>*Mrs.*</u>

How was that Honey, especially for you? Sel, I received two letters from you today dated February 3rd and 5th and it sure was good hearing from you again so soon. Honey you write such wonderful letters. I seem to be right next to you when I read them. Give anything if it were true.

Sel, don't worry about the cigars, the only reason I smoked them was because it was so damned cold with all the ice and snow. They actually did keep me warm, maybe it's just in my head. I don't smoke cigars though Honey, just used them when it was cold.

I heard from Bobby a few days ago and he seems to be having a swell life in the states. Sure glad that we all don't have to be over here or on the other side. Hope he stays there for the duration. Looks like quite a thing between he and Ruthie. Seems to think it's alright too.

Sel, I've skiied a few times since the last time I wrote you about it, but now all the snow is gone so I hope to be skiing at Timberline next winter.

Glad to hear that you heard from Hesh, what does he have to say? He's probably having a pretty rough time. Honey, how many boys do you write to besides me? I'm sure a jealous guy, aren't I? Well, do you blame me?

Sel, I'm going to keep numbering my letters to you unless you don't think it helps. Have they been coming in order?

Well Sweet, that's about it for now. Take care of yourself and write again soon.

I love you,
Bob

P.S. Sure glad to hear about Benny getting a furlough. Boy I'll bet that was really a surprise. Honey give him my regards and tell him we'll go on a good drunk once we all get home.

Pfc. B. D. Browne 39337016
Co. I, 410 Inf. A.P.O. 470
c/o Postmaster New York, NY

Miss Selma Nepom
716 S.W. Harrison
Portland, Ore.

··· *February 16, 1945*
Alsace

Dear Selma,

Just a line Honey to let you know that I'm fine and we're still here in a rest area. We had an inspection parade today for the General. He really gave us a going over too. He stopped and talked to about every 15th man. Thank goodness he didn't pick me out. We've gotten all repairs on weapons and a new issue of clothing, so I imagine we'll be moving out sometime soon.

Hope everything is going alright with exams Honey. Take it easy and I'm sure you'll do alright.

The weather really has made a change no fooling. It's really been wonderful. Just like summer. The people seem to think that it might start snowing again, but I don't see how because it's really been beautiful.

We had a band concert last night Sel and it was really alright. Went over in a big way. Sure sounded swell. We also went to a show and saw "Janie." Honey this rear echelon is really alright. Sure do hate to think of going up again. Don't know when it will be, but I've got a feeling it might be soon. The weather seems to be too good.

Well Doll, that's about it for now. Write soon and regards to all at home Sel. I'll keep numbering my letters until I forget the number. Does it help any? How about starting all over from scratch if it helps?

Yours with love,
Bob

Letter #16

PFC. B. D. BROWNE 39337016
CO. I, 410 INF. A.P.O. 470
c/o POSTMASTER NEW YORK, N.Y.

MISS SELMA NEPOM
PHI SIGMA PHI
4540 17TH ST. N.E.
SEATTLE 5, WASHINGTON

·· *February 19, 1945*
Alsace

Dearest Selma,

Hello again, this is me. Sel, I imagine by now you're right in the middle of exams. Make good Hon.

I haven't received any mail for the past couple of days, but I hope to get some tomorrow. Now that we're in the rear area we get mail every day, rather, it comes in every day.

Tomorrow we're scheduled to have a review for our battalion commander. They love to have their battalion parade for them.

It rained all day today which really makes things muddy. I sure feel for those fellows on the front. They must really be miserable. They must be going through hell.

This rest area is really swell Hon. We have a training schedule made out for the entire week so here's hoping we'll get to stay here for the week. If they want to move us though they'll do it regardless of the training schedule. Sure has been swell though.

It was sure good to hear about the bombing of Japan. That really means a lot. I'm sure this won't be the last time it happens. I hope they sink the whole damn island.

Here's hoping that everything is going along alright with you. Take good care of yourself Honey and have fun at school. Anything exciting been happening lately?

That's about it for now Sel. Regards to all at home and write soon. Send candy, cookies, dates, cake etc.

Yours with love,
Bob

P.S. Selma, I'm still waiting for that picture for my billfold. It's the only place we've got to carry pictures especially while moving.

Pfc. B. D. Browne 39337016
Co. I, 410 Inf. A.P.O. 470
c/o Postmaster New York, N.Y.

Miss Selma Nepom
Phi Sigma Phi
4540 17th St. N.E.
Seattle 5, Washington

.... *21 February 1945*
Alsace

Dearest Selma,

I received your wonderful letter today which was dated the 8th of February. Sure was good to hear from you Doll. From now on I promise to make a request in every letter and right now I would like to request "A PICTURE" of you to keep with me. All I have is a snapshot. I had to send your big picture home because I had no place to take it with me. I could have put it in my duffle bag, but it would have been ruined by now.

Honey our rest ends tomorrow morning when we move up on line, relieving another outfit. I sure do hate to see it end. Sure was swell while it lasted. I may not be able to write for a couple of days, but the first chance I get I'll give you all the dope.

You asked about Dave. He's with the 1st Army in Luxemburg. He was with the retreating outfit when the Germans made the salient in Audemars and lost everything he owned except what he had with him. Thank goodness he's alright. He too is with a front-line infantry outfit and from his last letter he seems to be on the defense which is holding ground.

Sel, we get all the toilet articles we need with our rations. I get the Readers Digest, Newsweek, and Esquire every month from home. We get plenty of stationery, but when we run short I'll let you know. You can send canned fruits, fishes etc. I love licorice if it's possible to get. Also send cookies, (fruit) cake, dates, etc. I would like something personal of yours that I could wear with my dog tags or something like that. Something that will always keep you and I together while I'm so far away from you. Sentimental jerk, aren't I?

Sure was swell to hear about the grade on your exam. Keep up the good work Sel. You'll have a lot to teach me when I get home.

About that overseas wife deal. I think it stinks. It's different if your wife can come over and live with you during the occupation or something like that, but as for a visit—no deal. It's hard enough leaving the first time, why go through the same agony again. I also don't like the idea of having the wife see what hell one has to go through over here, especially when the husband is a frontline soldier. Hope you agree Sel.

Honey, I have to go on a quartering party for the company in about 30 minutes. Where to, I don't know, but wherever it is I'm going to try to get billets.

I'll write again Sel, the first chance I get. Write often and take care of yourself. I hope you get to see the folks when you go home. Regards to all Hon.

Love,
Bob

Pfc. B. D. Browne 39337016
Co. I, 410 Inf. A.P.O. 470
c/o Postmaster New York, N.Y.

Miss Selma Nepom
Phi Sigma Phi
4540 17th St. N.E.
Seattle 5, Washington

February 23, 1945
Alsace #19

Dearest Selma,

Honey, I received your letter today dated the 9th of February. Golly you're really on the ball.

I really went for that cartoon. It sure was cute. About 25 fellows agree with me too. Lots of truth in it though Sel. I know a couple of fellows who have already married a girl from Alsace. One was an officer. Don't worry though Honey, I've got too much to look forward to. Don't get a swelled head now. They have a lot of beautiful girls here, but the trend of them are really filthy. They just don't know any better, I guess.

Glad to hear that you heard from Hesh. I imagine he writes an interesting letter. No Sel, I don't write to him. I don't seem to have the time. I write to Bobby, Monte, Lew, Junne, Dave (my brother), 3 friends from Salem, you and the folks. How's that for a list? I write only when I have time though Sel. I try to write to the Folks once a day, time or no time.

Sel, we're now about 2 miles from kraut land. We'll probably move into position tomorrow or the next day. Sure hate to go back after such a nice vacation. Really was swell.

I got a letter from Monte a couple days ago telling me about his sister's wedding. He's with an ordnance section, the 9th Army. He's somewhere in Holland. It's strictly rear echelon stuff and he really enjoys it.

Well Doll, that's about it for now. I'll write again tomorrow if possible. Take care of yourself Honey and regards to all at home. Hello to Saralyn. Write soon Sel and study hard, you'll have a lot to teach me when I get home.

Love you,
Bob

Pfc. B. D. Browne 39337016
Co. I, 410 Inf. A.P.O. 470
c/o Postmaster New York, N.Y.

Miss Selma Nepom
Phi Sigma Phi
4540 17th St. N.E.
Seattle 5, Washington

··· *February 24, 1945*

Dearest Selma,

Just a line to let you know that I'm fine and getting along swell. Miss you a lot Honey and tonight I really feel like letting you know all about everything, but I don't know where to start.

A long time ago I had a dream about you which started our correspondence. It has lasted till now and it's going to last until I get home. I got my first and last furlough in the states and we went out together for the first time in our lives. It meant an awful lot to me because I've felt as if I've been foolish for not taking you out before. I've known you all my life and practically grew up together. Sel that date we had lasted till early in the morning and I learned more about you than I've ever learned about any other girl. You and I had a wonderful time that night. It was the night of my furlough aside from being with the folks. Sel it really wasn't much, but it was enough to I think teach us both a lot about one another. We have a lot in common. I only hope and pray that someday soon I'll be able to return and prove to you what I've said. Regardless though Sel, I'm a fatalist and what is to be will be. I only hope it will be soon. I miss you a lot Sel, your letters are wonderful.

Today it was really beautiful.

During our leisure time today, we had a football game. Really was swell. I'd give anything if this damn mess would end. Just think Honey, spending our weekends at the coast. Really was swell today. Plenty of hot sunshine and blue skies.

We've been put into battalion reserve which puts us about ¼ of a mile behind the line. Really is a break. It should last for about 3 or 4 days.

Well Honey, that's about it for now. Take care of yourself and study hard. Write soon and regards to all.

Yours with love,
Bob

P.S. Send dates, candy, cookies, etc.

Pfc. B. D. Browne 39337016
Co. I, 410 Inf. A.P.O. 470
c/o Postmaster New York, N.Y.

Miss Selma Nepom
Phi Sigma Phi
4540 17th St. N.E.
Seattle 5, Washington

February 25, 1945

Dearest Selma,

I received your letter today dated the 14th of February which is very good time. The mail system is really funny. Sometimes the mail comes in very good and other times very slow. I received a package from the Folks about a week ago which was sent out the middle of December. I guess it got lost somewhere along the way. I got it eventually though.

Honey, I was glad to hear about Ruthie's Sailor coming to Portland. What goes between them, anything serious? Is he good enough for her? He'd better be. I sure wish Selma's Soldier would get a chance to come to Portland. One of these days Honey. Golly, what a wonderful day that will be.

The reports on the Junne-Besse handicap is as follows. It looks as though Besse will lead the race by 2 or 3 months. Besse will have her child sometime in April and Junne will have hers in late June or early July. Golly, what a family?

Don't worry about your family not expanding. There's plenty of time yet, and with this war and all maybe it's a little more wise to wait.

We had another one of those beautiful days today. Really was swell. I hope it keeps up for awhile, but I think we're due for a little rain sometime soon.

I received a letter from Lew today and he seems to be well situated in London. He says that London is a filthy place due to the war. I guess that goes for most large cities. They call their beer "Bitters" and he says it tastes like the name says—bitter as hell! He also says that the people are very hard to understand at times. Must be the language Honey.

Well Sel, I guess that's about it for now. Take care of yourself Sel and study hard. Write often and give my regards to all.

Yours with love,
Bob

Pfc. B. D. Browne 39337016
Co. I 410 Inf. A.P.O. 470
c/o Postmaster New York, N.Y.

Miss Selma Nepom
Phi Sigma Phi
4540 17th St. N.E.
Seattle 5, Washington

February 26, 1945
Alsace

Dearest Selma,

Hello Honey. Got some spare time tonight so I'm catching up on my letter writing. I owed Lew a letter since last week—same goes for Banny.

Sel, I got hold of a souvenir today from one of the civilians here. All the girls aged 17 to 30 had to wear them when the Germans were here. They sewed them on their sleeves. The boys wore something similar, but was worn on a cap. They really had the younger set sewed up. They started training the boys at ten years of age. Girls at maturity age. Must have been quite a thing. Honey, just throw it away if you don't want it. It's not much of anything.

We had a few rounds of artillery (Kraut) thrown at us today but didn't do any damage. They seem to be after some artillery pieces that we have in our support. They didn't hit them though.

Started raining this evening but at present it's clear. I hope it doesn't start in again. It's miserable enough as it is, but rain really tops it all. Everything turns muddy.

Well Doll, that's about it for now. Take care of yourself and regards to all at home. Write soon Sel, and send plenty of dates, cookies, candy, etc.

I love you,
Bob

The filing time shown in the date line on telegrams and day letters is STANDARD TIME at point of origin. Time of receipt is STANDARD TIME at point of destination

EAA265 EFM=SANSORIGINE VIA SEATTLE WASH 27   1945 FEB 27 PM 12 01

EFM MISS SELMA NEPOM=

716 SOUTHWEST HARRISON ST PTLD=

DARLING MY THOUGHTS ARE WITH YOU GOD BE WITH YOU TILL WE MEET
AGAIN=

BERNARD BROWN.

No. 74231 To

By   At   To Be

NEPOM.

Pfc. B. D. Browne 39337016
Co. I, 410 Inf. A.P.O. 470
c/o Postmaster New York, N.Y.

Miss Selma Nepom
Phi Sigma Phi
4540 17th St. N.E.
Seattle 5, Washington

.... *28 February 1945*

Alsace

Dear Selma,

Just a line Honey to let you know that I'm fine and as far as I know the situation is well in hand.

I received your letter today Sel, dated the 12th of February. It was the letter with that so called "Funny Stationery." I like it Sel, it's really different. I still can't figure out how you keep writing in a straight line with lines going every which way on the paper. It's nice stationery though Honey.

I sure appreciate your trying to find licorice for me. It must be pretty hard because the Folks very seldom can find it anywhere. Junne seems to be able to get plenty of it though. They must have quite a bit of it in her part of the country.

Honey, don't worry about your schoolwork. I realize at times it really piles up but remember that a mountain looks much steeper than it really is. I'll bet you're hitting straight "A's" already. Sure wish I was going to school with you. Here I go dreaming again.

Golly, I'll bet Ruthie is all excited about her sailor boy. Sure hope he doesn't have to go overseas again.

Good to hear that Eric got permission to wait for his mother. Boy I'll bet he's really excited. Sure will be swell to visit the good old West. No doubt you will go home to meet them. Introduce them to me Sel—hope to meet them all one of these days.

Yes Sel, I do know Ray Veltman. Glad to hear that he got a furlough. Who does he claim in the house? I haven't seen him for an awfully long time.

Well Sel, that's about it for now. Take care of yourself and write soon. Regards to all at home.

Yours,

Bob

Pfc. B. D. Browne 39337016
Co. I, 410 Inf. A.P.O. 470
c/o Postmaster New York, N.Y.

Miss Selma Nepom
Phi Sigma Phi
4540 17th St. N.E.
Seattle 5, Washington

2 March 1945

Dearest Selma,

Just a line Honey to let you know that I'm fine and feeling swell. I didn't receive any mail at all today except for a package from home. I'm looking forward to some mail tomorrow though.

Weather was pretty bad today Sel. It rained all day and it's still raining tonight. It's been pretty bad but thank goodness we're not out in the field. It's really wonderful having a roof over your head, especially during bad weather. I sure hope it keeps up for a little while longer. We're due to go on-line (or push forward) any day now. These past couple of weeks have really been wonderful.

Honey, I had a typical German meal today. The people that we're staying with wanted us to try one of their meals with them. It consisted of ham, potatoes, (French fried) sauerkraut, and wine along with French bread as a chaser. It was really very good Honey, but I'll stick to G.I. hash. It was very tasty, but I must admit it was hot as hell. They seem to season their food quite a bit. They are very fond of coffee, so we got them a big pitcher of it for them. They're very good to us Sel. They sure do work hard. They all seem to be farmers (bauern in German) in the small villages and they really do work hard. If an American farmer had to do the work that they do, I don't think they would last very long.

Well Doll, that's about it for tonight. I'll write again tomorrow if possible. Take good care of yourself and give my regards to all at home.

Yours,
Bob

Pfc. B. D. Browne 39337016
Co. I, 410 Inf. A.P.O. 470
c/o Postmaster New York, N.Y.

Miss Selma Nepom
Phi Sigma Phi
4540 17th St. N.E.
Seattle 5, Washington

March 3, 1945

Dearest Selma,

I received your letter today dated the 17th of February, which tells me about the 8-ounce package that you sent me. It was sure mean of you though not to tell me what was in it. Thanks an awful lot though Sel, you're sure swell.

I was glad to hear about your yellow sweater. Boy I'll bet it's really sharp. You asked my favorite color. Honey, it all depends for what it's for. Sweaters I like powder blue, yellow, light green. Cars I like different colors and houses still different colors. It all depends for what it's for. I like the sound of that sweater though. Sure would be wonderful if I could see you in it. Golly Honey, what a day that will be. I promise to call you the first chance I get after hitting the states. I'm sure looking forward to a lot.

Honey, I got a letter from Lew today and he attended my cousin Bernice's wedding in London at my Aunt's house. They sure made a fuss over him. He really had a swell time. I think he's going to try to stay with them, but I don't think he'll be able to leave the field. He likes it a lot though. He says they have a beautiful home (small mansion) and live in the finest residential district in London. Poor guy is awfully worried about Junne even though he gets a letter everyday telling him that she's getting along fine.

Sel, I am more anxious to learn about Ruthie and her sailor now than you are, I think. I'm really curious to hear the outcome. Keep me informed Sel and give her my love in your next letter home. Also give my girlfriend Tillie a great big kiss.

Honey, don't worry about anyone finding out about Ruth. It's not going beyond me.

Sel, you mentioned in your letter that there were a lot of things you didn't know about me. Ask me any questions you want Hon. I promise to give you a truthful answer. Really isn't much to me Sel. I'm not very complex. Just an ordinary G.I. who is looking forward to an awful lot, including you. I only hope and pray that this damn thing will end soon so that I can get home to straighten out a lot of things. My first big job will be dating you every minute of the day so that no other wolf will be able to. Just think Sel, when the war finally ends everybody will be coming home including Hesh, big Sol, and all your other boyfriends. I can see that I'm going to have quite a time. By the way Miss Nepom, I would like to make a date with you at this time. You are coming to Salem with me and the second night home, we're really going to get stinking. The entire family. They tell me it's foolish to plan things, but I'm taking a chance. It will all work out for the best Honey regardless of what happens. Just pray that this mess ends in a hurry.

Well Doll, that's about all for now. I'll write again tomorrow if possible. Regards to all Sel and write soon. Send cookies, candy, and <u>A PICTURE</u>.

Yours with love,
Bob

Pfc. B. D. Browne 39337016
Co. I, 410 Inf. A.P.O. 470
c/o Postmaster New York, N.Y.

Miss Selma Nepom
Phi Sigma Sigma
4540 17th St. N.E.
Seattle 5, Washington

March 5, 1945

Dearest Selma,

Just a line to let you know that I'm fine and getting along swell.

Sel, I'm now the uncle of a 6-3/4 lb. boy. Junne had her child the 18th of February and I found out about it today. I sure was surprised—I guess I had my dates all mixed up. They didn't send me his name though darn it. I'll bet Lew is sure excited. He wanted a boy bad.

Honey, I got a letter from Bobby today and he sent me some sharp pictures that he took while in Seattle. He really sent some beauties of he and Ruth Shultz or whatever her name is. Looks pretty good Sel.

It started snowing here last night and it's been snowing all day today. It's wet snow though and it's not sticking thank goodness. Everything is wet and muddy though which is almost just as bad.

Well Sel, how have things been going at school? By now you should have full results from your finals. How about letting me know how you made out Honey. Were they very rough Sel or were they a snap?

Nothing new from here except for the weather. Received no (your) mail for the past couple of days but I'm looking forward to tomorrow.

Well Honey, that's about it for now. Take good care of yourself and give my regards to all at home. I'll write again as soon as possible.

Yours with love,
Bob

Pfc. B. D. Browne 39337016
Co. I, 410 Inf. A.P.O. 470
c/o Postmaster New York, N.Y.

Miss Selma Nepom
Phi Sigma Sigma
4540 17th St. N.E.
Seattle 5, Washington

March 8, 1945

Dear Selma,

I received another letter from you today dated the 26th of February. Keep up the good work Sel. Honey, I'm glad to hear that you're getting a good rest while you're at home. Bet it really feels swell taking it easy every once in awhile.

Honey, don't worry about Normie, he'll be alright. He and I understand each other wonderfully. He's a swell kid Sel. I haven't received his postal card yet but it should be coming in any day now. I'll keep sending him things like that anytime I can get hold of them. Once we start on the offensive, I should be able to get plenty of souvenirs. I don't seem very anxious to start moving though, because once we start, we won't stop.

Besse's husband is now somewhere with the 1st Army. That's the last I heard anyhow. I got a letter from him about 2 weeks ago and he seemed to be getting along fine. I should be getting another letter from him soon.

It stopped raining today Sel, and the sun is now shining. It sure is wonderful. I could really go for a good dose of Rockaway or Seaside.

Well Honey, that's about it for now. Take good care of yourself and write soon.

Yours with love,
Bob

Pfc. B. D. Browne 39337016
Co. I, 410 Inf. A.P.O. 470
c/o Postmaster New York, N.Y.

Miss Selma Nepom
Phi Sigma Sigma
4540 17th St. N.E.
Seattle 5, Washington

March 10, 1945

Dear Selma,

I received your letter today dated the 25th of February and it sure was swell receiving such a long letter from you. Honey we moved again today into position so we're now about 600 yards from the enemy. We are on the MLR which means Main Line of Resistance. I'll probably have a lot of interesting things to write to you while we're here.

Sel I'm awfully sorry I asked you to write to the folks. It was very foolish on my part and I guess, I just wasn't thinking. I didn't seem to look at it the way you did. You see Sel, I figure you just as a good friend until I prove otherwise to myself. As for a definite understanding, well that will just have to wait until I get home. Sel I wasn't thinking of you and I believe I was thinking only of the folks. They naturally worry about Lew and I, so I thought maybe you letting them know would make them feel a little better, but after thinking it over, it wouldn't be the best thing to do. You know how folks are and I don't want anything to happen until we both have the chance to spend a little more time with one another. You're a swell girl Sel, but after all we did spend an awfully short time with one another.

I also agree with you on competition. Sort of makes a person fight for things. Sel you'll have to excuse some of my letters, they are awfully forward at times, but it's only because I get so damn depressed every once in awhile. Just ignore those letters Sel. It's just like a house without a foundation. I'm sure you'll agree.

Sorry to hear about Dave not writing, but there's times when you're moving around that it's practically impossible to write. When I see him next time I'll tell him, though.

I got a letter from Monte Chusid today and he's getting along swell. He seems to be experiencing good weather in Holland. I'd like to trade because it's just muddy as H--- here.

I also got a letter from Lew and one from the folks. They're all fine and feeling swell. Sure does make me feel good.

Well Sel, that's about it for now. Take care of yourself and regards to all.

Bob

Pfc. B. D. Browne 39337016
Co. I 410 Inf. A.P.O. 470
c/o Postmaster New York, N.Y.

Miss Selma Nepom
Phi Sigma Sigma
4540 17th St. N.E.
Seattle 5, Washington

March 15, 1945

Dear Selma,

Well here it is Wednesday and it really is a beautiful day. The sun came up this morning and it's been shining all day. Really feels swell after the rain and everything. I hope it keeps up for a while.

Nothing too new Sel, except that I've got a feeling we'll be moving out one of these days soon. We've gotten all new equipment and clothing, so I imagine we'll be coordinating the offensive with the other Armies soon. At present we're still in the defensive which isn't so bad except for the artillery and mortar fire that comes in every once in a while.

Yesterday we got two prisoners who came walking into our lines with white flags in each hand. We got some pretty good information from them. They told us that they had enough of battle and that they just couldn't take it anymore. They were put into the Kraut Infantry only 2 months ago. They were in Anti-Aircraft for 5 years, so I imagine it was pretty rough on them. One of the two was in "Oberfeldwebel" which is equivalent to our first Sergeant. I am sending the insignia that they wear on their sleeve about 5 inches from the bottom. They call it "THE HAGENCROSSE" but all it means is swastika. It's really nothing Sel but thought you might like to see one. The Germans feel very honored in wearing one.

Well, that's about it for now. Give my regards to the gang Sel and write soon.

Bob

Pfc. B. D. Browne 39337016
Co. I, 410 Inf. A.P.O. 470
c/o Postmaster New York, N.Y.

Miss Selma Nepom
Phi Sigma Phi
4540 17th St. N.E.
Seattle 5, Washington

March 18, 1945

Dear Sel,

Please excuse the messy letter but it can't be helped. I'm sitting in a house that's been blown to hell. We started our drive 2 days ago and we've really been moving. Our battalion alone has taken 4 towns. The prisoners captured were young kids and old men. They gave us plenty of good information. I'm sending you some money taken from a prisoner. They're German Marks.

I received your letter written the 5th of March and it was a wonderful letter. Thanks for all the flattery Sel, it really comes in handy up here.

So far everything goes alright. I've lost a lot of good friends but thank goodness I'm still in one piece.

Sel, I don't have much time so excuse the short letter. We liberated this town last night before dark and we're planning to shove off this morning sometime. In fact we're waiting for the order right now.

Honey, take good care of yourself and write often. If you don't get much mail from me it's because we'll be out in the woods somewhere. I'll write though whenever possible. Regards to all at home Sel.

Yours with love,
Bob

P.S. Hope you like your new roommate

Pfc. B. D. Browne 39337016
Co. I 410 Inf. A.P.O. 470
c/o Postmaster New York, N.Y.

Miss Selma Nepom
Phi Sigma Sigma
4540 17th St. N.E.
Seattle 5, Washington

March 21, 1945

Dear Selma,

Just a line to let you know that I'm fine and getting along alright. We're at a lull in the push now due to the Siegfried Line. It's really a tough baby to crack. Seems almost impossible to get through. The only thing that could knock it out is a 2000 lb bomb hitting directly on top of the pill boxes. They really are solid. We're trying everything in the world to break through though. We've moved quite a way since I last wrote to you.

We've been living in the woods for the past three nights, but it hasn't been too bad. Thank goodness the weather has been favorable. I haven't received any mail for the past couple of days because it hasn't had time to catch up with us. If we don't move today, we should be getting some mail.

We've been living on cold "K" rations ever since the push off. I guess the kitchen is stranded somewhere about 10 miles back.

What's new with you Sel? Anything exciting been happening?

Sel that's about all the time I've got to spare now. I'll write again whenever possible. Regards to all at home.

Bob

Pfc. B. D. Browne 39337016
Co. I 410 Inf. A.P.O. 470
c/o Postmaster New York, N.Y.

Miss Selma Nepom
Phi Sigma Sigma
4540 17th St. N.E.
Seattle 5, Washington

March 22, 1945

Dear Selma,

Just a line to let you know that we're still moving, but all goes well. This morning we moved about 3-1/2 miles which puts us about ½ mile away from the German border. We're sitting on top of a mountain waiting to move up tonight. We haven't been in the fight for the past 3 days, but we made the jump off and formed the spearhead which was very costly. Our company alone took in about 50 prisoners which is pretty good. Our division took in about 1000 since the push started. Most of them were young fellows ranging from 15 to 20. Really were kids, but their minds have been poisoned with Hitlerism which makes them reckless with their weapons.

I received your letter yesterday (#10) and it was very good to hear all the news, especially that you're getting along fine at school.

Nothing much new here Honey except I miss you a lot but your letters do me a world of good.

Sel you asked me a lot of questions, so I'll now attempt to answer them. (1) I like a modern home with everything new and light colored. (It also depends where the home is) (2) I think blue is a very substantial color for a car. I also like maroon. (Both with white sidewall tires) (3). I've often wanted to have a home by a lake or at the coast. That's beside the home in the city in an exclusive residential district. It all depends though Honey on a lot of things—for instance—what are your ideas? I am very much in favor for a place at the coast or by a lake just to spend weekends at.

Well Sel, that's about it for now. Take good care of yourself and regards to all at home. Tell your Mom not to worry about your Post War problems—I'm sure things will all work out for the best.

Write soon Honey.

Yours,
Bob

Pfc. B. D. Browne 39337016
Co. I, 410 Inf. A.P.O. 470
c/o Postmaster New York, N.Y.

Miss Selma Nepom
Phi Sigma Sigma
4540 17th St. N.E.
Seattle 5, Washington

March 23, 1945
—Germany

Dear Selma,

Honey just a short time to let you know what gives. I'm writing you while sitting in a fox hole at the base of the Siegfried Line. We're about 5 or 6 miles into Germany.

Last night about 11:30 we relieved Dave Gold's outfit and it sure was good to see him. It was pitch dark but he really looked good. He told me about Irv Potter being killed when we first jumped off. It's very hard to believe Honey and I won't believe it until I find out for sure. He was a wonderful kid and I just can't believe it.

We've been pinned down here ever since last night by small arms and mortar fire and we're trying to break through today, but it really looks impossible. Honey, I received four letters from you yesterday, no.'s 4, 6, 7, and the letter to San Francisco. Those snapshots were really swell Sel, thanks a lot. You sure are a doll, did you know that?

Sel I've got to sign off for now. Excuse the note, but it's better than nothing. I'll write again when possible. Regards to all Sweetheart and congratulations on the good grades. I knew darn well you'd do it. You'll probably be doing all the work for the other girls soon. Write soon Sel.

I love you,
Bob

Pfc. B. D. Browne 39337016
Co. I, 410 Inf. A.P.O. 470
c/o Postmaster New York, N.Y.

Miss Selma Nepom
Phi Sigma Sigma
4540 17th St. N.E.
Seattle 5, Washington

March 24, 1945
—Germany – Letter #31

Dearest Selma,

Honey we got through the last defenses of the Siegfried Line this evening about 5:00 P.M. with the capture of about 200 prisoners by our
company alone which is very good pickens for one day. We marched
about 6 or 7 miles, blowing pillboxes every few hundred feet. That damn
line was full of them. Sel we got one prisoner today who was 54 years
old so you see they must be pretty desperate. I feel very optimistic for
one reason or another, but we still have plenty of fighting ahead of us,
including the Rhine.

I received your letter no. 8 last night when we got rations and it
sure was swell hearing from [you]. You mentioned something about not
being able to write for a week or so because of 'Hell Week" coming up.
Have lots of fun Sel. Must be quite a deal. Hope you're not too busy
so that you won't be able to drop me a line. Just a note Sel is better
than nothing. I imagine "Hell Week" comes first, but a note would be
greatly appreciated. Whether you know it or not (and you should) this
guy seems to like his Doll quite a bit and the more he hears from her
the closer they seem to be together. Understand Honey?

Sel, we took this Kraut town tonight and if we want a house, we just
run the people out. It's an order from "Ike" that no civilians will be in
the same house with soldiers. Germany is much nicer than France, the
roads, the country, the people etc. They are a smart, clean, witty people
but they don't know when they're well off. I talked to quite a few in town

241

and they're the same if not worse than a Kraut soldier with a rifle. The sooner they're all gotten rid of the better. They are a very clean people though compared to the French—who are filthy in all ways!!

Well Honey that's about it for now. Excuse the scribbling—I'm in a hurry. Take care of yourself and have fun. I'll write again when possible.

Bob

P.S. We're still pushing on.

Pfc. B. D. Browne 39337016
Co. I, 410 Inf. A.P.O. 470
c/o Postmaster New York, N.Y.

Miss Selma Nepom
Phi Sigma Sigma
4540 17th St. N.E.
Seattle 5, Washington

BOB TO SELMA

March 24, 1945
—Germany— #32

Dear Selma,

Honey I received two letters from you today no.'s 13 & 14 so I have now received all of your letters up to date. This numbering system really helps out. I hope you're getting all of mine. Sel, thanks an awful lot for sending those campus pictures, they sure did look swell. Sort of made me homesick, and then that wonderful stationery topped it all. I really go for stuff like that. It was the cleverest I've ever seen. Sure did make me feel good. Sort of made me feel like I was the one and only which I know I'm not, but we're both "optimistic fatalists" so in time we'll find out. I've also got my campaign planned so you'd better be prepared. I still think that stationery is the best I've ever seen—thank you Honey.

Well Sel, we took another town today because the last one was pretty well crowded. We captured about 15 more prisoners and I'm enclosing an emblem which they all wear above the pocket on their jacket.

I am writing you from the dining room of a German house, also on German stationery. Our kitchen moved up this evening so we're hoping to have hot meals tomorrow. We've been living on cold rations for the past week.

As you've probably seen in the papers, we met Pattons 3rd Army and formed a pocket around the Saar Basin. We really bagged a lot of prisoners.

Sel, I want you to thank your sis for dropping me the note she did. She seems to be a very nice girl and I'm sure glad to hear that she's taking good care of you. She'd better!! Glad to hear that she knows the family. Just like one of the family now.

Well Honey, I think we push on again tomorrow sometime toward the Rhine. I'll write you again whenever possible. Take good care of yourself Doll and regards to all.

Thanks again for the pictures and I love that stationery.

Love,
Bob

Envelope signed by Lt. Keogh

Pfc. B. D. Browne 39337016
Co. I, 410 Inf. A.P.O. 470
c/o Postmaster New York, N.Y.

Miss Selma Nepom
Phi Sigma Sigma
4540 17th St. N.E.
Seattle 5, Washington

March 26, 1945
#33

Dear Selma,

Just another line to let you know that I received 4 letters from you today and one was no. 15 so they seem to be coming in order except for the 1st few. Sel I'll now attempt to answer your questions. I received Normie's card today and it was very nice. He wants some stamps so I'll see what I can do for him. I like light blue stationery very much—it's my favorite—for a girl of course. I like Sororities and I think they have very good standards. Pi Phi has always been my favorite because I've had friends in that Sorority. I think I'm gradually changing though. They are quite complicated I know. Many times though, girls often get to think they're pretty good though just because they're a member of a Sorority. They seem to change though.

Sel, it's still impossible to carry our own stationery. It's not really impossible but after it's been carried through battle in one day there wouldn't be too much left to it. We just write on anything we get ahold of. As you'll notice this stationery isn't too fancy.

The officers who censor my mail have never read my letters once. We're all together in headquarters so all I do is give him the envelope and he signs it. Many times, I sign them myself with their permission. At present I have 6 envelopes signed and I hope to write all the letters today. The 1st Lt. you mentioned is also an I & R man, so we are always together. When we take a town and move in – Co. headquarters takes a house of their own so we're always together.

Sel, please don't send any cigars. I only wanted them when there was ice and snow on the ground. They actually could keep a fellow warm, but they taste awful.

I'm glad you set me straight on all my competition. At least I now know just how I stand. Sort of like a well-liked stranger. I hadn't heard of this fellow Mal before. Sounds like a nice fellow. Glad to hear you and the folks like him. He must be quite a fellow. I'll bet you've really had some wonderful times together. Too bad he had to leave Portland. As for you and Hesh—I don't know what gives but whatever it is—it's your business. As for knowing Mal better than I, that's probably true because I've taken you out only once and as you say we've still got to get acquainted. He's probably spent more time with you than I've seen you in my entire lifetime. No doubt you know him better.

You mentioned writing to some other fellows just to keep up their morale. That's very sweet of you. Sel I want you to promise me that if you write to me just to keep up my morale—quit now. I write to you because I like you and I want you to like me. I want you to write just like you feel. When you feel bad, tell me about it. I want you just like you are, not with a bunch of flowers thrown in for morale. That's the last thing I want. Understand Honey?

I write to approximately 10 or 11 people. The family most often, next you (just as often), Lew, Banny, Junne, Bobby, a friend at Annapolis, another at Pensacola Naval Air Base, Monte, and a couple of other friends in Salem. I try to write to you and the folks as often as possible. I write to the others only on receiving letters from them.

You're probably wondering when I got all the time to write lately. Well we've been fortunate enough in having a house in almost every objective, so I took full advantage of it.

Well Doll, that's about it for now. I hope I straightened you out on a lot of things. I still won't be satisfied until I can get home and take care of you myself—regardless of Mal or any other guy.

Take care of yourself Honey and write often. I love your new stationery. I'll write again when possible.

Bob

P.S. I like mints very much. Send candy, cookies, etc.

Excuse the messy paper—it's all I could get hold of.

Pfc. B. D. Browne 39337016
Co. I, 410 Inf. A.P.O. 470
c/o Postmaster New York, N.Y.

Miss Selma Nepom
Phi Sigma Sigma
4540 17th St. N.E.
Seattle 5, Washington

March 28, 1945

Letter #34

Dear Selma,

Just a line to let you know that we're still here in the same town and it looks as if we may be here for the next 2 or 3 days before we shove off again.

I received no mail from you in the past couple of days but I'm expecting some tomorrow.

Our shower unit moved up last night, so we got to take showers today. Really felt wonderful.

I got hold of some stamps yesterday, so I sent them to Normie this morning. Hope he gets them alright.

My Newsweek and Readers Digest came in today, so we've now got reading material to last for a while. We got a P.X. ration last night which included beer, peanuts, hersheys, stationery etc. We get them every time we settle down for a few days. They come in about once every 3 weeks.

I got a letter from the folks today and they tell me that Frieda and Ben bought a home in Salem, so I guess they plan to stay there awhile.

The war looks good Sel but I'm afraid the Krauts are fanatic enough to fight till the last man is killed or captured. I certainly hope I'm wrong.

Well Sel, that's about it for now. Take good care of yourself Honey and have fun.

Bob

Pfc. B. D. Browne 39337016
Co. I, 410 Inf. A.P.O. 470
c/o Postmaster New York, N.Y.

Miss Selma Nepom
Phi Sigma Sigma
4540 17th St. N.E.
Seattle 5, Washington

March 31, 1945

Letter #35

Dear Selma,

This is the first chance I've had to write since I left our last position. Honey from where I'm sitting now, I get a full view of the Rhine River. We moved into position here 3 days ago and we really moved. About 28 miles altogether. We took trucks most of the way.

We're sitting on the west bank of the river and the Krauts are on the east bank—very well dug in. They keep throwing mortars and artillery at us but not half as much as we throw back at them. The nights are full of enemy sniper fire from across the river. Last night we got two prisoners who rowed across the river to give up. They claim their hometown had been taken by American troops so they thought if they gave up to us, they would be released to go home, but they were assured differently. Honey we've received no mail in the past couple of days but hope to get some today or tomorrow.

The weather has been pretty lousy. Plenty of wind and rain. It looks as if it may clear up a little today.

I got a letter from Lew a couple of days ago and he just missed me before we made the jump off. He visited my last position in Alsace after riding 50 miles by jeep and he found out that we jumped off a day before. Sure burned me up. May be quite a while now.

Well Sel, that's about all I have time for now. I'll write again as soon as possible. Take good care of yourself and have fun.

Bob

Send plenty of cookies, candy, etc.

Love

Pfc. B. D. Browne 39337016
Co. I 410 Inf. A.P.O. 470
c/o Postmaster New York, N.Y.

Miss Selma Nepom
Phi Sigma Sigma
4540 17th St. N.E.
Seattle 5, Washington

April 1, 1945
Letter #36

Dear Selma,

I received your letter today Sel—no. 16—and we all appreciated those jokes very much. They were very clever.

Sel I was very sorry to hear about you falling down and bruising your knee. What happened Honey did you trip or something like that. Golly I'll bet you looked cute—I'm sorry Sel—just kidding. Next time—darn it— watch where you're going. I want you to thank all the girls in the house—for me—for taking such good care of you.

I got a letter from Bobby today and also two from the folks. Bobby is getting along fine and thinks he'll be leaving for overseas soon. I sure hope not. Aaron is at P.O.E. now with some infantry outfit. He's in a heavy weapons company (3 rifle companies, 1 heavy weapons company make a battalion) which is a much better set up than a rifle company. All they do is support the rifle companies with heavy mortars and machine guns. I'm sure he'll make out alright though if I know him. I'll bet it's pretty depressing though going from a teletype operator in the air corp to a combat soldier in the infantry. I feel for the poor guy.

Sal, Besse tells me that (THE LATEST GOSSIP) Frieda and Ben are moving back to Portland to stay. He's selling his house which he bought in Salem. He plans to work for Gilbert Bros in the furniture department. I guess he didn't like his job in Salem or something. He left a beautiful little town though.

Sel I just love that new stationery of "ours." That's the cleverest I've seen in a long time. Everyone here admires it. It looks so swell to have both of our names together.

I'm looking forward to that box of dates you sent. I like dates an awful lot Honey—especially yours—WOW! I'm sure fresh, aren't I?

Well Sel, that's about it for now, I'll write again whenever possible. Take good care of your knee Honey. Regards to all at home.

Bob

Pfc. B. D. Browne 39337016
Co. I 410 Inf. A.P.O. 470
c/o Postmaster New York, N.Y.

Miss Selma Nepom
Phi Sigma Sigma
4540 17th St. N.E.
Seattle 5, Washington

April 2, 1945
Letter #37

Dear Sel,

Just a line Honey to let you know that by the time I write my next letter we'll be on our way again. As for us I know we're supposed to move from here in two or three hours so as soon as I've finished scribbling this note to you, I'm going to pack up and get ready to move again.

Honey I received your letter today dated the 20th of March—no. 17—and it was sure good hearing so often. That's just the way I like it. Honey, I'm sorry to say that I don't like that new stationery. It's different and all that but it's sort of sickening. Reminds me of doilies. It's very different though. I like our stationery much better.

Let me know how the inspection comes out Sel. Did you show them a good time?

Yes Honey, Bertha Klorfein is a Salem girl. She always used to tell me how wonderful U. of W. used to be. She was really a swell kid—always full of fun.

Well Doll, I'd better call it for today because I've got an awful lot to do. I'll write again whenever possible.

Take care of yourself. Send mints, dates, cookies etc.

Yours,
Bob

P.S. Excuse the note Sel

Pfc. B. D. Browne 39337016
Co. I, 410 Inf. A.P.O. 470
c/o Postmaster New York, N.Y.

Miss Selma Nepom
4540 17th St. N.E.
Seattle 5, Washington

April 4, 1945
Letter No. 38

Dear Selma,

Honey I haven't had a chance to write to you for the past couple of days because we've been moving all that time. At the present time we're about 35 miles behind the front lines and it really feels wonderful. Our division was due to go to rest camp but instead they send us up in the mountains to occupy some small villages that we by passed on our way through the line. It's really not a bad deal, but a rest camp is much better. Our company alone has about 75 square miles to take of which includes 5 small villages which are practically totally destroyed by artillery. It's right in the middle of the Siegfried Line and there are pill boxes all around us. They have all been blown up though so that all that are left are big blocks of concrete scattered everywhere. They really had a wonderful defense system. Thank goodness it didn't work.

I received your letter number 18 just before leaving. Glad to hear all the good news. Your new dress sounds wonderful. I was glad to hear about Sol Menashe—hope he got a nice girl. I guess I can cross one off of my list now. Just kidding Honey.

Sel I can tell you that we spearheaded the drive to Mannheim all the way up to the banks of the Rhine. We stopped there and let the 44th Inf. Div. push through to take the city which looks like all factories and beautiful homes. The Rhine is a beautiful river Sel.

I'm enclosing a news summary that we got our name into. We get these news summaries every day and they give us the straight dope. The news contains no flowers at all.

Well Doll, that's about it for now. Take care of yourself and write often. Regards to all. Keep sending fruit juice, canned fruit, candy, cookies etc.

Love,
Bob

Pfc. B. D. Browne 39337016
Co. I, 410 Inf. A.P.O. 470
c/o Postmaster New York, N.Y.

Miss Selma Nepom
Phi Sigma Sigma
4540 17th St. N.E.
Seattle 5, Washington

April 6, 1945

Dear Selma,

I received your letter #21 today so 19 & 20 must be drifting around somewhere between here and Seattle. Honey I was glad to hear from you so soon.

Golly I didn't think I had written so many letters to you, but I imagine they do pile up. One of these days we'll read them together Sel, that should be fun.

I'm enclosing a couple of pictures that we took with a captured German camera. One of the fellows got it from a prisoner along with 2 rolls of film. The film was very poor though and very few of the pictures came out at all. The fellow with me is a Jewish fellow from Penn. And he's really a swell kid. He's still kicking himself in the pants for not marrying his girlfriend. They've been planning it for the past 3 years.

The little puppy that you see is our company mascot—"Tippy" by name. He travels with the kitchen while we're in the field. Sure is a cute little mutt.

Nothing much new here Sel. The rest sure is wonderful. We have our everyday garrison routine but it's wonderful compared to the front. Sort a wish it would last for the duration. It should last for a couple of weeks anyhow.

Sel I'm taking the best possible care of myself so don't worry. Sure makes me feel good though.

We had fried chicken today for dinner and it sure was wonderful. Now that the kitchen is with us we should be having some wonderful meals. Food has been swell Sel except for those damn cold rations which play hell with everyone. They taste good though when you haven't eaten for a day or so.

Well Doll, that's about it for now. Take good care of yourself Honey and I miss you a lot.

Yours with love,
Bob

Tippy with the guys, Oberammergau, Germany

PFC. B. D. BROWNE 39337016
CO. I, 410 INF. A.P.O. 470
c/o POSTMASTER NEW YORK, N.Y.

MISS SELMA NEPOM
4540 17TH ST. N.E.
SEATTLE 5, WASHINGTON

April 7, 1945

Dearest Selma,

Honey, just a line to let you know I'm fine and taking full advantage of this so-called rest. I received your letter no. 20 today so all that is missing now is no. 19. They've really been coming in pretty good though Sel.

I received a package that Lew sent to me. It contained a lot of English stuff—sox, towels, soap etc. It's all he can get over there. He doesn't mind it though because he spends most of his free time at my Aunt's house. He claims it rains more in London than it does in Oregon. Doesn't seem possible does it Sel?

It was sure good hearing about your invitation. I'm sure proud of you Honey. Golly I'll bet you're a popular girl up there. Only wish I could find out for myself. What a day that will be. I think the first thing we'll do is go for a nice long drive and just talk about one another. Do you like to drive Honey? We'll go off on some road where there is very little traffic and just drive along and talk—real peaceful like. Sure will be swell being with you Doll.

Honey, it's been raining here for the past day and a half but I don't mind it so bad as long as we have a nice dry place to go to.

The war news looks very good, but I still think it will be quite a while until hostilities have ceased. I've talked to a lot of P.W.s including many officers and they all seem very determined that it will be a fight to the end. I just keep hoping Sel.

It won't be long now until I'll be an uncle for the third time. Besse is expecting junior about the middle of April. Sorta hope it's a boy myself. Dave is pushing with the 1st Army and he hasn't been able to write for the past month. I guess he's pretty busy while on the go.

Well Sel, that's about it for now. Take good care of yourself and have fun.

Bob

P.S. Send plenty of canned fruit and fruit juices.

Pfc. B. D. Browne 39337016
Co. I 410 Inf. A.P.O. 470
c/o Postmaster New York, N.Y.

Miss Selma Nepom
4540 17th St. N.E.
Seattle 5, Washington

April 9, 1945

Dear Selma,

The last letter I wrote to you was written about 45 miles away from where I'm at now. We moved yesterday and crossed the Rhine on a pontoon bridge at Mannheim. At present we are 9 kilometers (about 6 miles) from Heidelberg, on the other side. Sel we took over a castle 300 years old. A German Baron & Baroness were living there with 5 servant families and it was really a pleasure to put them out. They thought being of German royalty we had no right, but we sure changed their mind in a hurry. Honey, I just can't explain this castle, it's just beautiful. We have our entire company in it so you can imagine how large it is. I only wish I had a picture of it to send you. It's just like you read about in fairy books and see in movie pictures. It has a moat, drawbridge, and the entire works. The furniture just can't be beat. This stationery was taken from the library. It's set up high on a mountain and looks over the entire country. It's really something Sel. Sure hope we stay here awhile.

We made quite a move Honey, straight into Germany. We've got 5 towns to police and control, so we'll be a little busy but it's much better than being on-line. Boy it will really be rough when we have to go back.

Well Honey, that's about it for now. Hope everything is going good at school. Take good care of yourself Doll.

Send fruit juices & canned fruit (Do you need points for them?)

Love,
Bob

Pfc. B. D. Browne 39337016
Co. I, 410 Inf. A.P.O. 470
c/o Postmaster New York, NY

Miss Selma Nepom
Phi Sigma Sigma
4540 17th St. N.E.
Seattle 5, Washington

April 10, 1945
Letter No. 42

Dear Selma,

Just a line Honey to let you know that I'm fine and received your letter no. 19 today so I've gotten all of your letters now.

We're still living in the castle and it really is wonderful. We went through our towns today and made them turn in all Nazi weapons, uniforms, equipment, etc. They also had to burn all of their swastikas. You have no idea how much they had Honey. They were really loaded down. Tomorrow we start screening all men within military age and find out when they were discharged from the Army and why. Those that have no discharge papers are considered prisoners of war. You'd be surprised how many of them have deserted. All they do is put on civilian clothes and consider themselves civilians.

Anything new at school Sel? I thought that was pretty funny about the old dried up gardenia. I'll bet the poor guy was really embarrassed. Do you like orchids Sel?

Otherwise Honey, nothing much new. The weather has been wonderful the past couple of days. Golly Doll, sure will be wonderful when homecoming comes. You have no idea how much I look forward to it. The war news looks good, but I still seem to think it will be quite a little while yet. We've got a long way to go in the Pacific yet. The Japs are preparing for the invasion of China which will undoubtedly come one of these days.

Well Doll, that's about it for now. Take good care of yourself and have fun. Give my regards to all at home.

Love,
Bob

P.S. Send plenty of canned fruit if no points are needed.

Pfc. B. D. Browne 39337016
Co. I, 410 Inf. A.P.O. 470
c/o Postmaster New York, N.Y.

Miss Selma Nepom
Phi Sigma Sigma
4540 17th St. N.E.
Seattle 5, Washington

April 11, 1945

Dear Selma,

Honey here I am again still alright and miss you a lot. Sel the company got no mail today, but we expect it tomorrow. Packages came in today and guess what was there? Your package came Honey and that candy was delicious. I like your taste very much. Those licorice caramels were delicious. Five of my closest friends wish to send their personal thanks to you. The darn hogs—they wouldn't take one or two pieces, but they had to take 6 or 7. They saved me a couple of pieces—god bless them. It was delicious Sel, thanks an awful lot. It was sure swell of you.

While screening a town today I bumped into a Jewish family. Their name was Bach. He has a daughter (married—2 children) in Minneapolis, Minn. His son was killed by the Wehrmacht because he was a German Jew. The only reason he wasn't killed was because he married a non-Jewish girl. He's an elderly man (about 64 years old) and he's really been through hell. We fixed him up pretty good and you have no idea how happy he is that the Americans have come. He is a merchant and sells women's clothes. He claims he had quite a business in Mannheim but it was blown to pieces by bombs and artillery. He plans to start up again the first chance he gets, but it will be quite a while before he'll be able to return to Minnesota, and it will be years until Mannheim is rebuilt. It was really blown to pieces.

Well Doll, that's about it for now. The weather was very nice today, plenty of sunshine.

Sel take good care of yourself and have lots of fun. I'll write again tomorrow if possible. Regards to all at home. Send canned fruit & fruit juice—goes better with this hot weather.

Love,
Bob

Pfc. B. D. Browne 39337016
Co. I, 410 Inf. A.P.O. 470
c/o Postmaster New York, NY

Miss Selma Nepom
Phi Sigma Sigma
4540 17th St. N.E.
Seattle 5, Washington

April 13, 1945
Letter #44

Dear Selma,

Just another line Honey to let you know that I'm still over here sweating this damn war out. The company received no mail for the past two days, so I hardly know what to write about.

The Red Cross visited us here in the castle today and gave us all the doughnuts we could eat. They really had a lot of them. They visit us quite often now that we're in the rear, but while on-line we hardly ever saw them. Sure is good to talk to an American girl again.

Sel, I sent you a Nazi flag and an arm band today. We found them while screening one of the towns. It's a brand new flag, I believe. They're not much Honey but thought you might like to have one. If you don't want it, just throw it away. We've scattered them all through Germany. Seems that the people hung them from every window they had in the house. You should receive it in 3 or 4 weeks.

Today is the first time it rained for quite a while but thank goodness it didn't last very long. Golly a castle is sure a dreary place when the weather gets blue. I'll take a modern home any day.

Well Honey, what's new at school? Anything exciting happening? How have things been going?

Doll, that's about it for now. There's really nothing new. We finished screening our towns and I think we'll be starting a training schedule in a couple of days if we're here that long.

I'll write again tomorrow if possible. Send plenty of canned fruit.

Yours,
Bob

Pfc. B. D. Browne 39337016
Co. I, 410th Inf. A.P.O. 470
c/o Postmaster, New York, N.Y.

Miss Selma Nepom
Phi Sigma Sigma
4540 17th St. N.E.
Seattle 5, Washington

April 15, 1945

Dear Selma,

Just a line Honey to let you know that all goes well. We found out today that the reason we aren't getting our mail is because the front-line troops have priority and there's only one bridge crossing here which is constantly full of supply trucks trying to keep up with the troops on-line. We should be getting some mail in a few days though. I really don't mind Honey because those poor guys up there slugging it out need all the morale builders they can and mail from home tops the list.

We finished screening civilians yesterday so today we started a training schedule which includes mostly fishing and hunting. Boy this life in the rear is really alright. Our job is over in this town, so I imagine that we'll be moving again soon. It's really going to be rough when we go back on-line because we're getting flabby and lazy back here where the life is so soft. Sel, there's just nothing worse than front line duty.

Anything happening at school Sel? How's the weather up there. It's really swell here. It rained for a day and a half, but the sun has been out most of the time. From the castle we have a beautiful view of the river. Sure is a beautiful place. Practically all of us have a bed to sleep on. They sure are hard things to get used to.

Well Honey that's about it for now. Take good care of yourself Doll and give my regards to all at home.

Love,
Bob

Pfc. B. D. Browne 39337016
Co. I, 410 Inf. A.P.O. 470
c/o Postmaster New York, NY

Miss Selma Nepom
Phi Sigma Sigma
4540 17th St. N.E.
Seattle 5, Washington

April 16, 1945

Dear Sel,

Still no mail Honey but we're all expecting some tomorrow. Sure hope it comes in.

We had a retreat formation tonight in the honor of President Roosevelt. He was a wonderful man Honey, and it sure hit us hard when we heard about his death. He is a loss to the entire world and mainly to the fight for freedom. That's fate though Honey—it does funny things at times.

Sel we're still at the castle enjoying this wonderful life but we expect to move any day now. This life is too good to last.

We learned tonight that the 9th Army had [to] withdraw one of its bridgeheads across the Elba, which isn't very good news, but it's better that way than losing a lot of men.

Three of us went hunting today but all we got out of it was a good walk in the woods and a lot of target practice. We fired at everything that moved including butterflies. We didn't see any game at all. If we have time tomorrow, we're going out again. Some of the fellows went fishing and had pretty good luck. I don't remember what kind of fish it was. It had some peculiar name just like everything else over here. They claim it tasted pretty good.

Anything new at school Honey? How's all the girls making out? Any good dates recently?

Well Doll, that's about it for now. Take good care of yourself and regards to all at home.

Love,
Bob

Pfc. B. D. Browne 39337016
Co. I, 410 Inf. A.P.O. 470
c/o Postmaster New York, N.Y.

Miss Selma Nepom
Phi Sigma Sigma
4540 17th St. N.E.
Seattle 5, Washington

April 17, 1945

Dear Selma,

Just a line honey to let you know that we moved about 15 kilometers today (9 miles). We moved to a little town on the other side of Heidelberg and I think we'll do the same thing here that we did there. As far as I know we start screening civilians tomorrow morning. Golly, I sure hated to leave the castle. It was really wonderful there. We moved into a very nice home here. We have electricity, hot and cold water, etc. Really is alright, but the castle was really the Ritz. I brought some of this stationery with me because it seems to be pretty good stuff. We received no mail today due to the move that we made. We're all hoping to get some tomorrow. Do you know that it's been 6 days since I've gotten any mail? Really is rough. When we do get it though we should really get a lot of it.

Honey, from where I'm sitting, I have a full view of a cherry orchard and it really is beautiful because all the trees are in blossom. Just like a white carpet of snow.

Well Doll, that's about it for now. Take good care of yourself and have fun. I'll write again tomorrow if possible.

Love ya,
Bob

Pfc. B. D. Browne 39337016
Co. I, 410 Inf. A.P.O. 470
c/o Postmaster New York, N.Y.

Miss Selma Nepom
Phi Sigma Sigma
4540 17th St. N.E.
Seattle 5, Washington

April 18, 1945

𝒟*ear* 𝒮*elma,*

Honey the mail finally came in today and I really hit the jackpot. I got 5 letters from you and also the package you sent containing licorice, mints and glazed fruit. Selma you're a Doll and that's all there is to it. You're my Doll too, nobody else's.

Your letters were beautiful Sel. You write just like I want you to. We're both old enough to understand one another and I want you to write just like you feel. If you have things you want to tell me just put them forward because that's what I'm doing to you.

Honey, you and I seem to have an awful lot in common especially in the trend of our thoughts. We both seem to feel the same things the same way. It seems so funny that I take you out such a short time and yet I seem to know so much about you. Honey I've just got to get home to you, that's all there is to it.

Now about Hesh. I'm awfully sorry to hear that he's going overseas. I hope you showed him a nice time—NUFF SAID!!

Sel you sent me some kind of stationery with flowers on the top and I liked it very much. It was very nice stationery Honey.

We started screening today and we've already found 9 deserters from the German Army. They put on civy clothes and just sweat the war out. Tomorrow we should be getting some more. We turn them over to regiment who in turn sends them to the P.W. cages.

Honey, this rear echelon life is really tops. I don't think it will last long though. You see, we were due for a 30-day rest at a rest camp and instead they gave us this rear echelon detail. So, I figure we'll be here for a couple of more weeks at least. I'm taking full advantage of it too Honey.

Sel last night we had another fraternizing case. I always have to go along because I do the talking to the damn Krauts. The company (I & R officer), executive officer (Lt. Keough), first Sergeant, and myself and jeep driver went along. It's the 3rd case we had since we hit the rear area. We went into this house and we found this G.I. in bed with this German girl. After questioning the girl, she exclaimed that the G.I. made her get into bed at the point of a rifle. She didn't seem to mind it though. The G.I. was a little drunk and claims that his emotions ran away with him. Well, he'll probably get 6 months pay taken away because it's his first time. Second & third time though they usually go to jail for a year or so. We sure do hit a lot of funny cases and 9 times out of 10 it's the girl's fault. They know darn well that the soldier will get into trouble. Last week we had a case of rape when all the soldier did was kiss the girl. She swore up and down that he raped her, but after a 4-day investigation we found out all he did was kiss her. He paid for it, and I think he's cured now.

These German people are still our enemies and they'd kill us the first chance they'd get. They're sneaky and mean and can never be trusted. I have so many stories to tell you when I get home that you'll hardly be able to believe them.

Well Doll, that's about all the time I have now. Take good care of yourself Sweetheart and give my regards to all at Home. Thanks again for the package. Keep sending canned fruit and fruit juices.

Your lover,
Bob

Pfc. B. D. Browne 39337016
Co. I, 410 Inf. A.P.O. 470
c/o Postmaster New York, N.Y.

Miss Selma Nepom
Phi Sigma Sigma
4540 17th St. N.E.
Seattle 5, Washington

April 23, 1945

Dear Selma,

Honey I have very little time now, but I'm trying to get this note off to you anyhow.

We've been pushing the enemy for the past two days along with an armored outfit and about half of the way we've been riding on tanks and walking the rest. It's been pretty rough Honey, because it's been raining so hard. The first night we had to sleep out so we got drenched through and through, but last night we took a town so we got to stay in houses which gave us a chance to dry off. The Krauts have been throwing mortar & tank fire at us and plenty of small arms but thank goodness no artillery. All I can tell you of the situation is that we are in the area of Stuttgart and are closing in on a formed pocket containing SS infantry troops and panzer (tank) units. Thank goodness we've got them on the go, sure hope it stays that way.

Sel, I've got to leave soon so I'd better sign off for now. Take care of yourself Doll and don't worry about me. I'm taking the best possible care of myself and I'll write whenever possible.

Love,
Bob

P.S. We spent about 2 hours in a bank yesterday and found some old German money. Notice the high amounts.

Pfc. B. D. Browne 39337016
Co. I, 410 Inf. A.P.O. 470
c/o Postmaster New York, N.Y.

Miss Selma Nepom
4540 17th St. N.E.
Seattle 5, Washington

April 27, 1945

Dear Selma,

Honey we just took this town about an hour ago and we were lucky enough to stay here tonight. At present I'm writing you from a Kraut Beer Hall which we made our C.P. The trouble is they don't have any beer.

We've been cleaning out pockets of resistance for the past week and they have really been playing hell with us. This is the first chance I've had to write for the past 3 days. They seem to hold out in the mountains more because they have such good observation. The last one we cleaned out had enough supplies to last at least a year. They were really loaded down with ammo and weapons. Every once-in-a while they would come out at night and attack our supply convoys so they had to be cleaned out.

We went after one Tuesday at dawn which was made up of civilians as well as soldiers and they threw everything in the world at us including anti-tank weapons. Casualties were heavy but thank goodness I was only bruised from hitting the ground so often. Well we finally cleaned it out by taking this last town this evening. Thank goodness it's over with. We start for a new one tomorrow and I sure hope it isn't as bad as this last one.

Honey, I got a radiogram yesterday telling me of my new Nephew. Yep Sel, Besse had a boy. Golly that was sure good news to me. I'm not sure of the name but I believe it is Millard Alan. Golly that family of mine has really grown in the past six months.

Sel I've received all your letters up to & including no. 36. Your letters are wonderful Honey. Thank Shirley for writing to me. That was very nice of her and she wrote a very nice letter. She sounds like a swell kid Honey. Tell ya Sel, the four of us should throw a big fling when we get home. Really have a party. How does that sound?

Well Doll, I'd better get some sleep now because I'm really all in. Thanks for the jokes. Take <u>good</u> care of yourself and write often.

Love you,

Bob

P.S. NOTE KRAUT STATIONERY!

Letter No. 50

Pfc. B. D. Browne 39337016
Co. I, 410 Inf. A.P.O. 470
c/o Postmaster New York, N.Y

Miss Selma Nepom
4540 17th St. N.E.
Seattle 5, Washington

April 28, 1945

Dear Selma,

Just a line Honey to let you know that we're here in a small town waiting to make a crossing across the Danube River. At present we're about a mile away from it and the mortars and artillery have really been coming in. Must have another pocket formed on the other side. I hope the crossing won't be too rough.

Honey, I'm sending you a little Kraut helmet which I imagine was used as an ashtray. I thought you might like it. Hope you get it in good shape.

Sel, I have very little time, but I figure a note is almost as good as a letter. I doubt whether I'll be able to write for the next couple of days because we should be pretty busy moving. I sure hope we make the crossing in good shape.

Honey I've got to go and get ready to move. I'll write the first chance I get. Take good care of yourself Doll and keep the letters coming. Regards to the folks and say hello to Shirley. Don't forget to tell her about our post war party.

Sel, I'm glad to hear you're playing golf. I like it a lot myself, I'll try to beat you when I get home.

Yours with love,
Bob

PFC. B. D. BROWNE 39337016
CO. I, 410 INF. A.P.O. 470
c/o POSTMASTER NEW YORK, N.Y.

MISS SELMA NEPOM
4540 17TH ST. N.E.
SEATTLE 5, WASHINGTON

April 31, 1945
Letter #53

Dearest Selma,

Well here it is another day Honey, and we traveled 18 miles today clearing a very small part of the Bavarian Alps and I'm telling you I've seen some of the most beautiful scenery I've ever seen in my life. It reminds me of the pictures you often see of the Swiss Alps. The people still wear their customary dress and it really is picturesque. Just like pictures. It's actually hard to believe.

We found an awful lot of Krauts who took to the mountains for refuge, but we caught up with them. I think we got close to 1000 of them today. Really was a field day.

Sel, the mountains remind me very much of some of the mountains in Oregon and Washington. They are really beautiful. I only wish I could get some pictures to send you.

We moved into this village a few hours ago which is directly at the foot of a high snow- capped mountain. Sure is cold, but we took over a very nice house so that's all that counts. It seems that our rat race sort of slowed down a little since we hit the mountains so we're hoping to stay here tonight. The way I understand it, we might even get a hot breakfast in the morning.

As for the war we haven't hit any resistance for quite a time, thank goodness. All the German soldiers seem to do is wait for us to come after them and then they come out with their hands on their heads. Reason is I guess is because they are not at all organized. Really is funny. They have all just seemed to quit. I sure hope it stays that way. I had enough of combat, in fact I never want to see any more if possible. I'm ready to do anything though to end this damn mess. I've got so much to do at home??

Sel, I received two letters from you today, no.'s 37 & 38 and it sure was good hearing from you. I was glad to hear that you helped entertain all the service men. Really helps. As for Wally Schneider, I don't know where

270

he is now. The last I knew he was in England in a general hospital. I could probably get a letter to him through our mail clerk. He should be on his way back unless his wound was bad enough to keep him out of combat.

Well Honey, that's about it for now. I'm going to bed after I finish this letter and try to catch up on some lost sleep. We've really been on the go this last week.

Take good care of yourself Doll and have fun.

Love,
Bob

Pfc. B. D. Browne 39337016
Co. I, 410 Inf. A.P.O. 470
c/o Postmaster New York, N.Y.

Miss Selma Nepom
4540 17th St. N.E.
Seattle 5, Washington

May 2, 1945
Letter #54

Dear Selma,

Honey we received word today that we leave here tomorrow morning to rally one of our regiments that hit resistance farther along. We looked everywhere to try to get some pictures of this place because it's so beautiful. I'm enclosing what I found in the attic of our house. Sel, we're staying in what was a guest house for tourists and it really is a beautiful place. This country here just can't be beat. I've often read about the Bavarian Alps, but I didn't think they were actually so nice. I hope you like the pictures. We sure hate to leave here because for one thing we'll be getting into the fight again, and another it was really a beautiful village to stay in.

I got a letter from Monte today and he is now in Germany somewhere far in the rear. He's set up good and likes it. He claims that his sister had a baby boy—Mazal tov, he's an uncle.

I sent some more stamps to Normie today because I really got hold of some beauties. They looked nice anyhow. Hope he gets them alright.

Honey, we move tomorrow morning before daybreak so don't be worried if you don't hear from me for a couple of days. I think we go farther into the mountains which will make things rough as hell. I hope it won't last long.

Well Honey, that's about it from this side. Anything new at home? How's school coming along? You can count on a darn good licking from me when I get home because about 2 months ago, I asked for a picture and as yet you haven't come through. That's not very nice Sel. Just wait til you want something real bad. See, I'm pouting now.

Well Doll, that's it for now. Take care of yourself and have fun.

Love,
Bob

Oberammergau, Germany

Pfc. B. D. Browne 39337016
Co. I, 410 Inf. A.P.O. 470
c/o Postmaster New York, N.Y.

Miss Selma Nepom
Phi Sigma Sigma
4540 17th St. N.E.
Seattle 5, Washington

May 5, 1945
Letter No. 55

Dearest Selma,

Honey, we've really been traveling in the past few days. This is the first chance I've had to write in the past 3 days. It looks as if we may spend the night here in the little village in among the Bavarian Alps. Honey at the present time we are deep into Austria and close to Brenner Pass which we took early this morning with very little resistance. Sel, the only resistance we're having now are these small groups of SS troops which hide out here in the mountains. The regular Army troops are glad to surrender but those damn SS fanatics still keep us ducking. We should have them cleared out in time though.

Sel, on our way here we liberated 2 concentration camps full of Jews and all they are is skin and bones. Those poor guys really went through hell. I hate to tell you what actually happened. I'll tell you all about it when I get home.

I haven't received any mail for the past 3 days because we've been moving so fast and it just hasn't had time to catch up with us. We should get some tomorrow or the next day.

Sel, I'm enclosing an arm band that was worn by those people employed by the German Army. They did not wear uniforms but were civilians working with the Army. Quite a set up. The words "Deutsch Wehrmacht" mean "German Army." I got it early this morning when we took a small city.

Well Doll, that's about it for now. Take good care of yourself Honey and have lots of fun at school.

I'll write again whenever possible.

Love,
Bob

274

Two Holocaust Remembrances

Two Mirabella residents have personal experiences of German World War II concentration camps, one from the inside and one from the outside. Frieda Grayzel is a survivor of Auschwitz and Bernard Brown is a liberator of Dachau. Here are their stories.

Bernard Brown Remembers Dachau Liberation

by Nancy Moss

Mirabella resident Bernard Brown's most vivid memory of World War II was the liberation of Dachau. His U.S. Army infantry unit was the first to reach the concentration camp.

Bernard saw the camp's inmates, who were "all skin and bones," fall on their knees, calling out "Wasser! Bitte!" (Water! Please!).

The American soldiers, who each carried two canteens, poured water from one of them into their helmets and gave them to the inmates. It was a "tough memory," Bernard says. He adds that trucks that followed the army took the camp survivors away to food and clean clothes.

Bernard joined the army after graduating from high school. His high test scores meant he would be sent to college, but after a short stint at Oklahoma State and the University of Colorado, the demands of war meant he was sent overseas to Marseille, France, on Oct. 20, 1944.

Bernard and the 103rd "Cactus" Division fought their way north to the Vosges Mountains. Bernard was a light machine gunner, working in a team with two other men who carried ammunition; he was the shooter.

During a particularly heavy engagement on April 2, 1945, artillery shrapnel wounded Bernard in his back and legs. His wounds treated, he returned to his unit. "I wanted to get back with my group," Bernard says, calling them a brotherhood that protected and looked out for each other.

During the Ardennes-Alsace Campaign, a sergeant asked if anyone on the front lines could speak and understand German. Bernard, who had studied German in high school, said that he could. He then assisted in the interrogation of captured German soldiers. Worried at first that they would not understand his high school German, Bernard found that "I learned in a hurry," and "the more I did it, the easier it became." He was happy to leave the front lines, he says.

During his first days in the army, as a "frightened young kid," Bernard needed someone to help him get over his homesickness. He wrote two girlfriends from high school and another girl, a family friend he had known all his life, Selma Nepom.

"Selma's letters grabbed me," Bernard says now. Home on furlough, he dated her, and in February, 1946, he married Selma in Portland. In 2016 Bernard and Selma celebrated 70 years of marriage; she is now on Mirabella's second floor.

Honorably discharged from the army on November 28, 1945, Bernard earned a number of military honors including the Bronze Star, Purple Heart, World War II Victory Medal, European-African-Middle Eastern Campaign Medal with two bronze service stars, the Combat Infantry Badge and Good Conduct Medal. He received the two service stars for participation in two major battles.

Licensed as an optometric physician, Bernard maintained a practice in Salem for 57 years before retiring in 2007. He and Selma have three children, Shelley, who works for the guitarist Santana, Jordan, who runs the eye clinic that Bernard founded, and Eden Rose, a lawyer.

Bernard has compiled and is proud of a legacy family book, a reminder of his exemplary participation in our great and good war.

But the liberation of Dachau remains his most vivid memory. ❁

Bernard at Mutters, Austria, 1944

Pfc. B. D. Browne 39337016
Co. I, 410 Inf. A.P.O. 470
c/o Postmaster New York, NY

Miss Selma Nepom
Phi Sigma Sigma
4540 17th St. N.E.
Seattle 5, Washington

May 8, 1945
Letter No. 56

Dearest Selma,

Just a line Honey to let you know that I'm fine and thank goodness the war over here is over with. I only hope the other will end soon but I'm afraid we're going to have to go over there and help out. I only hope I'll be able to come to the states on furlough first.

Sel, I received your letter today no. 39 and it was good to hear from you. Those 5 days without mail were really rough. I turned in the letter to Wally Schneider and it should be on its way to him by now. I hope he gets it alright.

I received a letter today from Normie thanking me for the stamps and he also sent me a copy of the Service edition of the Oregonian which was very nice of him. He's a swell kid Sel. He's very fond of stamps so I'll do what I can for him. I think I sent him all that's possible to get through. Maybe now that I'm in Austria I'll be able to get him some Austrian stamps.

Honey, today I took a few hours off and a few of us went hiking to a lake about 3 miles away. It was really swell up there and the sun was good and hot. I think I swam myself out. It was really wonderful.

I'm enclosing a circular which shows the town that we're staying in. It's only a Winter pamphlet but you can get an idea of what it's like.

Well my Doll, that's about it for now. Take good care of yourself, have fun and write often. Pray for my home-coming now Honey.

Love,
Bob

Innsbruck, Austria May 45

Mary Lou Schaffer – Detroit
    Our Red Cross Doughnut
girl. She followed the
Div. all through combat.

Pfc. B. D. Browne 39337016
Co. I, 410 Inf. A.P.O. 470
c/o Postmaster New York, N.Y.

Miss Selma Nepom
4540 17th St. N.E.
Seattle 5, Washington

May 10, 1945
Letter No. 57

Dear Selma,

Well Honey, the war over here is officially over and it sure is wonderful. We had a big victory parade yesterday in downtown Innsbruck, Austria and it really was nice. I took some pictures of it and will send them to you if and when they're developed. Developing is a problem over here. Golly, I only wish the whole damn thing was over with.

Sel, I leave tomorrow night on a furlough to England. I'll spend seven days in England and I already wrote Lew. I only hope he's there rather than flying around the world somewhere. Sel if you don't get any mail from me for a few days you'll know why. I'll write to you from England though. I only hope Lew will be there. We'll really have a wonderful time together. We catch a plane tomorrow night in Munich and change planes at Dijon, France to England—where in England I don't know but I sure hope it's London. I'm not too sure about the plane schedule but that's how they think it will work. I'm going with 2 others from our outfit so we're really going to have one hell of a time. I'll write you all about it.

I got a letter today from Bobby and he's still in New Mexico hoping that he'll be there a long time. A person is a damn fool to want to come overseas—especially a combat man.

Well Doll, that's about it for now. I'll write tomorrow before I leave if possible.

Love,
Bob

Pfc. B. D. Browne 39337016
Co. I, 410 Inf. A.P.O. 470
c/o Postmaster New York, N.Y.

Miss Selma Nepom
4540 17th St. N.E.
Seattle 5, Washington

May 14, 1945

Dear Selma,

Just a line Honey to let you know that I'm writing you from a little A.R.C. club in a small town called Etratat located on the French Riviera and it's really beautiful. We stay here for about 48 hours getting ready to go to England. We get all new clothing, necessary papers etc. here. We embark at LaHavre and 5 hours later debark at Southhampton in southern England. We go across the channel on an English boat. I'll write and give you all the details later.

As yet I haven't been able to wire Lew because we are both military men. I will be able to write him when I hit England though so here's hoping that he'll be there. He'll probably be flying all over the country.

Well Doll I'm awfully tired because we traveled all night on one of those damn French trains. I'll write again when possible. Right now, I'm going to bed and I'm not going to get up until tomorrow at noon. Golly that's really going to be wonderful.

Take good care of yourself Sel and have fun at school. Regards to all.

Love,
Bob

Pfc. B. D. Browne 39337016
Co. I 410 Inf. A.P.O. 470
c/o Postmaster New York, N.Y.

Miss Selma Nepom
4540 17th St. N.E.
Seattle 5, Washington

May 17, 1945
London – No. 58

Dear Selma,

Well here I am in London and the ole place is really pretty nice. It's far from being modern, but I guess that's what makes it so beautiful.

I arrived yesterday morning and Lew met me at the train. Sure was good to see him. We went to his apartment (English call them flats) and I got cleaned up and settled. He works during the day, so we went out last night with two of my English cousins. I was surprised at the number of relatives I have over here. About 15 of them. Tonight, we're having a big party at my aunt's house and over the weekend we're all planning to go to a coast town called Bournemoth where my aunt has a summer home so you can see what I'll be doing. Monday Lew is flying to a port in France and I'm going with him. We'll be gone two days which will give me one day in London before I leave. Honey, it's really wonderful here. Lew's apt. is beautiful. He stays with another captain and a major. Both good Joe's. All I do is sleep—sure is wonderful. I had my first real glass of milk in 9 months in Lew's apt. yesterday. What a life.

Honey, the Air Corp in general is the cream of the service. A man's rating changes on an average of every 5 months whereas a Dog Face can stay in one place for years. In the infantry they have what they call T.O. (table of organization) and a man cannot advance unless the opening is there. If no opening—then no advance. It's strange the way two branches can be so different.

Well Doll, I hope everything is going alright in school. Are you having lots of fun? Just wait till I get home Sel—I've got so much to tell you. We've got an awful lot to talk about Honey.

I'll write again soon. Regards to all at home.

Love,
Bob

Enclosed will find a sixpence coin (same as a dime)

281

Pfc. B. D. Browne 39337016
Co. I, 410 Inf. A.P.O. 470
c/o Postmaster New York, N.Y.

Miss Selma Nepom
4540 17th St. N.E.
Seattle 5, Washington

May 20, 1945

Honey,

Just a line to let you know that I'm out here on the beach enjoying myself. I wish you were here. It's very similar to Seaside. We leave for London tomorrow. Will write you from there.

Love,
Bob

Pfc. B. D. Browne 39337016
Co. I 410 Inf. A.P.O. 470
c/o Postmaster New York, N.Y.

Miss Selma Nepom
4540 17th St. N.E.
Seattle 5, Washington

May 26, 1945
Southhampton, Eng.
Letter No. 59

Dear Selma,

Well Honey, our wonderful vacation ended yesterday morning and we leave for France at noon today. We left London yesterday and will leave from Southhampton today by boat.

Sweetheart I had one wonderful time just being with Lew and learning how to be a white man again. It really felt funny to sit down at a beautiful table in a beautiful night club and eat with real silverware. I spent most of my time with Lew except for those 3 days that I went to the coast with the rest of the tribe. Lew and I flew to Ireland, Scotland and in general he flew me all over England. Sure was wonderful.

England is very nice, and London has some advantages over New York. It has the finest subway in the world. Better cab and bus service, but New York has its advantages over London. It's really a very beautiful city though.

Sel the English people are all very envious of Americans & America. They see how the Americans live & what they have. As you probably know England is still very much held down by tradition and can hardly wait to let their hair down and live to enjoy life. They are a very rigid people. It's the hope of every English girl to latch onto some American boy so that she'll be able to come to America, and strangely enough some jerks, because of lonesomeness or something else, are marrying these girls which someday they may regret. The English girls love the way we live. Every one of them hopes to get to America one way or the other. I've really got some funny stories to tell you once I get home.

London is a very beautiful city, but I'll still take the modern way of life in the U.S. These people just don't seem to know how to enjoy life. Those G.I.'s stationed here though are teaching them slowly but surely.

It was really wonderful though Sel. Next to coming back to the states it's the best I could have hoped for.

Lew has a wonderful job and is getting along swell. He has a beautiful apt. and plenty of Black & White and Haig & Haig scotch which he gets in Edinborough so you can imagine the time we had.

We should arrive in Paris in a couple or three days and if we stay there any time at all I'll write you from there. I sure have missed your letters Honey. How has everything been going? Been having fun? Anything new with school?

Sel I'm enclosing a bracelet which I got in London made of thrupences (nickels). I'm also enclosing 3 regular coins their values are –

3 pence (thrupence) - 5¢
6 pence (tener) - 10¢
shilling - 20¢

A pound is a bill—amount of about $4.40. A person is weighed by stones—a stone weighs 14 lbs>.

Well Honey, that's about it for now. Write often as usual and I'll write from Paris if possible.

Love,
Bob

Pfc. B. D. Browne 39337016
Co. I, 410 Inf. A.P.O. 470
c/o Postmaster New York, N.Y.

Miss Selma Nepom
4540 17th St. N.E.
Seattle 5, Washington

June 1, 1945
Letter #60

Dearest Selma,

Honey I arrived in Innsbruck today at noon after a 9-hour ride from Strasborg and awaiting me were 3 of your packages along with 8 letters and it sure was wonderful. I really missed your letters an awful lot. I was so glad to hear that everything was alright and that you were planning to leave for San Francisco.

Sel now that I'm back the rumors are flying fast and furious. The latest one is that we leave for the states sometime in July and spend about 3 months there training for the Japanese theater. Just think Sel, if we were married and had 2 children, I'd be a civilian. This point system practically excludes me. I have exactly 38 points. Golly Honey if I do get home, I've got a lot of plans to put forth but as we've always said what's to be will be—and I'm sure hoping. When I know for sure about returning to the states—you'll be one of the first to know about it. Golly Doll, just think what it will be like when we actually see one another face to face. Honey, if you only knew how much I've thought of you. I've learned so much about you through your letters. As you put it, I want to be frank in everything I say and ask me whatever you like because I want you to know just how I feel about everything.

Well Sweetheart, that's about it for now. Take good care of yourself and write soon.

Yours with love,
Bob

P.S. I sent you a little gift from Paris—hope you get it alright. Thanks an awful lot for the packages—the candy is delicious.

PFC. B. D. BROWNE 39337016
Co. I, 410 INF. A.P.O. 470
c/o POSTMASTER NEW YORK, N.Y.

MISS SELMA NEPOM
4540 17TH ST. N.E.
SEATTLE 5, WASHINGTON

June 2, 1945
Letter No. 61

Dear Sel,

Honey we got some pictures returned today from Paris which we took while on the move through Germany. One picture shows the castle which I told you so much about. It's about 12 miles out of Heidelberg and was really a beautiful place. All three pictures are very poor, but I guess it's the film we use. It's very old German film.

Sel pictures 2 & 3 were taken while we were moving and they are really rough. You can see just what a doughboy looks like most of the time in battle.

Picture number two shows the jeep driver on the left and the other I & R man on my right. The three of us always travel together. We'd just came 74 km and we were all very tired, dirty & unshaven. I must have bit my lower lip just as the picture was snapped.

Picture no. 3 shows you a house in the background where we got two Jerries. We have their helmets on display. I was fiddling with a Kraut pistol at the time when picture was taken. Honey, if you'll notice on my pistol—the handles are made of plexiglass (transparent) and on one side I carry your picture and on the other side the folks. It's really swell. That way I can always keep you with me. If you only knew how many times you slept with me in fox holes—Golly Honey you'd blush.

They're terrible pictures but I thought you might like to see them. Strictly combat pictures—everything but the shooting.

Well Honey that's it for today—take care of yourself Sel and write often.

Love,
Bob

Pfc. B. D. Browne 39337016
Co. I, 410 Inf. A.P.O. 470
c/o Postmaster New York, NY

Miss Selma Nepom
4570 17th Ave. N.E.
Seattle, 5, Washington

June 5, 1945
Letter No. 62

Dear Selma,

I just returned from a little town way up in the mountains where I got billets for the company. We leave here Thursday and move there about 68 km. from Innsbruck.

It's a very nice little place but it's not half as nice as it is here. It really is swell here. We are relieving the 44th division who are going to the states for training. We hope to follow them so don't be too surprised if you see this kid in your arms in a couple of months. Golly that sure sounds wonderful.

Honey on our way over we stopped to take a look at Berchtesgaden and it is really bombed to hell. It must have been a beautiful place at one time. His chateau was built on a steel turntable so that he could have the sun in his library all day. It's very clever and very well built, but now it's not worth a darn. In his cellar he has 2 1500 gal. wine barrels but all the wine has turned to vinegar. The ruins resemble all the others I've seen. It was quite a place though at one time.

Nothing much new from here Sel. How are things at school? Did you have a good time in California? I'll write again tomorrow or the next day.

Send me some pictures of yourself Honey.

Love,
Bob

Pfc. B. D. Browne 39337016
Co. I, 410 Inf. A.P.O. 470
c/o Postmaster New York, N.Y.

Miss Selma Nepom
4570 17th Ave. N.E.
Seattle, 5, Washington

June 6, 1945
Letter No. 63

Dear Sel,

Just a line to let you know that I received your letter today telling me about Ruth getting married. Golly that's sure swell—congratulations Sel. One more addition to the Nepom family. Isn't it funny the way things happen? He must be a nice fellow. I know he's a lucky boy to latch onto Ruth. Send her (them) my best Honey. That's sure swell. I was glad to hear that Normie and Tillie got there for the wedding. I'll bet it was really swell.

Well Sel, we leave for our new hang-out tomorrow at 5 in the morning. We're supposed to have the relief completed by 12:00 o'clock noon.

I sure hate to leave this place because it's exactly like a summer resort in the mountains. It really is beautiful.

Well Honey, that's about it for now. I hope to be seeing you in a couple of months so keep your fingers crossed Sel.

I'll write again as soon as we get settled. Regards to all at home.

Yours with love,
Bob

PFC. B. D. BROWNE 39337016
CO. I, 410 INF. A.P.O. 470
c/o POSTMASTER NEW YORK, N.Y.

MISS SELMA NEPOM
716 S.W. HARRISON ST.
PORTLAND, 1, OREGON

June 9, 1945
Letter No. 64

Dear Selma,

I left the company yesterday Honey to work with Military Government here in Austria. Lt. Keough and I both got the job and we're making a swell time of it. It's only temporary and should last about a week to 10 days. Altogether there are 3 of us. Lt. Keough, myself, & a jeep driver. We are strictly on our own which makes us very happy. Our job is to go around and contact all the large farmers in our sector and see that they have equipment enough, plenty of help, & a market for their crops. It's up to us to see that they have all of that. All the help used is prisoner help who are happy enough just to get 3 meals a day.

At present we are living in a beautiful home in the town of Imst, Austria. It's a small town but we have a very nice place to stay.

Being that today is Saturday we quit work at 12:00 Noon (ahem!) Tomorrow we don't do anything, but Monday we have to travel about 180 km to contact the Secretary of Agriculture of Austria. It's really interesting stuff Honey and I like it a lot. Too bad it can't be permanent, but no luck I guess.

All I do is the interpreting and see that all the forms are filled out correctly. Best part about it is that we're on our own and we can do anything we want to. Tomorrow morning, we are going to a ski school in the mountains and go skiing. Hope the weather stays nice.

Well Doll, how are things at school? I hope you're all caught up by now so that you'll have time to get a little rest. I'm certainly counting on seeing you soon Sel because I've got a lot to talk over with you, but if that time doesn't come soon, I'm sure things will wait. There's nothing definite about coming home soon, but the rumor goes that we'll be home by the end of August. Sure would be wonderful.

Well Sel, that's about it for now. We won't go to the company after rations until Tuesday so that means no mail until Tuesday. I'll write though every chance possible.

Take care of yourself Honey and have fun at school. Regards to all at home.

Love,
Bob

Pfc. B. D. Browne 39337016
Co. I, 410 Inf. A.P.O. 470
c/o Postmaster New York, N.Y.

Miss Selma Nepom
716 S.W. Harrison St.
Portland, 1, Oregon

June 13, 1945
Letter No. 65

𝒟*ear* 𝒮*elma,*

Honey I received two letters from you No's 50 & 51 and it was very good hearing all about your trip to San Francisco. It's very fortunate that Hesh was there so that you could see so much of the city. I'm glad you like it, because I like it myself. I seem to like the Los Angeles area a little more though. Especially the city of Santa Monica which is just out of L.A. Also, glad to hear that you got the bracelet in good shape. I want to make sure that you have souvenirs from every country I've been in. I imagine between me and all the rest of your boyfriends you are really loaded down with souvenirs. They're always nice to have though—aren't they?

About my trip to London—I went there and back by truck, train, & boat. Lew and I flew after I got to London. We flew to Edinburg, Scotland, and saw where Haig & Haig Scotch was made. Sure is a beautiful place. We also flew to Ireland and I saw the original Irish Potato fields. We really had a swell time. We made the hop in a C-47 which made things all the more exciting.

Well Sel, I suppose you know by now that the 3rd & 7th Armies are going to occupy Germany—but this kid isn't. They're taking all the men under 24 years of age with less than 85 points and sending them to different outfits which are going to the Pacific. This coming Saturday 600 men & 2 W.O.s are leaving to join the 5th division who are in La Havre waiting to be filled. I'm keeping my fingers crossed Honey because to be frank with you I don't want to leave until I have to—which I know will be soon enough. The names of those men leaving Saturday will be posted tomorrow. They are taking 39 from I Co..which is an awful lot. One good thing though and that is these men will go home for furlough before going to the Pacific.

I was glad to hear that Ruth & Bob are getting along fine. I certainly hope he won't have to go across. Its hell leaving and especially now that he's married.

Well Doll, that's about it for now. I was sure surprised hearing about all the engagements. I guess they know what they're doing though. Bobby told me all about the breakup. It's probably for the best though—who knows.

I'd better get some sleep now Sel—it's getting pretty late. I'll write again when possible.

Love,
Bob

Pfc. B. D. Browne 39337016
Co. I 410 Inf. A.P.O. 470
c/o Postmaster New York, N.Y.

Miss Selma Nepom
716 S.W. Harrison St.
Portland, 1, Oregon

June 18, 1945
Letter No. 66

Dear Selma,

I returned to the company this morning after finishing our job with M.G. I was in hopes that it might last another week or so, but no luck. There just wasn't enough work. It was swell though while it lasted. Just like a vacation.

When I got back today, I found out that all of the division was transferring their low point men to Pacific bound divisions and that they in turn send the high point (85 or above) men to this division which in time will deactivate. Thirty men have already left our company (about 1800 from the division) and another shipment is expected at the end of the week. I may be home sooner than I expect—nothing definite though.

I was glad to hear that Ruth & Bob were getting along fine. I only hope that he doesn't leave because you have no idea how hard it is for a married couple to break away. I've seen an awful lot of fellows suffer, but badly.

Well Sel, that's about it for now. I imagine by now all exams are over with and you're getting ready to go home. Did you find your finals very rough?

Take care of yourself Honey and give my regards to all.

Yours,
Bob

P.S. How about some pictures of yourself?

Pfc. B. D. Browne 39337016
Co. I, 410 Inf. A.P.O. 470
c/o Postmaster New York, N.Y.

Miss Selma Nepom
716 S.W. Harrison St.
Portland, 1, Oregon

······· *June 21, 1945*
Austria

Dear Selma,

Just a line to let you know that I'm fine and managing to keep pretty busy. I haven't heard from you for a couple of days, so I imagine those finals are really keeping you busy. I hope you made out alright Honey. I think you will.

The weather had been pretty bad around here the past few days, but I think it will clear up soon. Boy, when it rains in these mountains it really pours down. This Sunday I and another fellow are going skiing up in one of their highest mountains. We are going with some of the civilian people who are going up at that time. I hope the weather is good by then because it should really be beautiful up there. There's snow on that mountain all year around and it is supposed to be wonderful for skiing. At the present time we are located in a town 4,200 feet high (1400 meters). So, I imagine we'll be a lot higher if we ever get there. Honey, do you like to ski? If you don't, I'm going to see that you do when I get home. Sel, they've got little kids up here 10 & 11 years old and they can really ski. Reason is that that is their only means of getting around in the wintertime. They sure are wonderful skiers though.

I got a letter from the folks today and they all seem to be getting along fine. Besse says that her boy seems to look more like Dave every day. They say he's not a very big fellow but I guess that doesn't mean anything.

Nothing definite on moving yet Honey, but when it comes it will come fast.

Well Honey, that's about it for now. Take care of yourself and write soon.

Love,
Bob

Pfc. B. D. Browne 39337016
Co. I, 410 Inf. A.P.O. 470
c/o Postmaster New York, N.Y.

Miss Selma Nepom
716 S.W. Harrison St.
Portland, 1, Oregon

June 23, 1945
Austria Lt. No. 67

Dear Selma,

Just a line to let you know that I'm fine and haven't heard from you for the past couple of days. Hoping to get a letter from you tomorrow though.

Well Honey, we got the latest news lately (about an hour ago) and here it is. Within the next 3 weeks all of the men in the division will be sent to other combat divisions in section 1 or 2. Section one is going to CBI direct and section 2 is going to CBI via the states. Honey, I'm really sweating it out. They're putting us all in rifle companies and giving us jobs where we are needed. So I'm expecting the worst. It doesn't look good Sel, but the best I can hope for is to get home before I go fight another damned war. Boy oh boy, seems like they never end. I'll tell you Selma, it's going to be awfully hard if I don't get a chance to get home. I've got an awful lot planned—I just hope things work out right.

The weather is much nicer now. The sun is very hot, and it really is swell. I'm taking advantage of every day of grace over here because I don't like the looks of the future.

Well Doll, nothing much else to write about—I just can't think of anything to say. I'm just praying that I'll be home within the next 60 days.

Take very good care of yourself Honey and write soon. Regards to all.

Love,
Bob

Pfc. B. D. Browne 39337016
Co. I, 410 Inf. A.P.O. 470
c/o Postmaster New York, N.Y.

Miss Selma Nepom
716 S.W. Harrison St.
Portland, 1, Oregon

June 27, 1945
Letter No. 68

Dear Selma,

Received your letter today dated the 16 of June and it was good hearing from you. You must be undoubtedly very busy with finals because your letters haven't been coming in as regular as before. Boy they must really be rough. I hope you make out alright Honey, I'm sure you will. I'll bet it's wonderful being home knowing that it's all over except for the grades. Be sure to let me know the outcome.

I was sorry to hear about Bob leaving so soon. The fact of him getting a house looks very promising. I hope they stay there. I'd sure like to know how those guys manage to stay in the states. I guess some have to stay though. I'm glad for Ruth. Golly I'll bet she's changed a lot since the last time I saw her. I imagine the same goes for you also. Honey, how about sending me some pictures. I asked you for a billfold size quite a while ago. But you never came through. Now that you've got some time how about fulfilling my request?

We started sending displaced persons out today and will continue sending 2 truck loads every 4 days. Today they all went to the Berlin Area. We sent close to 50 of them, packed like sardines. They're all very anxious to go though.

Well Sel, that's about it for now. Rumors are flying high and wide about shipment, but rumors are very seldom true. It should be happening soon though. I'm keeping my fingers crossed.

Take care of yourself Doll and regards to the family.

Love,
Bob

Pfc. B. D. Browne 39337016
Co. I, 410 Inf. A.P.O. 470
c/o Postmaster New York, N.Y.

Miss Selma Nepom
716 S.W. Harrison St.
Portland, 1, Oregon

July 1, 1945
Letter No. 69

$\mathcal{D}$*ear Selma,*

Well Honey, we were alerted this morning for a movement within 48 hours. They took about 80 of us from the company and the rumor is that we are going to some other active division and replace high point men. I know now for sure that it won't be occupation because those divisions have been filled already. I only hope we'll come to the states, first. It's the best I can hope for now.

I'm enclosing a map showing our advances since we hit combat. It should coincide with my letters, except for a couple of small places. These maps were given to all the men that are leaving this division. It will eventually go back to the states with high pointers and deactivate. It's a shame to break up a good division like this because we really thought a lot of it and had a very good record in combat. Everyone's running around here not knowing what's happening, but it looks like all low point men are being shipped out to active divisions. It's not much to look forward to in fact it's doing a lot of harm because after getting all settled here, they have to ship you out. Really messes things up.

Well Honey, there really isn't much more to say. I hope you're getting a good rest at home by now. I'll bet it's swell getting away from the grind of study.

Sel, it's pretty late now so I'd better get some sleep. Write soon and send some pictures.

Love,
Bob

WORMS

ARMY RESERVE & OCCUPATION
2-7 APRIL-45

MANNHE

NEUSTADT

XX 103

XX 103

SPEYER

DEFENSE
28 MARCH-2 APRIL

LANDAU

SIEGFRIED LINE

FORBACH

BREACHED SIEGFRIED
23 MARCH 45

KLINGENMUNSTER

HAARDT MTS.

DEFENSE
24 DEC-17 JAN

SARREGUEMINES

ENTERED GERMANY
15 DECEMBER 44

WISSEMBOURG

14 DEC 44

DEFENSE
17-21 JAN 45

DEFENSE
21 JAN-15 MAR 45

XX 103

SESSENHEIM

19-21 JAN 45

XX 103

Rhine R.

STRASBOURG

BARR

STEIGE

ERFIG

ST DIE

FOUCHY

SELESTAT

2 DEC 44

21 NOV 44

XX 103

5 DEC 44

23 NOV 44

11 NOV 44
DIVISION COMMITTED
TO ACTION

COLMAR

F R A N C E

VOSGES

MTS.

Meurth R.

Rhine R.

S W I T Z E R L A N D

ALPS

Rhine R.

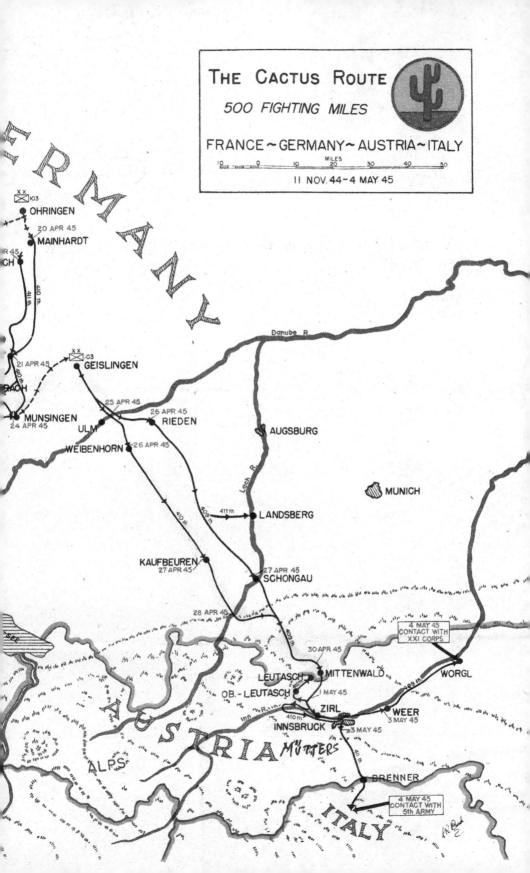

Pfc. B. D. Browne 39337016
Co. I, 410 Inf. A.P.O. 470
c/o Postmaster New York, NY

Miss Selma Nepom
716 S.W. Harrison St.
Portland, 1, Oregon

July 6, 1945

Dear Sel,

I landed in the 45th division and should be in the states around the early part of Sept. I'll send you details in a later letter. Write soon Honey.

Love,
Bob

Pfc. B. D. Browne 39337016
Co. I, 410 Inf. A.P.O. 470
c/o Postmaster New York, N.Y.

Miss Selma Nepom
716 S.W. Harrison St.
Portland, 1, Oregon

July 8, 1945
Letter No. 70

Dear Selma,

I'm now writing you from a little town about 9 miles from Munich where
I Co. 157th Inf. Regt. 45th Inf. Div. is located. It's a nice little town but
I liked Austria much better. This town is located on one of Germany's
famous Superhighways—it's really a beauty and stretches all the way from
Mannheim to Munich.

The situation is as follows. It seems that this division will be home
around the middle or end of September. We were slated to be home in
August, but our priority wasn't high enough. We're supposed to train in
the states from 2 to 6 months before going to Riceland. An awful lot can
happen in 2 months Honey.

It will sure be swell coming home, but I just won't believe it until I
get there. I don't really mind the slow up though because every extra day
over here prolongs our other voyage.

I haven't received any mail for the past 5 days and don't expect any
for another because it takes quite a while changing it all around. I hope
by now that you have received my change of address.

What have you been doing at home lately? Anything exciting been
going on? I'll bet it's really wonderful being home to stay for a while.

I'm hoping to get at least a 21 day furlough on arriving. Golly that
will be the fastest 21 days I've ever spent.

Well Sel, that's about it for now. Take good care of yourself and write
soon. Regards to all at home.

Love,
Bob

PFC. B. D. BROWNE 39337016
CO. I, 410 INF. A.P.O. 470
C/O POSTMASTER NEW YORK, N.Y.

MISS SELMA NEPOM
716 S.W. HARRISON ST.
PORTLAND, 1, OREGON

.... *July 9, 1945*

Dear Selma,

I received your letter today dated 24 June and it was good hearing from you and that you're enjoying being home. I imagine it is quite a relief getting away from school for a while. I was very surprised when the mail came in today. They're doing much better than I ever would.

Thanks an awful lot for sending Bobby's address but I received a letter from him just before coming here and answered it the next day. I was glad to hear of his promotion and also that he got into such a good outfit. It sounds very interesting.

I didn't know that Eric was born in Vienna. I talked with a lot of people from there but didn't visit it while in Austria. It's supposed to be a beautiful city and very bright and lively, similar to Paris. I've always heard a lot about Vienna.

I was glad to hear about Betty and Eric coming home for a few days. I'll bet that was really nice. If and when you write to Eric tell him that I heard an awful lot about his hometown. I also heard that many Jews were taken into Germany as slave labor when the Germans were there. Boy I've really seen the Jews suffering over here. They sure have gone through hell.

Sel, you ended your last letter with some kind of talk about me expecting something of you. Well I can straighten you out right now and that is I don't expect a thing of you and I never did. At times my letters might have been a little sentimental, but I doubt whether they would give you any idea like that. I want you to know now that I don't, and I never have taken anything for granted and I don't think that time will ever come, so don't worry your little head about it. You're a very nice girl to write to and we had a very nice time the last time we were together but please don't worry about me expecting anything because believe me, I don't, and I don't want to. I had a lot of nice plans about having a good time if I ever get home, but I don't think I explained myself well enough. I'm awfully sorry you wrote that little note in your letter. I'm certainly sorry if I gave you that impression.

I got a letter from Dave today and he's in a little town by Kaiserlauten. He expects to leave for the states within the next 3 weeks. I imagine we'll follow them back. He's in the 28th Division.

Dave Gold expects to be coming to the 45th soon but doesn't know when.

That's about all for today Sel. Regards to all.

As ever,
Bob

PFC. B. D. BROWNE 39337016
CO. I, 410 INF. A.P.O. 470
c/o POSTMASTER NEW YORK, N.Y.

MISS SELMA NEPOM
716 S.W. HARRISON ST.
PORTLAND, 1, OREGON

July 16, 1945
(With the 45th Division)

Dear Sel,

This is the last letter I'll ever be writing from Germany because we will soon be in our staging area in Reims, France. Don't write to me from now on Sel because your mail won't reach me until I get back to the states. I hope to be in New York around the early or middle part of September. We may hit it around the end of August, but I doubt it very much.

I received two of your letters today and it was good hearing from you as always. Glad to know that you're having a good time at home. I'll bet it was really funny seeing that man take his butter to lunch. I guess it's really hard to get stuff there. You're right about having it all planned and it's all rest and having a good time and doing things which I dreamt about over here. Sel, excuse the V-Mail but our last mail goes out in less than an hour. Take care of yourself.

Love,
Bob

Pfc. B. D. Browne 39337016
Co. I 410 Inf. A.P.O. 470
c/o Postmaster New York, N.Y.

Miss Selma Nepom
716 S.W. Harrison St.
Portland, 1, Oregon

July 26, 1945
Reims, France
Assembly Area Command

Dear Selma,

I received two letters from you today postmarked the 17th & 18th of July which is exceptionally good time. Sure did surprise me.

Sel I've been working as an asst. company clerk ever since I joined this organization and when we got here we were put directly to work getting ready for our final processing. Well we finished tonight and believe me we were really busy. We start processing tomorrow morning and will (should be) through about Sunday afternoon sometime. Sure is a swell feeling Honey knowing that we're actually on our way. It sure makes me mad though when I think that when we were at war here, I was front line stuff but when the war ends, I get clerks jobs. That's just like the Army though. I don't mind though Sweetheart. I'm really so fortunate that I came out of this side without a scratch after seeing fellows 20 ft. away from me getting blown to pieces. Thank goodness it finally ended.

Sel, when we leave here we go to La Havre where we will spend 1-6 days before getting on the boat. We should leave here about the 14th of August if not sooner. We should hit New York by the 1st of September. I'm hoping to be home for Labor Day weekend. When we get to New York we spend from 24 to 48 hours there. From New York we go to Fort Lewis where we are given furloughs from. Golly, what a day that will be. I'll call you from New York Sel, if it's at all possible.

Honey, it's just like a very bad dream and then waking up and finding out that it was really a dream. I'll tell you now though that we are Pacific bound. We should spend from 2 to 6 months in the states. How would you like to visit me at camp or is it improper? I hate to say this but the rumors lead to some Post in Texas which is no good, but I really don't mind, just so it's in the states. Sel, I'll tell you for sure that you'll find out that I've changed quite a bit. I've seen so awfully much over here that it's really hard to realize certain things.

About us Sel, as we've always said let fate play its part. It will be wonderful to see you Honey. Something I've always thought about. Sel, we spent so little time together that I just don't know what to say or do. Please help me out.

Sel, don't write to me anymore because I'll be on the boat when I receive your letter.

Love,
Bob

Pfc. B. D. Browne 39337016
Co. I, 410 Inf. A.P.O. 470
c/o Postmaster New York, N.Y.

Miss Selma Nepom
716 S.W. Harrison St.
Portland, 1, Oregon

July 27, 1945
Reims, France

Dear Selma,

I received 3 more of your letters today and it was good hearing from you. Honey, I'm glad you liked the gift I sent you from Paris. I hoped you would. I liked it an awful lot myself Sel.

Well Hon, we found out today that we won't leave here until the 25th of August which puts things back quite a bit. I don't know what the reason for it is, all I know is that we have to make up training schedules up to and including the first week in September. It doesn't mean anything though Sel, things can change in minutes at this stage of the game. It's good knowing we're going home though. I still think we'll hit N.Y. around the early or middle part of Sept. I guess the longer we stay over here the better off we are, but I'm sure anxious to get back.

Selma, I'm enclosing some pictures that were taken in Austria and I just got them after having them enlarged. I hope you like them. They give you an idea of how beautiful the country was around there. I didn't mind leaving it though.

Keep writing to me Sel but don't write after the 15th of August because your mail will just follow me to the states. I'll keep you as well informed on our movement as possible.

Love,
Bob

PFC. B. D. BROWNE 39337016
Co. I, 410 INF. A.P.O. 470
c/o POSTMASTER NEW YORK, NY

MISS SELMA NEPOM
716 S.W. HARRISON ST.
PORTLAND, 1, OREGON

July 27, 1945

Dear Sel,

Just a note to let you know that we won't leave here until the 28th of August. Keep writing to me Honey but don't write to me any later than the 15th of August. Will write tonight.

Bob

Pfc. B. D. Browne 39337016
Co. I, 410 Inf. A.P.O. 470
c/o Postmaster New York, NY

Miss Selma Nepom
716 S.W. Harrison St.
Portland, 1, Oregon

July 31, 1945
Reims, France

Dear Selma,

I received your letter no. 66 today and it really made wonderful time. It got here in 7 days Sel which is very very good time. Keep it up Honey. I'm awfully sorry to hear that my mail isn't coming through. I try to write you every chance I get. For a while though we were pretty busy, and I didn't have too much time to write but I hope you at least got a couple of letters explaining the situation.

Selma, I just got back from hearing Shepp Fields and his orchestra and it was really a swell show. Every night they have something else and I've got to give them credit. The U.S.O. is doing a bang-up job over here. They really have some wonderful shows. Tomorrow we're having a show including the Rocketeers from New York, and Thursday night an all colored show from New Orleans. They're really pretty good though. We also have movies every night with a new film change every 3rd night. It's really not a bad set up except for the tents and the dust. Sure does remind me of Texas.

I got a letter from Lew today and he just returned from a trip to North Africa. He enjoyed it very much. Especially Cairo—he says the city itself is very similar to a big city in the states—neon lights and all.

I found out today Sel, that we leave here for a staging area at Le Havre anytime between the 12th & 19th of August. I doubt whether I'll get home for Labor Day but I sure hope it's nice and warm because I would really like to go to the coast for a few days—how about you? Well Sel, that's about all I can think of for now. Please write soon Honey and keep your fingers crossed. It's sure going to be good seeing you after such a long time.

Yours,
Bob

Pfc. B. D. Browne 39337016
Co. I, 410 Inf. A.P.O. 470
c/o Postmaster New York, N.Y.

Miss Selma Nepom
716 S.W. Harrison St.
Portland, 1, Oregon

August 3, 1945
Reims, France

Dear Selma,

Just a line Honey to let you know that we're still here in the assembly area sweating it out and it looks like we'll be leaving in a couple of weeks. I know for sure that we leave here sometime in August. We're still going through the usual routine of processing before we move into our staging area. They really are strict about taking an excess of stuff to go with you and everything other than that is excess and has to be turned in. Believe me though Honey it doesn't hold to record.

I didn't receive any mail for the past couple of days but I'm hoping to get some tomorrow. It gets here in very good time.

The weather has really been terrible these past few days. Very cold, rainy, and windy and it's really miserable in these tents but they're just like castles compared to fox holes so I'm really not complaining.

The company has been training these past couple of weeks with the main idea of just keeping them busy. A lot of the fellows would get pretty restless if they didn't have something to do.

Well Sel, that's about all I can think of at present. With so little happening around here it's pretty hard to think of anything to write except that I miss your letters and can't hardly wait till we meet. You'd better have something planned Sel because I'm leaving it all up to you. I hope it's nice and hot. We'll go swimming at the coast. I would really like to go to the beach for a weekend or so.

Write soon Sel and I'll do the same.

Love,
Bob

PFC. B. D. BROWNE 39337016
Co. I 410 INF. A.P.O. 470
c/o POSTMASTER NEW YORK, N.Y

MISS SELMA NEPOM
716 S.W. HARRISON ST.
PORTLAND, 1, OREGON

August 7, 1945
Reims, France

$\mathcal{D}ear\ \mathcal{S}elma,$

Well here it is another day and the rumors are still flying high and wide. Today we heard that we're due to dock in New York or Boston on or about the 15th of September which means we'll be leaving here around 25th August. I thought we would leave much sooner, but it doesn't sound that way does it? It's sort of tough just hanging around here not knowing when or any of the details. If you believe all these rumors around here, you could really go wacky.

Nothing new around here Sel, in fact things are pretty quiet. Very little has been happening except for a few sneak inspections every now and then.

The mail seems to be coming in very well, but I haven't heard from you for a couple of days now. I'm sure getting awful. I seem to expect to hear from you every day. I think by the time I get home the Summer will be pretty well to a close. Means nothing though Sel. If and when we get there means nothing just so I know we're coming for sure within the next 6 months.

I got another letter from Lew today and he's hoping to fly home soon. He's trying to fix it up so that he'll be home when I am. Sure would be swell but I doubt it very much.

Well Sel, that's about it for now. Write real soon and keep hoping Honey.

Love,
Bob

Pfc. B. D. Browne 39337016
Co. I, 410 Inf. A.P.O. 470
c/o Postmaster New York, N.Y.

Miss Selma Nepom
716 S.W. Harrison St.
Portland, 1, Oregon

August 8, 1945
Reims, France

Dear Selma,

Just a line Honey to let you know that I'm still here and waiting. Not really much to say but I did want to write to you. I try to get a note off to you every chance possible.

Sunny day today and very hot. It's really surprising. I never thought it would get this hot in this section of France but the longer I stay here the more it reminds me of Texas—hot, dry, and dusty. I don't mind it though Sel, believe me. My mind is full of what's before me and that's all that counts. Selma, there's so many things I want to talk to you about, but I can't think of where I'm going to start. I'll have to race against time, I think. Things can always change though. This word fate is beginning to stare right at me.

At present I'm sitting here in the orderly room tent taking it easy. The company is out getting a lecture on military discipline. As soon as I finish this letter to you, I'm going over to take a shower. It's an outdoor job, G.I. version but it's not too bad in this hot weather.

Well Sel, that's about it for now. I hope to be well on my way next month at this time. Write soon Honey.

Love ya,
Bob

Pfc. B. D. Browne 39337016
Co. I, 410 Inf. A.P.O. 470
c/o Postmaster New York, NY

Miss Selma Nepom
716 S.W. Harrison St.
Portland, 1, Oregon

August 9, 1945
Reims, France

Dear Selma,

Just a line Honey to let you know that I'm fine and getting more and more impatient as the days go by. It shouldn't be too long though, if things are starting to cook around here already. We got our train bulletins today giving us full details about leaving here for our staging area which will be just outside of La Havre. It will be at least 2 weeks though Sel before we leave here.

Well we received the very good news early this morning about the Russians joining us in the fight for that everlasting freedom. Honey along with this Atomic Bomb the Japanese can't, absolutely cannot last long. If they decide to choose the suicide aspect, they may be able to hold out for 6 months at the most, and if so the entire island of Japan should be under water. This new bomb is quite a thing isn't it? It will have to be watched closely.

The weather came to quite a change in the past 24 hours. It rained almost all night last night and part of the morning this morning. It's pretty cloudy now and it looks and feels as if it's going to start in again soon.

Nothing much new around here. I plan to go to the show with some of the fellows as soon as I get this letter off to you.

I haven't gotten any mail in the past few days due to some hold up along the line. Very little mail has been coming in.

Well Sel, that's about it for now. Write soon Honey and regards to all the family.

Love,
Bob

Pfc. B. D. Browne 39337016
Co. I, 410 Inf. A.P.O. 470
c/o Postmaster New York, N.Y.

Miss Selma Nepom
716 S.W. Harrison St.
Portland, 1, Oregon

.... *August 11, 1945*
Reims, France

Dear Selma,

Just a note Honey to let you know that the good news reached us yesterday about 1:00 P.M. Everyone in the entire camp practically ran wild until we found out the details. Truthfully, I don't know whether or not the U.S. will accept the surrender terms, but it does show one thing and that is the Japanese War Machine is through. They cannot carry on any longer unless they all want to be killed. Golly it sure is a swell feeling. I only wish we were already on that boat on our way home. It won't be too long though and something tells me that it's going to be for good this time.

Sel, Dave Gold and I finally got together yesterday. We didn't know what happened to one another and we didn't know where to write. So, thanks to that crazy jerk we found out. He went to the Red Cross and gave them full details on me. They wired 103rd who in turn wired back telling them what outfit I was in. He came up last night and boy was I surprised. I didn't know whether he was transferred or remained with the 103rd. He's in 180th Inf. Regt. Same division. We'll both be coming back together.

The weather has really been terrible these last two days. It's been raining awfully hard and believe me it really pours down here. Sure hope the sun comes out soon because things are getting awfully muddy and damp. Otherwise nothing much new.

The present rumors lead to us leaving here the 19th or 20th of August. The sooner the better as far as I'm concerned.

I still haven't received any mail, so I imagine they're holding it up at our staging area.

Well Sel, that's about it for now. Keep writing Sel and maybe I'll get one of your letters soon. I'll write again as soon as possible.

Love,
Bob

Pfc. B. D. Browne 39337016
Co. I, 410 Inf. A.P.O. 470
c/o Postmaster New York, N.Y.

Miss Selma Nepom
716 S.W. Harrison St.
Portland, 1, Oregon

August 13, 1945
Reims, France

Dear Selma,

Just another line Sel to tell you that I spent this past weekend in Paris and had a wonderful time. It's only about 140 miles from here. I'm enclosing some pictures of the city and when I get home, I'll tell you all about them. The group picture is a touring group (2-1/2 hours) sponsored by the R.C. and they show you all the highlights of the city which is very beautiful. This picture was taken at the base of the Arch of Triumph. The last night Sunday night I went to attend Mass at Notre Dame just to see what it was like. Sel, there are no words to express the beauty of that beautiful cathedral. It's magnificent. As we entered the organ was playing softly and all the civilians were kneeling and praying. It's something that's hard to forget. It really was beautiful. I also attended the finest stage show in Paris called Follies Bergere. Your cheapest seats are 75 francs $1.50 and they are high in the balcony. We got very good seats 220 francs, thanks to the Red Cross and it really was a wonderful show. I'm enclosing a small program.

Well Sel, we should be leaving for La Havre this coming Saturday or Sunday because we got notices today from ye ole grapevine. Our training schedule stops on Thursday, so it looks like the real thing. It shouldn't be too long Sel once we get there._

Well Honey, that's about it for now. We're receiving no mail at all here so it's either being held up at New York or La Havre. Keep writing though.

Love,
Bob

Pfc. B. D. Browne 39337016
Co. I 410 Inf. A.P.O. 470
c/o Postmaster New York, N.Y.

Miss Selma Nepom
716 S.W. Harrison St.
Portland, 1, Oregon

August 17, 1945
Reims, France

Dear Selma,

Up to now the news has really been running all ways. Our entire division is really sweating out getting on that boat. It's very possible that they jerk us out here or at our staging area in La Havre in order to make way for high point men. Boy I'm really keeping my fingers crossed and praying constantly to get on that boat. We're really sweating it out now.

Sel, today at 3:00 P.M. our outgoing and incoming mail stops so this will be my last letter from here. I don't know now whether or not we'll have facilities to write from the staging area. If possible though I will write. Just keep praying that we don't get put aside for high pointers.

We are supposed to leave here for the staging area at La Havre tomorrow, Saturday 18th of August. We leave at 2000 (8:00 P.M.) and arrive about 1700 (5:00 P.M.). We go on French trains which are slow as hell. All of the organizational equipment and supplies are packed, sealed, and checked for shipment to U.S. so here's hoping they don't change their minds.

Sel I'll have to close it for now if I want to get it off in time. If you don't hear from me for quite a while, you'll know that we're on the way. Don't write anymore Sel. Keep your eye on the newspapers.

Love,
Bob

Pfc. B. D. Browne 39337016
Co. I 410 Inf. A.P.O. 470
c/o Postmaster New York, N.Y.

Miss Selma Nepom
716 S.W. Harrison St.
Portland, 1, Oregon

··· *August 25, 1945*

La Havre, France

𝒟*ear* 𝒮*elma,*

Well, we finally got to our staging area in La Havre with the hopes of leaving right away but it looks as if we're going to be here for about another week. There are about 7 or 8 such staging areas here which we call cigarette camps because they're all named after cigarettes. We're in camp Herbert Tareyton. All we do here Sel is eat, sleep and repeat. The weather has been very bad though. It's rained everyday so far and we're living in tents which doesn't add to its pleasure. It's not bad though Honey, in fact it's swell just taking it easy.

We have no mailing facilities here but I'm taking a chance and giving this letter to one of the camp cadre compliment to mail for me. No mail is coming in but it's being held up in New York so we should get it all when we get there.

This camp as all staging areas have their own station compliment and it's their job to run the troops through. Troops are usually here from 2 to 7 days but due to the Japanese capitulation things were slowed up for a while.

Sel, the latest dope is that we sail from port on the 1st or 2nd of September which means we should arrive in New York around the 10th or 11th. The name of our boat is Athos #2, it's an American troop ship with a merchant marine crew which is much better than a Navy crew for numerous reasons. Honey I should be home around the 15th of September if things go right. I certainly hope no more changes occur. I was hoping to be home by New Year's but it doesn't look like I'm going to make it. We were originally supposed to sail on the 26th of August, but it was changed, damn it!

The other two regiments are sailing from England which means they will travel on a much larger ship. Maybe one of the Queens. We should pull into New York together though.

I received no mail for quite awhile and I would sure like some, but I don't think we'll get any until we get home.

We turned in all of our French money the other day to be converted into American money. We also took our physical and had our final inspections which means all we're doing now is waiting.

The city of La Havre is still pretty well banged up. The port isn't half as large as the one in Marseilles and isn't nearly as good. The Germans did a pretty thorough job of bombing it. The port isn't large enough to hold larger boats. All of the larger boats leave from Southhampton, England.

Well Sel, that's about it for now. I hope you had a good time at the beach. You'll have to tell me all about it. I'll phone you from New York—if possible.

Love,
Bob

Coming Home

⸺⧓⸻

CAMP BOWIE, TEXAS

FROM

39337016

TO: Miss SELMA NEPOM

716 S.W. HARRISON ST.

PORTLAND, 1, OREGON

Pfc. Bernard D. Browne

Co I, 410th Inf. A.P.O.470

c/o Postmaster, New York,

New York

(Sender's complete address above)

(CENSOR'S STAMP)   SEE INSTRUCTION NO. 2

Dear: Selma

PLEASE ADDRESS ME AS SHOWN BELOW UNTIL OTHERWISE ADVISED:

Pfc.   Bernard   D.   Browne   39337016
(grade)   (first name)   (initial)   (last name)   (A.S.N.)

Co. I   157TH INF.
(Company)   (Regiment)

A.P.O.No.   45   c/o Postmaster   NEW YORK, N.Y.

The above COMPLETE ADDRESS should be placed on ALL MAIL sent to me.

Normal Signature Bernard D. Browne

Dear Sel,
  I landed in the 45th division and should be in the states around the early part of Sept. I'll send you details in a later letter. Write soon Pony.
                                        Love, Bob

HAVE YOU FILLED IN COMPLETE
ADDRESS AT TOP?

REPLY BY
V---MAIL

HAVE YOU FILLED IN COMPLETE
ADDRESS AT TOP?

GPO U. S. GOVERNMENT PRINTING OFFICE : 1943 16—28143-3

Brown's Jewelers-Optometrists
Libert and Court Streets
Salem, Oregon

Miss Selma Nepom
4540 17th St. N.E.
Seattle 5, Washington

··· *October 30, 1945*
Salem

My Darling,

You have no idea how hard it is to write this letter to you. I'm so used to having you right next to me that it really is hard. Honey, I miss you so awfully much now that I can't imagine how rough it's going to be when I get farther than 250 miles away. I've got your picture in front of me and it's going to stay there until I'm back for good. I love that picture. Thank goodness they can't send me out of this country. I only hope and pray they kick me out soon. After all what good am I to them now? Believe me, my heart's not in it. It's with you where it belongs. Sweetheart, it's me that's dreaming this time but it's such a wonderful dream that's really coming true.

Honey, I was sure glad to hear that you're rooming with Saralyn—she really seems to be a swell girl and as far as I'm concerned, my wife deserves the best. I was rather surprised to hear about Rose—I seemed to understand that she would have no trouble at all, but if they didn't like her I guess that's all that counts. You surely did your part anyhow. I hope to be up this weekend Sweetheart and I'll take care of her typewriter then.

Lover, your watch is fully covered so if you need any extra spending money just use it. Dad took care of it Monday, so you don't have to worry about it.

I'm enclosing two of your pictures Honey and if you want anymore, let Besse or me know and we'll get them for you. I think it turned out very good and I've gotten congratulations and pats on the back all day today. You have no idea how popular you've made "us." Everyone tells me I have very good taste—ha! they're telling me. Think you're pretty good now, don't you?—well keep it up because we aren't going to disagree on anything.

I'm enclosing the dates of all the birthdays except Junne's which we'll get later.

That's about it for now Lover. I'll call you tomorrow night and every night possible.

Say hello to all the girls and especially Saralyn. Also say hello to Marvie.

Sweetheart, there's one thing that should never leave your mind and that is that I love you so much that it's hard, awfully hard, to express at times. Just being with you, close to you with my eyes looking into yours expresses it better than anything else. We see in each other our future lives together as one complete life and the happiness and contentment shown there is enough to keep a world going around.

Good night Sweetheart.

Your lover always,
Bob

February 8	Blanche Sharff
February 18	Gary David Brown
April 14	David B. Sharff
April 16	Millard Solotar (Pivi)
May 19	Dad
July 25	Mom
September 14	Alene Sharff (Eeny)
October 20	Lewis Brown
November 5	Besse Solotar
December 5	David Solotar

Pfc. B. D. Browne 39337016
Co. I, 410 Inf. A.P.O. 470
c/o Postmaster New York, N.Y.

Miss Selma Nepom
4540 17th St. N.E.
Seattle, 5, Wash.

November 6, 1945

En route
Having a short layover here in a one-horse town—traveling Pullman—
should arrive Wed. Take good care of yourself. I love you,

Bob

BERNARD H. BROWN
DENVER, COLORADO

MISS SELMA NEPOM
716 S.W. HARRISON ST.
PORTLAND 1, OREGON

November 6, 1945
Denver, Colo.

My Darling,

We have a four hour lay-over here in Denver so I'm taking full advantage of it. This trip has been very slow and monotonous even though we're traveling with civilians. The way it looks it will take us 4 days to get to Texas—if not more. We took the northern route to Denver, so now we will start going South.

Coming through town I stopped and got you a Jewel Box. I hope you like it Sweetheart—you should get it in about a week.

I hope you and Edith got back without any trouble. Can hardly wait to hear from you.

Denver is quite a city. You can do practically anything you wish. It really is a pretty place though. It's jammed with soldiers and sailors though which takes a lot out of any city. Sure is beautiful country around here though.

Well Lover, that's about it for now. We're going right back to the depot. I'll wire you as soon as we get there. I'll always love you.

Your own,
Bob

Pfc. Bernard D. Brown 39337016
Co. I, 157th Inf., 45th Inf. Div.
Camp Bowie, Texas

Miss Selma Nepom
4540 17th St. N.E.
Seattle 5, Washington

November 8, 1945
With U.S. Occupational Forces in Texas

Sweetheart,

We finally got in this morning after spending five nights and four days on that damn train. It sure was a monotonous trip. Connections going south are really terrible.

Well Honey, we found out today that men with 50 points or more are due for discharge and I found out that I only have 48 points. The division is breaking up in a few days into three categories. Men with 1 to 38 points are being sent to Camp Swift, Texas to train for overseas duty with the 2nd Inf. Div. Those with 39 to 49 points will be held in the 8th Services Command as cadre until discharge time. Those with 50 or more points will be discharged. I don't expect to be here after 4 or 5 days, but I don't know where I'll be sent. They may send me to camp hdqts. here at this post but I won't know anything for a few days yet. I hope to be out for good in 2 or 3 months at the most.

Honey, we're about four miles out of a small town called Brownwood, population 18,000. We're as close to the middle of the state as you can get, and it still is rather warm here when the sun shines. They say it was 87 degrees yesterday and I don't doubt it at all. The nights are cool though so it shouldn't be too bad. The camp itself is very similar to Howze. There really isn't much difference in any of these camps. Sweetheart I'm sure the Army won't find me good for anything because I'm just waiting for the day to come back to you.

Honey, I'm terribly in love with you and I miss you more every minute I'm away from you. Someday soon we'll be together for good, lover and then let somebody just try to keep us apart.

Well funny-face I hope school is alright and that you're making out alright. I'll write again tomorrow if it's at all possible. Take the best care of yourself and write real soon.

Your lover always,
Bob

Pfc. Bernard D. Brown 39337016
Co. I 157th Inf., 45th Inf. Div.
Camp Bowie, Texas

Miss Selma Nepom
4540 17th St. N.E.
Seattle 5, Washington

November 9, 1945

Dearest Darling,

Well here it is another day and we already lost one shipment of men who went out this morning. They were low point men and will soon be overseas.

I've been working in Bn. Hq's helping them screw things up. Boy, things are really a mess around here. You see, the division will be broken up in a week or so and nobody knows anything about anything. It will work out though—it always does.

We got some old mail today sent from New York and in it were a couple of letters from Bobby so I wrote to him today for the first time. He'll forgive me tho ugh.

Sure is funny around here. Everybody is running around not knowing just what's going to happen to them. I'm pretty fortunate getting in here because we get first-hand info direct from Div. Hq. I would love nothing better than to be sent close to our part of the country until discharge time, which I'm hoping won't be too long.

The weather took quite a change today. It really is cold and it looks like it may stay that way for a while. I like it better that way anyhow. The climate is really funny in this state. One hour it will be freezing and the next hour you can't keep from sweating. The Texans love it though.

Well Lover, I'm practically going nuts waiting to hear from you. I miss you terribly Sweetheart and can hardly wait to get out of this rat trap. It's really not too bad a place but it's just the idea being away from you.

I plan to go to the show tonight and see "She Wouldn't Say Yes." It's supposed to be a pretty good picture.

That's about it for now Funny Face. I'll write again tomorrow. Take good care of yourself Sweetheart. I love you Honey.

Your own,
Bob

PFC. BERNARD D. BROWN 39337016
CO. I 157TH INF., 45TH INF. DIV.
CAMP BOWIE, TEXAS

MISS SELMA NEPOM
4540 17TH ST. N.E.
SEATTLE 5, WASHINGTON

November 10, 1945

Darling,

Here it is another day and as yet we have no news of being shipped out. I don't think we'll find out any sooner than a week or so. It sure is tough though not knowing just what's going to happen. We haven't been doing a thing around here—just waiting for news. As I said before I've been helping them out at Bn. because they really need it and it's better than just lying around doing nothing. Time goes much faster.

I'm going into town tonight to get a halfway decent meal. The food out here is really rotten. I think I've eaten only 2 meals in the mess hall. I go to the P.X. instead. It seems that the cooks here are just new ones and they don't seem to know much about it. They're getting plenty of good practice though.

We got all of our equipment in today from France and all we're doing is turning it over to the 8th Service Command who'll break it down and send it out to those units still training. I look to see this division deactivated inside of 2 weeks because they really are working fast aside from reassigning the men.

As yet Sweetheart I've received no mail except a few old letters and magazines. I don't expect any either until Monday or Tuesday because I don't think it comes in very fast down here in the heart of this stinking state.

It looks like it's going to be cold and wet for a few days because it sure got a wonderful start. Last night it rained practically all night, I think. This morning it was still at it and all we could see or feel was mud. Thank goodness it's not summertime Lover, because it would really be a scorcher. It's just like any part of Texas. It's as flat and open as can be. The camp reservation is made up of 120,000 acres of ranch land and it's really ranch land.

Well Doll, that's about it for today. Take good care of yourself and give my regards to Saralyn. By the way, how is she making out? I'll write again tomorrow Sweetheart.

Yours always,
Bob

Pfc. Bernard D. Brown 39337016
Co. I 157TH Inf., 45TH Inf. Div.
Camp Bowie, Texas

Miss Selma Nepom
4540 17TH St. N.E.
Seattle 5, Washington

November 11, 1945

Sweetheart,

Well here it is another day and still nothing happening. It's really funny Honey you can sleep all day if you want just so that you can be found in your quarters. I think tomorrow or Tuesday things will really start moving. The way I understand it is that by the end of next week the division should be pretty well broken up.

I went to town last night Honey and it's really quite a place. If it weren't for the soldiers it would be just like any other H I C K town. It has one main street with all the stores and restaurants on it. There are four U.S.O.'s there, one of which is run by the Jewish population of the town. Only one good theater and 5 REX type. There is one very nice hotel in town which really surprised me. It's really a very nice place. That's just about it. The people are typically Texans and most of them have ranches. Yesterday being Saturday most of them came to town so all you could see down the streets was khaki and ten-gallon hats and cowboy boots. It's really quite interesting to see. They have a big dance every Saturday night—upstairs is old time dancing and downstairs is ballroom dancing. I hope I get sent to a civilized part of the country this time. Sweetheart, how wonderful it will be when I get out of this outfit for good. The way the rumors go there'll be another cut in points sometime in December. It's only rumor though Honey.

I got a wire today from the folks telling me that I had been accepted into the Masons which was quite a surprise. They accepted me Wednesday after I had left. Golly, after that interview I thought I would never make it.

Well Lover, that's about it for today. I want to give this letter to one of the fellows who's going to town. It goes out much faster that way.

I'll write again tomorrow Honey. Take good care of yourself and remember that I'll always love <u>you</u> regardless of how far apart we may be.

Your loving,
Bob

Pfc. Bernard D. Brown 39337016
Co. I 157th Inf. 45th Inf. Div.
Camp Bowie, Texas

Miss Selma Nepom
4540 17th St. N.E.
Seattle 5, Washington

November 12, 1945

Darling,

Today was really my day Honey. I received all your letters today even the last one which was post marked the 10th which means it only took 2 days to get here which is wonderful time.

Sweetheart you can't realize how wonderful it is to hear from you. It's something I've looked forward to the minute I left you at Ft. Lewis. Lover, you mean everything to me and I miss you terribly.

It was so wonderful to hear all the news. Sure was nice of all those people to send us gifts—something I didn't expect. I was sure glad to hear of your driving so much. That's very good Sweetheart—I hope you'll be able to get your license when you get home. All you need honey is the practice—you know all the rest. Glad you took good care of our car. Don't worry about having it outside—as long as you have antifreeze in it, it will be alright. Maybe when I get back we'll trade it in for a new one. Rather than painting it and keeping it for a year or so—it might be cheaper to trade it in now. We'll see Lover, when I get back.

I'm glad you dropped accounting Brown—It sounds like a quick death and as long as you're not interested in it—don't bother with it. This Home Ec. course sounds very practical Honey—glad you decided to take it. Sounds like a modern course too.

Darling, you're so right when you say we were very fortunate. First of all, we were so fortunate in finding one another and thank goodness they can't send me away again. It shouldn't be too long before we're together again forever. The next cut in points will include me. I got a transcript of points this morning and it reads like this:

DUTY IN U.S. – 13 PTS.
DUTY OVERSEAS – 20 PTS.
BATTLES & AWARDS – 15 PTS.

So with a total of 48 points I hope to be out much sooner than I ever expected. They stopped counting points as of V.J. Day, which cheated me out of 4 points. As you said though Lover, we really have an awful lot to be thankful for. Sweetheart, you're such a wonderful person that I just beam all over when I think about you. So Brown, keep your chin up and it shouldn't be too long before we're together for good.

The weather sounds terrible there. It seems worse than here. At least here it's cold one day and warm the next. I'll take the west coast weather any day.

Glad you sent Mrs. Brodsky a little gift Honey—she is really a fine woman. Leave it to my wife to take care of things. God Bless you Sweetheart.

Sure is swell that Ruth & Bob are coming home for a little while. I wish we could be there when they come. Honey, maybe Bob won't be shipped, he may be stationed there. They don't seem to be shipping many now. The way I understand it most of the Navy would be stationed in the states but could be ready for action within 10 days or something like that. Let's hope he doesn't get shipped out anyhow.

Well Sweetheart, that's about it for today. By the way—thanks a lot for sending some stationery. I haven't received it as yet but I was planning to buy some soon myself because all I have is this pad which is practically all gone. It will probably get here in a day or so.

I'll write again tomorrow Honey. Good night Darling. I'll love you always.

Yours forever,
Bob

Pfc. Bernard D. Brown 39337016
Co. I 157th Inf. 45th Inf. Div.
Camp Bowie, Texas

Miss Selma Nepom
4540 17th St. N.E.
Seattle 5, Washington

November 13, 1945

Well Brown,

Here it is another day and still nothing new. I didn't get any mail today because very little mail came in today—mostly papers and magazines. I'm expecting some tomorrow Sweetheart.

Another shipping list came in today for Friday but only 15 men are going from the Battalion. They are going to some camp in Oklahoma. Looks like they really tie you down to the 8th Service Command. I expect to be leaving here in a week or so but there's nothing certain. They may keep me here for all I know. It shouldn't be for too long though Lover.

Honey, I read your letters over and over again, they're so wonderful. You have no idea how good they make me feel. Sweetheart, the more I'm away from you the more I miss you. It's such a good feeling though Lover when I get out we'll never be apart again. It's so wonderful to be with a person like you. You're so understanding and everything. You always seem to know just how I feel about everything. Honey, don't get a swell head, but I think you're tops—they just don't come any better.

I'm awfully proud about your driving and especially your parking. That's very good. I hope you'll be able to get your license soon. You can take me for a long drive when I get home Lover.

Well Sweetheart, that's about it for now. There really is very little happening here. Everyone just seems to be waiting to see what's going to happen to them. I'll write again tomorrow Sweetheart. Take good care of yourself and have fun at school. I love you Brown.

Your own,
Bob

P.S. One of the fellas is going into town tonight so I'm giving him this letter to mail. They go out much faster that way.

Pfc. Bernard D. Brown 39337016
Co. I 157th Inf. 45th Inf. Div.
Camp Bowie, Texas

Miss Selma Nepom
4540 17th St. N.E.
Seattle 5, Washington

November 14, 1945

Lover,

I received the anniversary card today and it sure made me feel swell. It was sure cute Honey and it expresses my feelings exactly. I didn't get any letters today at all. I guess it just hasn't started coming through regularly yet. I sure hope I get some tomorrow.

It's hot again today so I guess tomorrow it will be cold again. What a state. Only the people born here seem to like it.

Well Doll, we have a shipment of 243 men leaving tomorrow for different posts in the 8th Service Command and my name isn't on it so I guess I'll be on the next list. I sure hope they don't keep me here. This place really is a hole. When you go to town all you see are cowboys, soldiers, and Mexicans. I don't think I'll be stationed here though. Most of the fellows seem to be shipping out to other camps so I hope they don't make an exception of me.

Very little happened today Sweetheart except for that big shipping list. All we do is just lie around here waiting for something to happen. I'm still helping out at Bn. and if it wasn't for that I would really go nuts.

Just think Lover, a month ago today was our big day—golly it seems like years and I really mean years. I miss you so very much Honey that I find it hard to tell you in a letter. It's like being torn away from something that you've been attached to all your life. They've just got to drop the points again soon. So far, we've been very lucky Sweetheart and I don't think it will change now. Honey our entire lifetime will be full of luck because that's how it started out. Finding what we did in one another was the luckiest part of all.

Well Lover, that's about it for now. I want this letter to go out tonight, so I'll have it taken into town. Take good care of yourself Sweetheart and I'll write again tomorrow. I love you Sweetheart.

Yours,
Bob

Pfc. Bernard D. Brown 39337016
Co. I 157th Inf. 45th Inf. Div.
Camp Bowie, Texas

Miss Selma Nepom
4540 17th St. N.E.
Seattle 5, Washington

November 15, 1945
Thursday

Sweetheart,

I received the swell box of stationery today Honey and thanks an awful lot. You're sure a doll even though I do call you Funny Face. They did a swell job of printing as you can see. Thanks again Honey. I also got a letter from you postmarked the 12th of Nov. Getting your letters is just like taking a good medicine. Sweetheart, I always feel so good. You have no idea how I look forward to hearing from you.

Well Lover, at present there are only 270 men and officers left in the Battalion when originally, we had 850 so you can see that they are moving. We have a couple of more groups leaving tomorrow, but I don't seem to be on any of them. Maybe they'll keep me here until everyone else is gone. Just filled my (our) pen. At any rate Honey, it looks as if I may be here for a while yet. It's really hard to tell though because nobody knows nothing from nothing.

I was surprised to hear that you hadn't heard from me yet. I guess it takes about 3 or 4 days to get from this hole to any civilized part of the country. I've received no mail from the folks at all. Maybe I'll get some tomorrow. That's what I keep saying all the time. Everyone is complaining about mail. so I guess it's just not coming through. Reason must be the crew up in personnel. Practically everyone here is getting out on this 50-point cut. About 1/3 of the outfit are in my shoes—ranging from 44 to 49 points.

Honey, I turned in an application today for (college) credits while in the army. I know I got some while going to school in Oklahoma and I may get some others for various types of training. They'll always be good to have and to use if necessary. I won't use them though unless I really have to because I actually gained very little scholastically in the Army.

Well Lover, that's about it for now. I'll write again tomorrow. Take good care of yourself and have fun at school. I know you're popular Sweetheart, as far as I'm concerned, you're the most popular girl in all the world. I love you very much Sweetheart.

Bob

Pfc. Bernard D. Brown 39337016
Co. I 157th Inf. 45th Inf. Div.
Camp Bowie, Texas

Miss Selma Nepom
4540 17th St. N.E.
Seattle 5, Washington

November 16, 1945
Friday

My Darling,

I received another letter from you today so maybe they'll be coming in regularly now. It sure is wonderful to hear from you Honey, especially when you tell me what you do and how you feel and everything. I'm more concerned about you than anything else. I miss you Sweetheart, but one day soon I'll be back with you for always. It's the most useless thing I've ever done—just sitting around here doing practically nothing. They'll just have to lower the point score again soon because there's nothing to do around here. I've been helping them out in Bn. Hq. but if I didn't want to do it, I wouldn't have to. This army has really changed.

I placed an emergency call today home because I hadn't heard from them as long as I've been here. I couldn't understand it, because I would receive your mail but nothing at all from them. The only way I could get a call through right away was to place an emergency call through the Red Cross and even with that I had to wait an hour and fifteen minutes. Phone service is terrible down here. They just don't seem to be able to get through. Mom told me that you were taking the car when you went, which is a better idea. I hope you're driving all over the place, the practice will do you good. They said that they've been writing every day and still I haven't received a word. I guess it's screwed up along the line somewhere. Well, maybe I'll get some tomorrow!!

I'm going out to dinner tonight which is given by the Jewish people of Brownwood. I'm going with a couple other Yid boys from my company. They'll probably have services and a dance and the whole works. There are quite a few Jewish people living in Brownwood. I imagine they run the business end of the town. It will be nice to get away from this place for a while.

337

We had another shipment go out today and one more for tomorrow. They are 40 to 50 pointers and are being sent to Camp Polk, La. so thank goodness I'm not going with them. They seem to be shipping all over the 8th Service Command which includes Arkansas, Oklahoma, New Mexico, Texas, and Louisiana, so you can see that one is just as bad as the other. I may be able to work a little deal when my turn comes to ship, but it's just a very small chance that might work. Time will tell Honey.

Well Sweetheart, how has school been? I hope you're having a good time along with your studying. Take real good care of my wife please, because I'm so much in love with her that I tell everyone I see about her. I'll write again tomorrow Lover.

I love you Sel, you mean everything to me.

Your own,
Bob

PFC. BERNARD D. BROWN 39337016
CO. I 157TH INF. 45TH INF. DIV.
CAMP BOWIE, TEXAS

MISS SELMA NEPOM
4540 17TH ST. N.E.
SEATTLE 5, WASHINGTON

November 17, 1945
Saturday

Sweetheart,

I really hit the jackpot today when I got 3 letters from you mailed on the 14th and 15th of Nov. Mail has really started to come thank goodness. I also got a letter from the Folks and one from my friend at Annapolis. He's looking forward to meeting you.

Lover, if my letters sound a little sad it's only because I'm away from you. I love you more than anything Honey. As far as getting breaks—I got mine when I got you. Nothing really matters, as long as I know I have your love. Honey, it won't be long now before I'll be home for good. Time should fly by fast. Sweetheart, I just read your letters over and over again. You're such a wonderful person and the funny part about it is that everybody is telling me what a nice girl you are. Ha! Ha, they're telling me.

I was glad to hear that you received the jewel box and gum alright. Every once in a while they get some good gum in and I was just there when it came in. If you want anymore, be sure and let me know.

Honey, don't worry about the Folks not having the car—they always get one somewhere. Please don't feel bad Sel—there's no reason to.

I did expect to be transferred Lover and I still do but I don't know when. I'm still with the division and will probably be one of the last to get out which might be for the better. The 45th Division is to be finally deactivated on the 28th of November so I may be shipped out then. It's really hard to tell Honey, I'm just sitting tight and waiting for an opening, if you know what I mean.

I'm taking very good care of myself Lover so don't worry about me catching cold. The food has improved quite a bit but it's still G.I. food. It's much better though Honey.

Sel, I really don't need or want anything at present, but I promise you when I do, I'll write and ask you. I have everything I want here Honey except my wife, and it won't be long until I come back to her. I think it would be a good idea to order some thank you notes because eventually we're going to need them and if you can get nice ones get them. If not, Sweetheart we can always get them later on. Do what you think is best Honey. As far as I know there's nobody who needs any stationery. I imagine they all have plenty.

Honey, I'm planning to call you Friday night the 23rd around 4 or 5 o'clock your time in Portland. If I don't get through by 9 o'clock forget about it and I'll try again Saturday. I think I'll be able to get through alright. I haven't heard from Lew or Junne as yet, but the Folks tell me that he is now in Rome and will be there for a couple of months yet. He should be out by March at the latest. I'm expecting a letter from Junne any day now. I wrote to Pacific U. about a week ago and I'm still waiting for their answer. Should be here in a few days. I am very anxious to find out what the deal is up there.

Sweetheart, every night before I fall asleep, I think of you. It's so good falling asleep and you're always there close to me Honey. You're always with me Lover and you always will be regardless of how far we are apart.

Well Brown—that's about it for now. Take real good care of yourself and I'll write you again tomorrow.

I'm going golfing tomorrow with a couple of the boys. Golly I haven't golfed for such a long time. They have a very nice course right here on the post so it's pretty handy.

Well Lover—that's it for today. I love you Sweetheart.

Your own,
Bob

Pfc. Bernard D. Brown 39337016
Co. I 157th Inf. 45th Inf. Div.
Camp Bowie, Texas

Miss Selma Nepom
4540 17th St. N.E.
Seattle 5, Washington

November 18, 1945
Sunday

𝒟*arling,*

I received your letter today mailed on the 16th so it made good time getting here.

Golly, sounds like the house is full of wounded and sick. Honey, be sure to take good care of yourself and keep warm when you go out. It must be quite cold there now with plenty of rain too.

Lover I'm awfully sorry to hear about the car. Golly I always thought those hoses were in good shape. They are the originals, so I guess they were pretty rotten inside. Golly Honey, I hope it didn't cause you too much trouble. You see Sweet, that's why I'm in favor of getting a new car if possible. After you have a car for 3 years or more it starts giving you trouble. Not necessarily the motor but smaller parts similar to hoses and stuff like that. We'll talk it over when I get home and decide then. I'm glad to know that you're driving a lot. That's very good. Keep it up Honey.

At the present time we have but 72 men in the Battalion, so you see in a few days we'll all be gone. I think I'll be one of the last to leave though. It might be better and maybe not. I don't know yet.

We didn't go golfing this morning because the weather was pretty bad, and it looks like it might be that way all day. It will probably be hot as hades tomorrow. May go to a show tonight and see "A Thousand and One Nights." All depends how things go here. It's been busy all morning which isn't like most Sundays.

Well Lover, that's about it for now. I repeat—take very good care of yourself Sweetheart. Give Bob & Ruth my regards when you see them in Portland. I'll write again tomorrow. I love you Sweetheart.

Your own,
Bob

PFC. BERNARD D. BROWN 39337016
CO. I 157TH INF. 45TH INF. DIV.
CAMP BOWIE, TEXAS

MISS SELMA NEPOM
4540 17TH ST. N.E.
SEATTLE 5, WASHINGTON

November 19, 1945
Monday

My Darling,

Just a line to let you know that I'm still here alive and kicking and waiting to see what's going to happen. It's just like a ghost town around here—practically everyone has shipped out. We have but 54 men here and by Saturday most of them will be gone.

Well Lover, you'll probably be in Portland when this letter gets to Seattle, but I'll keep writing you there. We didn't get any mail at all today for some unknown reason. I guess they're losing their men over there also. This outfit is really breaking up in a hurry. As yet, I still don't know where I stand but should know in a few days. Nothing at all is happening around here except the moving. We had 47 move out today from the regiment who went to a P.W. Camp in New Mexico which is one of the worst deals you can get. So far, I've been pretty lucky Sweetheart.

We've had very little to do around here and I really like it because it gives me all the more time to think about you and make plans. Sweetheart I love you more than anything. You mean everything in the whole world to me and as long as I have you the rest will come with little effort or none at all. When I'm with you Lover I feel so sure of everything that all I want to do is tell everyone about it.

Well Doll, that's about it for today. I'll write you again tomorrow. Take good care of yourself Sweetheart. As ever, I love you always,

Yours,
Bob

Pfc. Bernard D. Brown 39337016
Co. I 157th Inf. 45th Inf. Div.
Camp Bowie, Texas

Miss Selma Nepom
4540 17th St. N.E.
Seattle 5, Washington

November 20, 1945
Tuesday

Hi Brown,

Just a note to let you know that I received your letter today and also a copy of the Columns and I want to thank you Lover. I read it from cover to cover already. Sure is a nice magazine and some of the jokes can't be beat. At present it's being passed around by the Bn. Officers.

Honey, it was sure nice of Mrs. Benden to invite you to dinner. She is a wonderful person.

Sweetheart, I want to explain this point system to you. You see all Army Ground Force men who are considered surplus can get out with 50 to 59 points. That includes us because we were originally slated to go to the Pacific theatre but the war ended so they kept us in the states without any assignment with a result that the division is being deactivated and all those eligible for discharge are getting out and the others are being trained for occupational duty and others 40 to 49 points, are being reassigned to Army Service Forces which means they'll be out of the surplus category. Then they'll have to have 55 points to get out. That's the reason I'm trying to stay here as long as possible. Maybe something will happen before I get shipped.

Lover, it's been raining for the past day and it looks as if it might stay that way for a while. Sure is miserable down here when it rains.

Well Sweetheart, that's about it for now. There's really very little to write about except that I love you Brown and you're always with me wherever I go and whatever I do. You mean everything to me Lover. Take good care of yourself and thanks again for the Columns. I'll write again tomorrow.

Your own,
Bob

PFC. BERNARD D. BROWN 39337016
CO. I 157TH INF. 45TH INF. DIV.
CAMP BOWIE, TEXAS

MISS SELMA NEPOM
4540 17TH ST. N.E.
SEATTLE 5, WASHINGTON

November 21, 1945
Wednesday

Hello Sweetheart,

I got two letters from you today and I was sure glad to hear the good news. I was actually sweating it out, but I feel much better now. Yes Honey, I guess we were both a little confused.

Lover, as for Christmas, well I don't even know where I'll be then, but when I find out for sure you'll be the first to know about it. Things are so uncertain now. Golly the weather really sounds bad there. Be sure to take good care of yourself and keep warm when you go out. We're having a so-called windstorm now. Everything blows everywhere and the wind really blows here because there are no trees to hold it back, just flat land with cacti all over the place. It must be much worse there, Honey because we haven't had any windows blown out yet.

Glad they did a good job on your watch. They had better. Is it keeping good time Honey?

I got all the info today from Pacific and I'm sending some of it to you. I'll send the application from home and we'll fill it out when I get back. We may start this Summer Session if I get out in time. It all depends on a lot of things such as our wedding etc. We should be able to start by Fall at the latest. That might be better. We'll see when I get out. Honey, you can throw the letter and pamphlets away when you've read them. No need to save them. We'll make a trip up there when I get back.

Well Lover, that's about it for now. This place is dead as ever but it's as good if not better than being shipped out. I'll write again tomorrow Lover. I love you Sweetheart with all my heart.

Your own,
Bob

Pfc. Bernard D. Brown 39337016
Co. I 157th Inf., 45th Inf. Div.
Camp Bowie, Texas

Miss Selma Nepom
4540 17th St. N.E.
Seattle 5, Washington

November 22, 1945
Thanksgiving Day

My Darling,

Well it finally happened today of all days. Honey I have 5 more points added to my score which gives me a total of 53. Let me explain how it all happened. Last week I found out that my old company commander was here in the camp waiting to be reassigned. I went to see him, and we had quite a talk. He asked me if I wanted to get out and you know what I told him. Anyhow when we were in France last year I was wounded, but not seriously, by a shell fragment. I didn't want it to be known because the Red Cross always sends a telegram notifying the family, so I just had our own company aid man fix me up. It wasn't a serious wound at all. Because of that the C.O. put me in for a Purple Heart. I was sent to the medical officer and he looked at the scar and signed an affidavit to that effect. Honey, believe me, it was just a small cut on my right thigh. You can hardly tell it was ever cut. The order came down today awarding me a Purple Heart for that wound, so I guess it went through alright. Anyhow Sweetheart it gives me 5 more points and I'm still in the surplus category so I should be home for Christmas. I don't know when I leave here it will probably be a week or so. They have a separation center here at Bowie so I may get discharged from here. It won't be long at any rate Lover.

I got your letter today Honey and I love you so much that I think I'll be the first to burst. Your letters are wonderful Sweetheart.

I was sorry to hear about your watch. You should have left it and had it cleaned and oiled. If it gives you too much trouble ,we'll send it back to the factory.

Glad to hear you got mail from everyone. I haven't heard from Bobby as yet but should get a letter soon. Your letters as well as the Folks' letters have been coming in regularly. I guess it just had to get started. Sounds like that cousin of ours has changed quite a bit. That's what seeing what the rest of the world is like does for you.

I'm glad the weather is changing for the better up there. The weather is still windy and cold here. It will last about a week in all. It's good to know you're feeling better Sweetheart. As long as you feel good, I'll feel good and vice versa.

I'm going to try to call you tonight and if I don't get through, I'll try again tomorrow and if not then I'll live in the telephone booth the next day. I may not have any trouble at all Sweet—it all depends if they can get through or not.

Honey I sent the credit application home and when we start school, I'll use it then. They are to be submitted when you enter the school and they figure out how many credits you can get.

Glad to hear you're enjoying your home ec course Honey. That spaghetti really sounds delicious. Keep up the good work Lover. By the way Sweetheart, Dallas is the only nice thing about Texas. It's a very modern and beautiful city. It's the only good thing about this state.

Well Brown, that's about it for now. Give my regards to Charlotte. I'll write again tomorrow Sweetheart. I love you with all my heart Lover.

Your own,
Bob

Pfc. Bernard D. Brown 39337016
Co. I 157th Inf. 45th Inf. Div.
Camp Bowie, Texas

Miss Selma Nepom
4540 17th St. N.E.
Seattle 5, Washington

November 23, 1945
Friday

My Darling,

I received your letter today written the 20th so I guess it takes just 3 days. Your letters have been coming in everyday Lover and they sure are wonderful. I live by your letters Sweetheart. Honey I love you more than anything with a kind of love that I never knew existed and it's wonderful. Sweetheart you mean everything in the world to me and when I get home, we'll be together for the rest of our 50 million years. I can just imagine how happy we'll be Lover with a start like we've made. I miss you Sweet, very much but I hope it won't be for much longer. The old saying goes that words are power but believe me they're not powerful enough to express my love for you.

I sent your father some gum today because I think he likes it and it's still hard to get as a civilian. I hope he likes it. I got a wonderful letter from him the other day. Honey we've got the best family in the world and there's no doubt about it. I also have the finest wife in the world and I'm not kidding.

I tried calling you last night, but they couldn't get through. I'm going up early this time. Sweetheart, I hope you had a very nice Thanksgiving at home. I'll bet it was really nice with Bob and Ruth there. We'll all have a big reunion one of these days.

Golly these fellows sure are growing. The last time I saw Phil Gladstein he was just out of the baby stage. No doubt, he must be a cute kid. He always was.

Well Lover, that's about it for now. I'm going to have this letter mailed in town. I'll write again tomorrow Sweetheart. I love you with all my heart.

Your own,
Bob

Pfc. Bernard D. Brown 39337016
Co. I 157ᵀᴴ Inf., 45ᵀᴴ Inf. Div.
Camp Bowie, Texas

Miss Selma Nepom
4540 17ᵀᴴ St. N.E.
Seattle 5, Washington

November 24, 1945
Saturday

Hi Lover,

I got two wonderful letters from you today Sweetheart and one was from Portland.

Golly Sweetheart, it was more than wonderful talking with you last night and it only took a little over an hour to get through which is very good time. Lover, it made me feel as if I was in the same town with you. You sound so good.

I'm glad you're getting a good rest at home. I can imagine what that house is like with all those girls. I was surprised to hear that Sam was there. They'd better come to our wedding. Lover, it looks like we'll have every state in the union represented there. Sweetheart, you're going to have the kind of wedding that you've always dreamt about. Lover, remember always that whatever I do you're a part of. You're constantly in my mind and always will be. I love you with all I've got Sweetheart.

Don't worry about your Folks not writing back. I understand everything, but I still like to let them know what's happening down here. Besides, I have plenty of time now with very little to do so if anything of importance comes up I'll let them know. Golly Lover, that was sure wonderful of you to call Banny and also to Salem. You have no idea what they think of you Sweetheart. There's nobody better than <u>my wife</u> and that's all there is to it.

I'm glad you made the trip home alright and I'm sure happy about you getting your license. Boy that's wonderful. So Funny Face you are now my chauffeur. You'll have to take me for a long drive in the country when I get back. Honey, that's really swell. All you needed was the practice so keep practicing every chance you get. By the way Sweet, if that's the first time you locked bumpers, you're not doing bad at all.

Glad Ruth and Bob are alright. Is it certain that he's going out to sea yet? Maybe he'll just be stationed there.

I got the good news about Eric in your letter today. That sure is wonderful. Practically all of the Air Corp personnel are getting out. I met a friend of mine from Salem in Denver and he was getting discharged with 18 points. He was actually surprised. If Bobby was here, I'm sure he would get out right away. Looks as if everyone will be out soon. Sure hope so.

Thanks for all the gossip. Good to know that Shirlee and Ted are still hitting it off. I would like to see her get engaged. Too bad about Shirley Menovitch. I thought they were really solid with one another. She seems to be a very nice girl.

Well Lover that's about it for today. I went golfing this afternoon and really messed up. I was really off today. They're having a big dance tonight in town so a couple of the boys and I may go in and see what it's like. Think we'll go bowling tomorrow. As I told you there are very few men left here. The fellows that have their wives in town report in the morning to see if they're shipping and then leave again for home. It sure isn't like the Army. Things have changed quite a bit since the war ended.

I'll write again tomorrow Lover. I miss you Sweetheart. I love you Funny Face with all my heart.

Your own,
Bob

Pfc. Bernard D. Brown 39337016
Co. I 157ᵀᴴ Inf., 45ᵀᴴ Inf. Div.
Camp Bowie, Texas

Miss Selma Nepom
4540 17ᵀᴴ St. N.E.
Seattle 5, Washington

November 25, 1945
Sunday

Hello Sweetheart,

I received your Thanksgiving letter today and Lover if it weren't for your letters, I don't know what I would do. They always seem to straighten me up and make me feel so good. Honey, we've got to remember one thing and that is the worst part of this whole mess is over with. The danger point has been taken out and that's something we should be very thankful for. Lover, we're both very lonesome for each other but thank goodness when I come home to you this time it will be for good. I'll never have to leave you again. I miss you more than anything else, but I just won't let myself get blue because I really have no reason. I have you Sweetheart and that makes me feel better than anything else in the world. Honey, never in my life did I ever realize that I would feel like I do about any one person. I love you Sweet, you mean everything in the world to me. Lover, it won't be too long now I hope until I'm back for good. Sweetheart, the next time you go home I hope to be with you. Thank goodness the war's over Honey!

Lover, from now on I think I'll let you take care of our car. You do a much better job than I do. You're wonderful, Lover.

Sounds like you had a swell time at Aunt Sofie's. Must have been quite a crowd. Honey what is Sammy planning to do. I know he was going to take a long rest, but I didn't know what he planned to do afterwards. Sure like to see him latch onto some nice girl. He's a nice kid.

Sweetheart, the commanding officer I told you about was named Thompson. If you remember he censored or rather I signed his name to lots of my letters from Europe. He used to be a captain but is now a major. He's an old Army man and plans to stay in and make it his life's work. He's a perfect guy if he likes you. By the way Hon., Lt. Keough is discharged now. Thompson told me about it. He got out as soon as he got back from overseas.

The weather is very nice today. The sun is out but it's not too hot. I don't think there's anything more dead than an Army Post on Sunday. Everything just seems to stand still. I'm going to a show when I finish this letter to you. I think "Kiss and Tell" is on and I've heard it's pretty good. Went to a dance last night in town and it wasn't too bad. They had an Army orchestra and they were really alright. It was something to do anyhow Lover, and that's hard to find around here.

Well Honey, I guess that's about it for today. Take good care of yourself Sweetheart and remember that I'll always love you. I miss you Lover. I'll write again tomorrow. Regards to all.

Always,
Bob

Pfc. Bernard D. Brown 39337016
Co. I 157th Inf., 45th Inf. Div.
Camp Bowie, Texas

Miss Selma Nepom
4540 17th St. N.E.
Seattle 5, Washington

November 26, 1945
Monday

$\mathcal{D}$*arling,*

I got your Nov. 23rd letter today and I was so glad to read all the things you said. Lover I think you should withdraw from school when I get out because after all with you in Seattle and me in Salem, we'd both run ourselves down going back and forth and besides you'll have plenty time to go to school. Sweetheart, speaking of school, it's quite a problem. I really want to start as soon as I can, but I don't think I'll start before Fall. That way we'll start right off at the beginning rather than mid or Summer term and besides I want to work awhile so that we'll be able to get a new car. Dad and Mom really need a little rest and if I stay there, they'll be able to take a couple of weeks off. Honey I was going to wait and talk it over with you, but we'll do that anyhow. Tell me what you think we should do. I think they're planning to go in March sometime. As for our wedding well, the sooner the better for me, but later I don't want to think that we rushed it too fast and left out something. Lover I want you to have the finest wedding you've ever dreamed about because you're going to make the most beautiful bride in the whole world. Doll, if it's possible in Feb. we'll do it but if not, we'll have it in early April. I wish I were back so we could talk it over and figure it out. Honey, I can hardly wait to get back, but I haven't been put on orders yet so all I can do is wait. It may be some time yet or it may be down in a couple of days, but as yet I'm just waiting. Lover, if I'm discharged here, I'll wire you from Denver when I'll find out what time I'll arrive and what train and all the dope. If I get sent to Ft. Lewis, I'll wire from here. I'll wire only you on my arrival so that you can meet me alone but if you're in need of a car call Banny and Dave and get their car. Lover, I'll have to wire the folks and tell them that I'm coming home but I won't tell them when or the time. You call and tell them that you're meeting me. Sweetheart I'm so darn anxious to get home to you that I just can't sit still. I sure hope I get back before Christmas. I should Lover. Honey, you stay in school until you get a wire from me. I'll either call or wire as soon as my orders come down. I feel exactly as you do about everything.

Have you decided on any silverware or china as yet? I hope you're getting a lot of ideas because everyone will be asking you soon. Lover, I want to get a complete set of luggage (alligator) for both of us before we go on our honeymoon. We both need it. As far as my clothes, I doubt very much if I'll be able to find any suits that are worth buying. I have plenty slacks and shirts and stuff. Golly we've got a lot of things to do, haven't we? As for linen Sweetheart, I know very little about the stuff. I don't know one from another. Glad to hear you got a new skirt and sweater. I love you in sport clothes. How's my brown suit Sweetheart? I hope your trousseau has a real long train. I think they're nicer long. I'd give anything to be home with you now Lover—we've got so much to do together.

Glad you had your teeth checked. I've got to have a couple of small cavities fixed before long. I may go down tomorrow or the next day. All depends when they can take me.

I got a letter from Bob today and he hopes to be home in February sometime. I sure hope Lew gets home soon. Bobby seems to be working pretty hard, but he enjoys it so that's all that really counts. I also got a letter from my friend at Annapolis. He plans to be home in September. He's all excited about the Army-Navy game Saturday. He thinks Navy will win but I'll take Army.

Well Lover, that's about it for today. Take good care of yourself Sweetheart and you'll be notified as soon as anything happens. I was thinking maybe Besse and Dave could go to Banny's when I come in so that we'll have a way to go to Salem. We'll see Lover. I love you Honey with all my heart.

Yours always,
Bob

BERNARD D. BROWN
710 SO. WINTER ST.
SALEM, OREGON

PLEASE FORWARD TO:
MISS SELMA NEPOM
716 S.W. HARRISON ST.
PORTLAND, OREGON

November 27, 1945
Tuesday

My Darling,

This is it Lover—I started running through discharge processing today and I get my final papers tomorrow at 3:00 P.M. Honey, fate's really on our side I know now for sure. I never expected to be out so soon but we sure fooled em, didn't we Doll?

Honey, this will probably be my last letter because tomorrow I'm going to Ft. Worth and try to get a plane or a fast train, so I won't write anymore. Don't worry if you don't hear from me Lover. I'll let you know in plenty of time when, how, and where I'll arrive. Truthfully, I can hardly wait to get back to civilized country again. So far Sweetheart everything is working out wonderfully well and it's going to continue that way. Sure would love to be home for your birthday but I'm afraid I'll miss it by a few days.

I came into town tonight to mail some stuff home so thought I would write to you from the U.S.O.

Sweetheart I'll be home before you know it and this time it will be for good.

Excuse short letter Lover but it's awfully late and I've got to get back to camp.

Will be with you soon. I love you Honey.

Always,
Bob

Army of the United States

Honorable Discharge

This is to certify that

BERNARD D BROWNE 39 337 016 Private First Class

Company I 157th Infantry

Army of the United States

is hereby Honorably Discharged from the military service of the United States of America.

This certificate is awarded as a testimonial of Honest and Faithful Service to this country.

Given at SEPARATION POINT
CAMP BOWIE TEXAS

291279

28 November 1945

STATE OF OREGON
County of _____

I hereby certify that the within
was received at 8:10 o'clock A.M.
on the 4th day of Dec
1945 and duly recorded by me in
Marion County Records Book of
Military Records
Volume 7 Page 613

Herman W. n Lanke
County Recorder
_____ Deputy

JOHN W GRANTHAM
Major   FA

ENLISTED RECORD AND REPORT OF SEPARATION
HONORABLE DISCHARGE

1. LAST NAME - FIRST NAME - MIDDLE INITIAL	2. ARMY SERIAL NO.	3. GRADE	4. ARM OR SERVICE	5. COMPONENT
BROWN BERNARD D	39 337 016	Pfc	Inf	AUS

6. ORGANIZATION	7. DATE OF SEPARATION	8. PLACE OF SEPARATION	
Co I 157th Infantry	28 Nov 45	Separation Point	Camp Bowie Texas

9. PERMANENT ADDRESS FOR MAILING PURPOSES	10. DATE OF BIRTH	11. PLACE OF BIRTH
1710 S Winter St Salem(Marion)Ore	24 Aug 24	Portland Oregon

12. ADDRESS FROM WHICH EMPLOYMENT WILL BE SOUGHT	13. COLOR EYES	14. COLOR HAIR	15. HEIGHT	16. WEIGHT	17. NO. DEPEND.
See 9	Brown	Black	6 ¼	188 LBS.	NONE

18. RACE			19. MARITAL STATUS		20. U.S. CITIZEN		21. CIVILIAN OCCUPATION AND NO.
WHITE X	NEGRO	OTHER (specify)	SINGLE X	MARRIED	OTHER (specify)	YES X NO	Student O-X

MILITARY HISTORY

22. DATE OF INDUCTION	23. DATE OF ENLISTMENT	24. DATE OF ENTRY INTO ACTIVE SERVICE	25. PLACE OF ENTRY INTO SERVICE
23 Jul 43		23 Jul 43	Salem Oregon

SELECTIVE SERVICE DATA	26. REGISTERED YES NO	27. LOCAL S.S. BOARD NO.	28. COUNTY AND STATE	29. HOME ADDRESS AT TIME OF ENTRY INTO SERVICE
	▶	1	Marion Oregon	See 9

30. MILITARY OCCUPATIONAL SPECIALTY AND NO.	31. MILITARY QUALIFICATION AND DATE (i.e., infantry, aviation and marksmanship badges, etc.)
Light Machine Gunner 604	Combat Inf Badge GO 13 Hq 410 Inf

32. BATTLES AND CAMPAIGNS
Rhineland-Central Europe GO 40 WD 45

33. DECORATIONS AND CITATIONS
EAME Ribbon-Expert Inf Badge SO 18 Hq 410 Inf-Victory Ribbon WW II Purple Heart GO 366 Hq 45th Div-Good Conduct Medal GO 47 Hq 410 Inf

34. WOUNDS RECEIVED IN ACTION
France - 2 April 1945

35. LATEST IMMUNIZATION DATES				36. SERVICE OUTSIDE CONTINENTAL U. S. AND RETURN		
SMALLPOX	TYPHOID	TETANUS	OTHER (specify) Typhus	DATE OF DEPARTURE	DESTINATION	DATE OF ARRIVAL
7Jul44	7Jul44	7Jul44	13 Aug 45	6 Oct 44	France	20 Oct 44

37. TOTAL LENGTH OF SERVICE						38. HIGHEST GRADE HELD	4 Sep 45	US	11 Sep 45
CONTINENTAL SERVICE			FOREIGN SERVICE			Pfc			
YEARS	MONTHS	DAYS	YEARS	MONTHS	DAYS				
1	4	27	0	11	8				

39. PRIOR SERVICE
NONE

40. REASON AND AUTHORITY FOR SEPARATION
Convenience of Government AR 615-365 WDAGO Ltr AGPE-A-WDGAP 21 Sep 45

41. SERVICE SCHOOLS ATTENDED	42. EDUCATION (Years)		
	Grammar	High School	College
NONE	8	4	0

PAY DATA

43. LONGEVITY FOR PAY PURPOSES			44. MUSTERING OUT PAY		45. SOLDIER DEPOSITS	46. TRAVEL PAY	47. TOTAL AMOUNT, NAME OF DISBURSING OFFICER
YEARS	MONTHS	DAYS	TOTAL	THIS PAYMENT			
2	4	6	$ 300	$ 100	NONE	$ 113.05	231.28 I A BEALL MAJ FD

INSURANCE NOTICE

IMPORTANT IF PREMIUM IS NOT PAID WHEN DUE OR WITHIN THIRTY-ONE DAYS THEREAFTER, INSURANCE WILL LAPSE. MAKE CHECKS OR MONEY ORDERS PAYABLE TO THE TREASURER OF THE U. S. AND FORWARD TO COLLECTIONS SUBDIVISION, VETERANS ADMINISTRATION, WASHINGTON 25, D. C.

48. KIND OF INSURANCE				49. HOW PAID		50. Effective Date of Allotment Discontinuance	51. Date of Next Premium Due (One month after 50)	52. PREMIUM DUE EACH MONTH	53. INTENTION OF VETERAN TO	
Nat. Serv.	U.S. Govt.	None	Allotment	Direct to V. A.			Continue	Continue Only	Discontinue
				X	30 Nov 45	31 Dec 45	$ 6 50	X	

54.	55. REMARKS (This space for completion of above items or entry of other items specified in W. D. Directives)
RIGHT THUMB PRINT	Lapel button issued ASR Score 2 Sept 1945 - 50

56. SIGNATURE OF PERSON BEING SEPARATED	57. PERSONNEL OFFICER (Type name, grade and organization - signature)
Bernard D Brown	GEORGE E PRENTISS 2d Lt FA George E Prentiss

WD AGO FORM 53-55
1 November 1944

This form supersedes all previous editions of WD AGO Forms 53 and 55 for enlisted persons entitled to an Honorable Discharge, which will not be used after receipt of this revision.

WESTERN UNION

A. N. WILLIAMS
PRESIDENT

The filing time shown in the date line on telegrams and day letters is STANDARD TIME at point of origin.   Time of receipt is STANDARD TIME at point of destination

DA89

D.CG313 NL PD=BROWNWOOD TEX 27   DUPLICATE OF TELEPHONE TELEGRAM   1945 NOV 27 PM 5 04

MISS SELMA NEPOM=

4540 17TH AVE NORTHEAST SEATTLE WASH=

BEING DISCHARGED HERE TODAY NOVEMBER 28. WILL WIRE TIME OF
ARRIVAL FROM DENVER SHOULD BE SOON. DONT WRITE ANYMORE LOVE=

BOB..

358

WESTERN UNION

1201 .(03).

A. N. WILLIAMS
PRESIDENT

The filing time shown in the date line on telegrams and day letters is STANDARD TIME at point of origin. Time of receipt is STANDARD TIME at point of destination

.DA30 FWA84
FW.LB140 16 TOUR=HU FTWORTH TEX 29 1234P   1945 NOV 29 AM 11 09

MISS SELMA NEPOM=
    4540 17 AVE NORTH EAST SEATTLE WASH=

ARRIVING IN PORTLAND BY TRAIN 730 AM SUNDAY DECEMBER 2
ON PORTLAND ROSE FROM DENVER LOVE=
    BOB.

Ke-4443   *adse*

Ed AT 1026ª TO BE mail

730 AM.

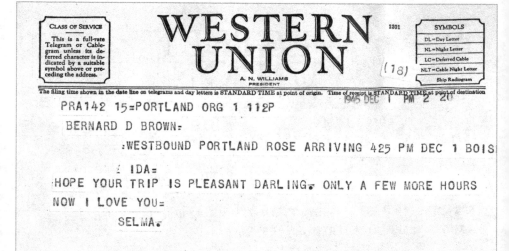

WESTERN UNION

1201

A. N. WILLIAMS
PRESIDENT

(18)

The filing time shown in the date line on telegrams and day letters is STANDARD TIME at point of origin. Time of receipt is STANDARD TIME at point of destination

1945 DEC 1 PM 2 20

PRA142 15=PORTLAND ORG 1 112P

BERNARD D BROWN=

:WESTBOUND PORTLAND ROSE ARRIVING 425 PM DEC 1 BOIS

IDA=

HOPE YOUR TRIP IS PLEASANT DARLING. ONLY A FEW MORE HOURS

NOW I LOVE YOU=

SELMA.

Epilogue

The Postwar Years

For service to his country as Private First Class (PFC), Bernard earned the Bronze Star, Purple Heart and the French Legion of Merit among other honors. He served in the 103rd infantry division and later the 45th infantry division of the United States Army during WWII.

Bernard was discharged from the Army on November 28, 1945 and he and his love Selma, were married a few months later in Portland, Oregon on February 9, 1946. They moved to Bernard's hometown of Salem, Oregon where they were the second married couple to attend Willamette University together. Selma majored in accounting and Bernard was in pre-med. After two years at Willamette, they moved to Forest Grove, Oregon where Bernard finished his studies at Pacific University College of Optometry and Selma worked at the local Ford car dealership.

After graduation, Bernard and Selma moved back to Salem, Oregon where Bernard joined his father's optometry practice. During the 57 years in his optometry practice in Salem, Bernard was appointed by the Governor to two 3-year terms on the Oregon State Board of Examiners in Optometry.

They had three children, Shelley, Jordan and Eden Rose. Jordan is the 3rd generation optometrist in our family, joining Bernard in his Salem practice where Jordan still practices today. Eden Rose is a successful estate planning attorney in Salem. Shelley's career took her to the San Francisco Bay area where she was a teacher and elementary school Principal for 25 years. She has been the Executive Director of musician Carlos Santana's non-profit Milagro Foundation since 2000.

Selma and Bernard were happily married for 72 years. Bernard currently lives in Portland. His sweetheart, Selma, passed away in 2017 at the age of 90. Bernard is a healthy 96-year-old (born August 24, 1924) who, along with his wife Selma, has always been a philanthropist. Throughout their lives, they donated to organizations near and dear to their hearts. Among the more recent bequests are a new children's cabin for B'nai B'rith Camp in Lincoln City, Oregon. Bernard spent many summers with his friends at the week-long Men's Camp to help raise scholarship funds for children. For his alma mater, Pacific University College of Optometry, Bernard established a scholarship fund for veterans interested in pursuing a career in optometry.

Bernard volunteers weekly at the Ronald McDonald house on the South Portland waterfront across the street from his residence at Mirabella. In honor of their daughter Shelley, who was ill as a child, Bernard donated funds for a family room in the new Rood Pavilion. Ronald McDonald House Charities offer a supportive, home-like community that keeps families with seriously ill children together and near the medical care they need.

All proceeds from the book sale of *Dear Selma* will be donated to Ronald McDonald House Charities in Portland, Oregon.

Bernard is beloved by all who know him.

"Till the End of Time"

Bernard and Selma's Wedding Song
Written by Buddy Kaye and Ted Mossman, Performed by Perry Como

Long as stars are in the blue
Long as there's a string of birds to sing
I'll go on loving you

Till the End of Time

Long as roses bloom
in May
My love for you will
grow deeper with every
passing day
Till the wells run dry
And each mountain
disappears
I'll be there for you, to
care for you
Through laughter and
through tears

Selma and Bernard on their wedding day, February 9, 1946

So take my heart in
sweet surrender and tenderly say
That I'm the one you love and live for

Till the End of Time

Brother Lew Brown, Bernard and Selma
at Rockaway Beach, Oregon, 1948

Salem, Oregon, 1971

Father and son optometry practice

Brown family in Lanai, Hawaii for 50th Anniversary, 1996

Selma and Bernard, 65th anniversary, 2011

Giving Back

Bernard Gets Almost Famous

MIRABELLA RESIDENT BERNARD BROWN WAS HONORED BY Ronald McDonald Charities for his service as a volunteer and for his donations with a "thank you" billboard.

It's part of a Ronald McDonald ad campaign celebrating its new shelter for cancer patients and their families in the Rood Family Pavilion.

Bernard is one of six volunteers selected for billboard fame. His billboard has been up by the east end of the Ross Island Bridge. It moves on Sept. 2 to SW Barbur Blvd. and SW 26th Ave.

Ronald McDonald Charities contracts with Oregon Health & Science University to run the housing site, including the accommodations provided for adult patients.

Bernard is available to talk with any resident interested in supporting or volunteering at Ronald McDonald House. ■

Volunteer Spotlight

A circle of giving

A father remembers and returns kindness as a volunteer

As a 31-year-old father, Dr. Bernard Brown experienced the fear and anxiety of having a very sick child. In 1955, his 4-year-old daughter, Shelley, was transferred from their home in Salem to OHSU Doernbecher Children's Hospital, where she would stay for four months until she recovered. The visiting rules then only allowed Brown and his wife, Selma, to visit their little girl three times a week for an hour.

An experience like that never leaves you, so now 64 years later, Brown volunteers as one of the friendly greeters to families arriving at the OHSU Rood Family Pavilion.

"When you have those experiences and you see families coming in, well, thank goodness we can help these children," he said. "This building is a wonderful situation. The rooms are wonderful, and the child and family can stay in rooms together. There's a lot of sadness in the families. You have to be there for them and give support. You recall what you went through."

A recent widower after 72 years of marriage, Brown could see the new pavilion under construction from his apartment at the Mirabella retirement community. The OHSU Rood Pavilion is a patient guesthouse providing affordable housing close to OHSU. The building has 76 guest rooms on the top five floors, half reserved for families of children who are patients and half for adult patients. Ronald McDonald House Charities of Oregon and Southwest Washington subsidizes and provides programming for the pediatric portion of the guesthouse. When Brown heard the mission, he immediately volunteered.

"Nothing could be finer than volunteering some of your time to an organization like Ronald McDonald House Charities," he said. "It takes 44 volunteers for every paid staff member at the house. It's wonderful to give a few hours every week to become a volunteer to help take care of families that need medical treatment."

The 95-year-old World War II veteran has recruited a few of his neighbors from Mirabella to volunteer at Rood by pinning a notice in the communal mailroom.

"You can cook, go to the bakery, clean rooms, clean things for the children," he listed. "They gave me a job at the front office to greet people. You have to go to some meetings to become a volunteer here, and then they match your interests. You're only allowed to work three hours a week, so I work every Friday morning."

Brown retired from his optometry practice in Salem after 57 years, though his son, Dr. Jordan Brown, continues to operate the practice. When Shelley was in the hospital for so long, Brown fretted how he would ever pay the bills, as he was barely out of school and just starting his practice. When Shelley was released from the hospital, he learned that there were no charges to him because the bill would be paid from donations of past patients. He resolved then to pay it forward, which his family did by sponsoring a treatment room at Doernbecher and a guest room at the Rood Pavilion. Both rooms have a plaque in honor of Shelley Nadene Brown. Shelley is currently the executive director of the Milagro Foundation (founded by Carlos Santana), and has guided the foundation in giving over $7 million to agencies serving children in 18 countries.

And Brown continues to give, finding volunteering is a gift that goes both ways.

"It's very gratifying to see the children and families getting all this care," he said.

If you are interested in becoming a volunteer at OHSU, please visit www.ohsu.edu/volunteer.

PEOPLE OF PACIFIC

PACIFIC UNIVERSITY

Pacific Optometry Alumnus, WWII Vet Establishes Scholarship for Other Veterans

By Mike Francis, photos and video by Robbie Bourland

Not everything in the life of Bernard Brown '49, OD '50 has gone as he hoped. Especially his military service during World War II.

He started attending the University of Colorado under an Army program that was canceled one month later. He qualified to serve as an instructor in the Army Air Corps — the forerunner to the U.S. Air Force — only to be reassigned to the infantry and told he was going to Europe. And he earned a Purple Heart — the honor nobody wants to get — when he was wounded by shrapnel during the fighting in France.

But many, many other things have gone right for the 94-year-old widower, who is a popular figure in his southwest Portland condominium.

He helped to liberate the starving people who were imprisoned at the Dachau concentration camp.

He married the love of life, Selma Nepom, and they remained together for 72 years, until she died in 2017.

He followed his father into the optometry business and made a successful living at it. Along the way, his son joined his practice.

And recently, he was able to give back to his alma mater, the Pacific University College of Optometry, establishing a scholarship to fund tuition and other expenses for military veterans.

"I've told this to all my family over and over again, I am so fortunate just to be where I am today, because I've been through a lot," he said from his living room, which overlooks the Willamette River. "And everything has been on the plus side."

The War Years

During his senior year at North Salem High School in 1943, Brown was drafted into the Army. The tide of the war had turned in favor of the Allies, but the fighting was far from over. After some temporary detours for his brief stint in college and preparing to be a flight instructor, he found himself assigned to an infantry unit bound for Europe, where the Axis powers were fighting to hold their gains from earlier in the war.

His overseas deployment amounted to 11 months, shorter than many, but still eventful.

When his unit was fighting through France, it came under artillery fire. One round landed nearby, killing a comrade and sending shrapnel into Brown's back and upper leg. He said he didn't care about being awarded the Purple Heart, but late in the war, it helped him qualify to come home a few months early.

"We were taught you either kill or get killed. We were trained that way," he said. "You're killing these young kids and you were a kid yourself, for no stupid reason at all.

"At that time, we didn't know that. We didn't think that way. You don't think that way until you've grown up a little bit and realize that life is very precious. Why take it away from people?"

Brown had two years of high school German, so as his unit fought its way into Germany and Austria, he was sometimes pressed into service as an interpreter. He said captured German troops, most as young as he was, usually were quite willing to tell the Americans all they knew about their own army's strength and movements.

At one point late in the war, Brown's unit arrived at the Dachau concentration camp in southern Germany after the German guards had fled, but the prisoners, wasted and weak, were still there. Brown's unit was ordered to help evacuate them, sending them back toward food, clothing and medical care.

It was a haunting scene. Brown, who was 20 at the time, still remembers the prisoners calling "Wasser, bitte" — "Water, please."

A little later and a little farther south, Brown and three of his buddies were hiding in the attic of an Austrian Gasthaus from the feared SS troops who were believed to be menacing the area near Innsbruck. They feared they would be overrun, so Brown, who is Jewish, did the best thing he could think to do: He buried his dog tags marked "H" for Hebrew and kept the backup tags he was given in case of being captured by Germans — tags embossed with "P" for Protestant. As it turned out, the SS troops never came.

Peacetime Life — and Optometry

Brown came home in the autumn of 1945.

Back in the States, Brown turned his attention to one of the women with whom he'd corresponded during the war. He'd kept up several steady correspondences with three young women he knew, but he was most intrigued by Selma Nepom of Portland, a childhood friend. Her wartime letters were friendly, newsy and direct before turning increasingly romantic. She and Brown exchanged hundreds of letters and, in February 1946, three months after his discharge, they married in downtown Portland's Multnomah Hotel.

Soon afterward they used his G.I. Bill benefits to enroll together at Willamette University in his hometown of Salem, the second married couple ever to do so. Two years later, he transferred to Pacific to enter the optometry program. In Forest Grove, the couple borrowed money to buy a new, $7,500 house on B Street. While Bernard was a student, Selma worked at a Ford garage.

He was all business as a student, he said. He didn't participate in Boxer tosses or engage much in college life. He was intent on becoming an optometrist as his father was.

He graduated from Pacific in 1950 and set up a practice in Salem that same year. The Salem Eye Clinic flourished, and Brown stayed until retiring in 2007. His son, Jordan, who joined him in the mid-1970s, now runs it. And it is still flourishing.

Giving Back

Selma Brown died in 2017, after 72 years of marriage to Bernard. Now he lives alone in the southwest Portland condominium they shared during her final years. It is full of their memories together, from the multiple photographs of her smiling face to the urn on his coffee table that contains her ashes.

With Selma's passing, Bernard has been preparing to manage their estate. He was drawn, he said, to the idea of donating to Pacific, which launched him on his long and successful optometry career.

The Bernard & Selma Brown Optometry Scholarship for Veterans will support military veterans studying optometry — people like him, using their G.I. Bill benefits to prepare for a career in the civilian workplace.

"Optometry really means a lot to me. And when I see that there are students who want to be optometrists, I want to help them anyway I can," he explained. And veterans, he said have "taken years out of their lives to do service for this country … I just have that feeling to help those, especially those who want to go into the same profession that I've been in.

"That profession has been so good for me and my family." ∎

This story first appeared in the Spring 2019 issue of Pacific Magazine.
For more stories, visit pacificu.edu/magazine.

Monday, Jan. 14, 2019

Personal Message from Author

There are no words to let you know how thrilled I am to see this very personal book completed. I want to thank everyone who helped put this book together. How fortunate it was that my wife Selma kept every one of the letters I sent to her.

My life with Selma was one of a deep, enduring love that began with her letters supporting me during the war. Her wisdom and strength led our family throughout her years with us. Gratitude was her philosophy and loving guidance was her gift.

A very special thank you to our daughter Shelley, who came up with the idea of putting all of these letters into a book. Shelley spent many hours, days and weeks working with other family members, publishers, artists and designers. Thank you to everyone for helping make *Dear Selma* a special part of my life.

—Bernard

Acknowledgements

This beautiful book of love letters would not have happened without our mother Selma lovingly saving these original handwritten letters from Bernard for over 75 years.

Thank you to granddaughter Natalie Brown and our friend, Shannon Bone, for scanning and organizing all 246 letters. Amy Kaufman did an awesome job transcribing and typing each handwritten letter. Claire Flint Last from Luminare Press was the designer responsible for using her talented skills to create the book format and capturing the essence of my vision on our beautiful cover.

Together with encouragement from my husband Jay, my sister Eden and my brother Jordan, along with invaluable memories and personal input from my father Bernard, *Dear Selma* will forever be a part of our family history.

—Shelley